THE TYRANNY OF THE MIND

THE TYRANNY OF THE MIND

A COMMON-SENSE PSYCHOLOGY

BY

BAMPFYLDE FULLER

GYAN

Published by

GYAN

Gyan Publishing House
5, Ansari Road
Daryaganj, New Delhi-110002
Phone: 011-47034999, 9811692060
E-mail: books@gyanbooks.com

Distribution Network
gyanbooks.com
India, USA, Canada, UK, Australia

ISBN: 978-93-6433-078-7 (PB)
First Published, 1935

2nd Impression 2024

Printed at: Gyan Press, Delhi.

THE TYRANNY OF THE MIND
Author: BAMPFYLDE FULLER

THE TYRANNY OF THE MIND

THE TYRANNY OF THE MIND

A COMMON-SENSE PSYCHOLOGY

By

SIR BAMPFYLDE FULLER

K.C.S.I., C.I.E.

Author of "Studies of Indian Life and Sentiment," "Life and Human Nature," "Some Personal Experiences," and other works

LONDON

T. WERNER LAURIE LTD.

COBHAM HOUSE, 24 AND 26 WATER LANE, E.C.4

PREFACE

PREFACE

This book endeavours to apply the "Common Sense" methods of Socrates to the vastly increased knowledge of the present day. Its arguments are, accordingly, drawn from experiences and not from beliefs.

It follows evolutionary lines. The doctrine of Evolution has hitherto been applied only to bodily changes. I now attempt to extend it to living forces, the most notable of which is the human Mind. To understand the development and working of the Mind is of the highest practical importance. For it has the faculty of enmeshing us in a veil of illusion. This may vastly enhance our enjoyment of the present. But, by mystifying the past and glorifying the future, it is of great disservice. For it obscures the causal successions amidst which we live, and prevents us from seeing signs of the future in experiences of the past. It is for this reason that the course of civilization has resembled the flight of an aeroplane in fog—soaring and diving without reckoning—and, at times, even crashing itself out of existence.

It is, then, only by analysing the mentality of mankind that we can hope to understand the extraordinary vicissitudes of human history—the development of civilization from barbarism and its relapse into barbarism, the overthrow of far-flung empires by marauding assaults, the occurrence of war and its inhumanities, changes of form in religions and governments, and of taste in food, dress, manners and art, popular revulsions from self-control to self-indulgence, and reactions towards puritanism that follow them, the substitution of conciliation for authority as the basis of social order, and the slumps and booms that distract commercial life. We dislike self-analysis, and endeavour to find explanations of these changes in environal or economic *circumstances*. Earthquakes and famines are, it is true, beyond man's control, as also are the influences of climate. But, for the rest, we are the offspring of our motives and emotions—such as likes and dislikes, desires and repugnances, extravagance and prudence, kindliness and hate, ambition and submission, respect and disdain, boldness and timidity, pride and humility, anger and tolerance. And these, again, are the offspring of *ideas*—ideas of present and prospective enjoyments or satisfactions, and their contraries, and of such abstract excellences as Unity, Kindness, Justice, Honesty and Truth and the duties that they impose: ideas of the multitudinous phases that Success assumes in tempting, inspiring, uniting and dividing mankind; and ideas of persons and things with which these ideas are associated as qualities, and are consequently liked or admired, feared, despised or hated. These ideas may be presented by memory, intelligence, imagination or experience. But they are, in great measure, instilled into us by the words of others, that is to say, by various phases of *propaganda*. They affect us as elements of the Mind, and the study of the Mind's evolution, capacities and workings is, then, of the utmost practical importance.

Ideas are as immaterial as "wireless waves," and in dealing with them—and with mental activities generally—we are subjecting to reasoning examination things that are commonly held to be "supernatural," and are left for religion to explain.

CONTENTS

CHAPTER I

MEMORY AND INTELLIGENCE

A PROFESSOR of psychology once told me—in the course of a drive through the hills beyond Brisbane—that his task consisted in explaining what everybody knew in language that no one could understand. We all know, intuitively, that we are composed of Body and Mind, both of which are inspirited by Emotional Energy. This knowledge is, however, confused by the language of psychology. It sharply distinguishes our "psychic," spiritual, or emotional endowment from our "physical" nature, and associates this endowment with the possession of a conscious Mind. But emotion inspirits creatures that lack minds. We can infer that an animal is mindless if it is unconscious of pain, since, when our minds are dormant during sleep, we become insensible to a toothache. Insects cannot feel pain as we know it. A wasp that has been grievously mutilated will contentedly occupy itself in sucking treacle. But insects, although mindless, are quite obviously energized by emotion. Curiosity, courage, anger and determination are emotions. Their possession cannot be denied to flies, bees and ants. Emotional energy must then be a *physical* endowment. But it is also, as we shall find, the evolutionary origin of Thought, and together with Thought, constitutes the Mind. It is, then, an energizing element on both the physical and mental sides of our nature, and acts as a uniting bond[1] between them. Consequently it can be stimulated through

[1] The Body, Emotion and Thought are deified by Hinduism as Siva, Vishnu and Brahma.

either one or the other. We can be inspirited by bracing weather, by a meal or a glass of sherry from one end of the combine, or by a compliment, by an ideal, or by "thoughts of her" from the other.

The Mind is, therefore, a combination of Emotion and Thought, as our physical life is of purely bodily activities and of emotional energies. But Emotion exercises its inspiriting influence intermittently. It is withdrawn during sleep or a fainting fit, and under the effect of an anæsthetic, although our *bodily* activities continue to function. And Thought vanishes with it. We must then conclude that although our emotional life runs in double harness with our bodily life, Emotion at certain times breaks away from its collar. When it is between the shafts—during our waking hours—Thought mounts upon it as its postilion,[1] sometimes urging, sometimes restraining it, and always rendering it "conscious."

We all know, again, that the course of thought is guided by the two marvellous faculties of Memory and Intelligence. But Psychology errs in classing them as purely "mental." For it will be shown that they control our physical as well as mental activities. It may seem preposterous to hold that forces which must be immaterial should occupy themselves with the management of the body. For we think of the body as a collection of tissues, nerves and organs. But—in so far as they are material—these are only the *instruments* of the immaterial energy of "Life." If life fails, they are as powerless as a closed-down wireless receiver. We can *feel* the emotional energies that are within us. But we are so dependent upon our senses that we are reluctant to admit the existence of anything which they cannot detect, and we therefore ascribe the multifarious activities of life to the "nervous system." But the nerves are merely cords of communication, and it would be as reasonable to call electricity "wirous" because it depends upon wires for its transmission. The existence of immaterial forces is, how-

[1] Mindless creatures have, of course, no such postilion in their service.

ever, indisputable, if only through our experiences of "wireless waves" and their reception. And, like them, Memory and Intelligence are only known to us by inferences from the effects that they produce. Similarly indirect is our knowledge of Gravity.

To begin with Memory. It can be defined as the repetitive reproduction by one thing of the *replica* of another thing that has become already connected, or associated with it. Its mental influence is sufficiently well known. It resuscitates a train of ideas that have become "familiarized" with one another either by deliberate "practice," or by the course of experience. We "link them together again"—a process which is admirably described by the literal meaning of "recollecting." We are conscious of this process. But it may occur spontaneously as well as deliberately. We figure a recollection as a "recall"—as a "record" of some kind, which is, as it were, brought out of storage and set before us. This materialistic explanation is easy to follow: it likens the Mind to a photograph album. But it is quite inadequate. What record can there be of a *movement*, as of a finger, for instance? Yet, after making it, we can recollect it perfectly well. What record can there be of a *thought*—of so abstract a thought as that a "ratio is a relationship between two numbers, or quantities, that is unaffected by their multiplication or division." Yet, if this occurred to me yesterday, it will occur to me to-day—quite automatically, if the subject that led to it presents itself again. There must, accordingly, be something, apart from the Will, that is its "recaller." An alternative explanation—which will gradually establish its truth as we proceed—is that an idea which is recollected is, in reality, reconstituted, or "reproduced," in mind: it is "regenerated" by an idea which in previous experience has preceded or followed it. That is to say, one idea has the faculty of regenerating another idea with which it has become connected in the past. We are quite unconscious of this process of regeneration: we are only conscious of its results in "remembering." But this is no good argument against its reality. For our vital processes are generally veiled from us. We are unconscious of the process of digestion; and even of the process of "seeing," we know no more than that its consequence is "sight."

It may seem preposterous to suppose that one idea can "give birth" to another—to imagine that generation is a mental as well as a physical faculty. We associate birth with sexual reproduction. But the living world around us demonstrates that living energy can reproduce phases of itself—quite apart from sexual breeding. How wonderfully is this illustrated by the regenerations of spring-time! Trees and plants—with nothing but earth, air and water to help them—reproduce leaves and flowers that are replicas of those which have grown and died during the year preceding. Nor is this faculty limited to plants. Stags annually repeat the growth of antlers that they have borne and dropped.

It is a notable fact that the formation of memorial *liaisons* is greatly facilitated by emotion. If, in reviewing past years, one calls to mind such a heart-felt experience as a declaration of love, for instance, its scene comes back in minutest detail. This is a fact of great evolutionary importance. For it materially assists us in profiting by experience. A successful effort is attended by a delightful glow of triumph: a failure by a pang of disappointment. The results of experience are, therefore, strongly impressed upon us. This association between memory and feeling may be artificially utilized. It is related of a professor of Botany that he impressed the name of a new flower upon his son by boxing the boy's ears when he told it him. The canings which one suffered at school had, no doubt, some instructional value as *aides-mémoire*. It was, indeed, to memories of pain that we owed our first step towards civilization —in becoming "house-clean." With advancing years emotion loses in delicacy of responsiveness. The lightly kindled glows of childhood "fade into the light of common day." Whilst emotional sensitiveness endures, it gives a memorizing power that is in amazing contrast with the difficulty that is experienced during later years in memorially fixing the botanical name of a new plant.

Mental recollections link themselves with memorized movements. Ideas of words, or musical notes, that present themselves, instantly and automatically provoke the muscular movements of speaking, singing and writing with no consciousness of these movements when they have once been "learnt." So the fingers of a pianist automatically reproduce on his instrument a tune that is "running in his head." Physical activities become associated with mental. They unite in forging the chains of Habit. The Mind repeatedly presents a series of ideas of conduct to which the muscles immediately give play. Ideas and movements are "associated" in a succession, and hence memory is commonly regarded as an *associative* process. It is by memorial association that doctrines, views or opinions, to which we are emotionally inclined or disinclined, immediately and automatically arouse the impulsive feelings of like or dislike which are termed "predilections," "beliefs," or "prejudices."

It is to the union of mental and physical memories that we owe the acquired sensibilities, or "tastes," that incline us to the influence of particular stimuli or "temptations." For the great majority of them are plainly founded upon habit. The taste for tobacco, for instance, is obviously acquired; and tastes in music vary with the fashions of the day. Some of these sensibilities are periodic: a lunch-time appetite is a sensibility which develops about one o'clock. After, however, a few days' residence, in France, it comes to us an hour earlier. Memory can, then, act rhythmically, and, provoked by the passage of time, can arouse sensibilities periodically: it is possible to awaken oneself, approximately, at a certain hour if this is impressed upon the mind overnight.

In these cases physical have become associated with mental processes. But, beyond doubt, Memory can be wholly physical, or unconscious. The accurate muscular repetitions, or reproductions, which constitute "dexterity" —as in piano-playing, for example—are exactly parallel with the mental repetition of a piece of poetry. A pianist's fingers will execute a familiar piece of music when the pianist himself is quite "absent-minded"—when his fingers are unguided by either ideas or by a music score.

Now these acquired automatic dexterities have a remarkably close resemblance to the intricate processes of our physical life—such as those of circulation, respiration and secretion. These also progress in regular repetitive succession, and it is difficult to avoid the conclusion that they are directed by a capacity for reproducing particular experiences of the past that has become heritable and can be passed from parent to offspring. This is illustrated by the curious repetitions of embryonic development—by the fact that, in gradually shaping itself, an embryo infant, for instance, rudimentarily develops the gill-slits of a fish, the brain of a reptile, and the disproportionately long arms of a monkey. It repeats the experiences of its forbears, acting upon memorial linkings that have been bequeathed to it. Variations occur, the source of which will be traced as we proceed. But, speaking generally, the growth of a living thing is a memorial repetition of stages through which its parents have passed. Unless the law of Evolution is untrue, these tendencies have been acquired, or evolved, by its ancestors. It is denied by some authorities that acquired characters are heritable. It is clear that artificial or accidental changes—the effects of circumcision, for instance —are not passed on from parent to offspring. But this fact has no application to changes that have come about naturally through circumstances that have emotionally evoked spontaneous new vital responses. English greyhounds imported into Mexico could not course hares successfully because they lost breath in the rarefied air. But their progeny were unaffected by it. English sheep that are domiciled in Argentine hereditarily change the character of their fleeces. And a study of the conditions of mankind in various parts of the world points very definitely to the conclusion that the effects of peculiarities of environment—of soil, climate, temperature and light—stamp themselves hereditarily—and memorially—upon a race.

These inherited physical successions are evidently the springs of the conduct that is called "reflex" or instinctive. They may take the form of habits—inborn sensibilities and promptings, which automatically initiate and direct certain lines of behaviour that are appropriate to certain conditions. They may be "timed," or periodic, such as the arrival of puberty, the break of the voice in boyhood, and the coming of hair on the face. Love begins as a physical sensibility to "sex-appeal." It is the Mind that glorifies it into admiring sympathy. Such, again, is the "call of the wild," which overmasters the education of the Australian aborigines. The life of an insect is a procession of periodic sensibilities, or "tropisms" as they are called. A caterpillar, for instance, is at first engrossed in leaf-eating: it then becomes obsessed with the construction of its cocoon; and, finally, as a butterfly, becomes sensible of the need of mating, and of the agreeable properties of flower nectar.

It is clear, on the other hand, that repetitive successions which *originate in the Mind* do not become heritable. Memorial—and intelligent—*capacity* may sometimes be passed on from parent to offspring. But particular mental acquirements and associations do not outlive the death of their possessor, unless they are stereotyped in writing. English children in India learn Hindustani as easily as their mother-tongue; and the changes that occur in human habits, tastes and fashions prove that Memory can obtain no heritable seat in our mental nature. In the life of each individual, thought must evolve itself from its beginnings. It is only the unconscious that naturally endures. Indeed it is to this that man owes his marvellous versatility.

Amongst the most fruitful of the differences between him and the lower animals is his lack of inherited, or instinctive, reactions, *so far as his external conduct is concerned.* A baby's only instincts of behaviour are to hold tight and to suck: it can, therefore, be brought up to any code of manners, language or religion. Man is, consequently, so far "free" in that he is left to develop his civilizing manners, industries and beliefs, either by learning them from others, or by the use of Intelligence. Memory alone would stereotype them. It is by Intelligence that they advance.

We apostrophize Intelligence as "The Intellect." The sciences accept it as the supreme arbiter of judgment. But they make no attempt to define or describe it, and leave its nature to be divined by intuition or guesswork. Like Memory, it is a *reproductive* force. But it reproduces through the familiarity, not of a past connection, but of a present resemblance, or analogy. The thing that is reproduced is *like* its producer, in some respect, and can be "fitted on" to it. Intelligence is, therefore, "adaptive," and consequently inventive. The resemblance, or analogy, may be of very various kinds—not merely one of appearance, character, quality, quantity or purpose, but (and this is a point of great importance) something that is similar in the origin or outcome—cause or consequence—of the two. A person's mind can, for instance, be adaptively styled "open," because, like an open door, it offers free admission to new ideas. Two things can even be analogically connected because both are irritating: hence a man may be analogically cross with his wife because he has mislaid his umbrella. There is an analogy between a thing and its contrary: hence Intelligence can summon illustration to contradict a superficial conclusion. An analogy may be a similarity between relationships in time and in space as, for example, "towards Bath" and "towards four o'clock."

We appreciate the similarity of the two things by consciously *comparing* them. But conscious comparison would be impossible did not one unconsciously reproduce an idea of the other. Mental Intelligence may, then, be defined as the analogical reproduction of ideas.

It is by Intelligence that we "comprehend" adaptations that have been made by others. By means of it we appreciate the similarities between the original and the metaphorical meanings of words—between two such things as an aeroplane and a dragon-fly, the tongue and a flame of fire, and a fit of temper and two cross sticks. Parables and metaphors are, then, comprehended as well as suggested by Intelligence. Metaphor contributes immensely to our vocabulary. When we think of the wind as "blowing," we are adapting ideas of our own expirations to its movement: when we think of the sun as "setting," we adapt the idea of "sitting" to its position on the western horizon. We apply the idea of "running" to a stream, a machine, the course of a month and a cold in the head. We use prepositions that apply to position in space to indicate points of time—"in a motor-car" and "in a minute," for example. In naming immaterial things we draw upon the material world: "the Spirit does but mean the Breath." If the verbs, adverbs and adjectives employed in speech are analysed, a surprisingly large number of them will be found to be metaphorically adapted from their original meanings.

The more emotional thought becomes, the "farther-fetched," picturesque, and imaginative are the analogies that it uses. The effect of emotion, it will be shown, is to express feelings, or general thoughts *figuratively*—that is to say, in particular images that are drawn from sensation. Picturesque analogies, therefore, abound in the thoughts of poets, essayists and rhetoricians. So Shelley could perceive a likeness between a skylark and a glow-worm, and Francis Thompson could sorrowfully liken his heart to "a broken fount in which tear-droppings stagnate." Musical composition is also imaginative when stirred by emotion, using successions of sounds that seem to be analogically connected with stresses of emotion—or with the rhythmic movements that may accompany them—as their expressions. Art begins as an expression of emotion, and develops into a demonstration of skill. In the latter stage it becomes deliberately effortful, but "uninspired."

Likeness culminates in identity. We "recognize" a person or thing by identifying it with a pre-existing idea of it. Recognition is involved in the perception of everything which is not quite strange, and it follows that a conscious sensation is ordinarily accompanied by the mental reproduction of an idea which it analogically recalls and with which it is identified. The idea may be one of the individual object, or of the class to which it belongs. The *process* of identification—that is to say, of "unifying" similarities—eludes consciousness. When there is a difficulty, we are conscious of a sense of hesitation, which ends in recognition. When no difficulty is experienced, we are hardly conscious of the process. But we can infer its nature from its results. Comparison is the fruit of identification. When we compare two objects, we must identify, or unify, the particular qualities or traits in respect of which comparison is made, and this results in the differentiation, or isolation, of differences, or degrees. Hence, through its appreciation of samenesses, Intelligence also appreciates differences. For these are qualities or quantities that stand out when two things are "merged together"—or identified through their samenesses. Comparison is not, of course, limited to objects that are before us. There can be comparison between an object and an idea that is reproduced by it, or between two ideas. We can compare a rose with the recollection of one we saw yesterday, or the idea of a rose with that of a hollyhock.

Analogical identification through a similarity of quality has a further result of momentous importance. It gives rise to the process that is variously termed "inference," "deduction," or "reasoning." This involves the identification of a sensation, or a thought with a *standard* of some kind, which may be drawn from experience, or has been elaborated by the Mind as a generalization. This is followed by the connecting of the sensation or thought with a quality of the standard or with something that precedes or follows it. Thus, going by experience, or "common sense," we infer that it is a slug that has eaten our seedlings, or that it will rain because the clouds are very low. Generalized standards may be of classes, rules or laws. We make use of them in deciding that a plant is poisonous if it belongs to a poisonous kind, that impure water is dangerous because it is the "source of disease," and that one suffering from a cold should be avoided because "colds are infectious." The attributes that are inferred in this fashion may be of quantity, or ratio. So we conclude that 2½ tons of coal, at 42s. the ton, will cost five guineas, because five guineas, being in the same ratio to 42s. as 2½ is to 1, corresponds analogically to 2½ tons.

Accordingly, reasoning inference runs from present experience to the past and back to the present, or from the particular to the general and back to the particular. Its course is "shuttle-wise." It ordinarily runs automatically and with great rapidity, so that we are hardly conscious of it and regard it as a "sixth perceptive sense." So we "know," at once, that it is raining if umbrellas are up in the street; and instantly convert visual perspective into mental impressions of solidity and distance, because experiences of sight and movement have shown that one is related to the other. But inference runs deliberately and slowly if a standard has to be discovered through a *clue* of some sort. It is this clue that is introduced into speech by a "because." The generalization from which the inference is drawn is, as a rule, too obvious to need expression. We use a clue when we think that a dog is scratching itself "because it has fleas." In the background is the general experience that scratching is the consequence of irritation.

Inferences may be very erroneous. Those drawn from

the successions of experiences fail if the experiences have been casual or exceptional; a mascot is not trustworthy because it has once been associated with good luck; "one swallow does not make a summer." Those drawn from mental generalizations are deceptive, if the generalizations have been made hastily, ignorantly, or under the influence of imagination or sentiment.[1] We are prone to accept as rules, or "laws," assumptions or doctrines that commend themselves as true by making an emotional appeal. Such, for instance, is the generalization that "the voice of the people is the voice of God," from which it is inferred that what the people demand in a particular case is best for them. The law that "action and reaction are equal and opposite" is contradicted by our experiences of elastic rebounds. Moreover we recognize as "laws" *averages* which are generalized from very diverse particulars and have only a mental existence. Many of the laws of Meteorology are of this kind. They indicate vague tendencies, not precise certainties. It is through the uncertainties—the gaps—in our knowledge that mystery-mongers and imposters of all kinds find their opportunities.

Nevertheless, amidst all its pitfalls, Reason is our only guide to the unknown. It enables us to appreciate possibilities—that is to say, future eventualities. It also enables us to appreciate degrees of intensity. If we cannot open a drawer, we pull it more strongly because, on previous like occasions, an increase of strength has helped us. If we have to catch a train, we infer from experience the time we should allow ourselves. It is to his reasoning capacity that man owes his civilizing progress. For he can enlarge his opportunities for reasoning by the artificial experience of experiment. And his lack of inherited instincts is of immense advantage to him, since it allows his reason full play.

The lower is the degree of intelligence the more pointed

[1] Such as that of the child who concluded that a family was not well off "because two of them played upon one piano together."

must be the resemblance that sets it working. A dog that has learnt by trials, or instruction, to unlatch a particular gate with its nose, is baffled by a gate of slightly different pattern. A lively intelligence can appreciate analogies that appear to be very remote—such, for instance, as that between the rotary revolution of the earth round the sun, and the similar movement of an inclined orange round a candle. This is a commonplace in these days but seemed quite fantastic to the contemporaries of Copernicus. Intelligent capacity appears to vary very greatly from individual to individual, and, in the individual, to vary with the matter to which it is applied. An ingenious mechanician may be puzzled by analogies in literary expression. The "point" of a joke is an analogy: some persons see it much more quickly than others. But natural intelligence may be most effectively blunted by sentiment or prejudice. We do not appreciate analogies that conflict with our self-esteem, our patriotism or our religious beliefs; in the course of education intelligence loses ground against these feelings. Children are disconcertingly quick in the perception of resemblances.

Mental intelligence, like mental memory, allies itself with physical processes. This is strikingly illustrated by the faculty of *imitation*. It clearly involves the analogical adaptation to oneself of the manners, feelings, ideas and language of others. As "acting," imitation develops into deliberate impersonification. But it is, primarily, quite spontaneous, although we are conscious of its effects. Children are passively "infected" by their surroundings; and, consequently, imitation is an educative instrument that endows one generation with the accomplishments of its predecessor. "Fashion" and "public opinion" are at once models for imitation and the modelling which follows them. Their immense influence needs no illustration.

Mental is associated with physical activity in the ingenious *experimenting* to which we owe the progress of material civilization. For experiment involves the adaptation of movements, or mixtures, to novel purposes, through a chain of analogies. We owe to it the growth of the art of cookery—the first of the arts—as well as of the "fine" arts: also the elaboration of the artificial complexities of cultured life, in language, dress, manners, buildings and furniture, the invention of tools and machines, and the great majority of the scientific discoveries that have laid open natural forces which are such energetic substitutes for manual labour. These discoveries have, for the most part, been made by experiment—not by philosophy or mathematics.

By a further logical step in our argument, it must be concluded that Intelligence, like Memory, is also a purely physical faculty which can act independently of the Mind. Perhaps the most convincing illustration of this is the effect of the sound of running water upon the action of the bladder—well known in hospital practice. An audience, or congregation, may become automatically "infected" with coughing. Such stimuli to imitation act upon us quite unawares—in the mental blank which psychology styles "subliminal consciousness." It is clearly physical intelligence that absent-mindedly, or "mechanically," directs the course of our movements, regulates the strength that is used on different occasions and balances us in various positions against the stress of Gravity. It adaptively reproduces activities without ideas of them, so that we are unconscious of its assistance. In running upstairs we unconsciously adapt our steps to the windings of the staircase. It appears, indeed, that the greater part of our life of active movement is automatically guided by physical intelligence. It is this that endows us with the adaptability of eye and hand which wins success in playing games. They are "played" by physical Memory and Intelligence, although they are invented and learnt through the Mind, and it is the Mind that offers their incentives in thoughts of victory. One is "nervous" when the Mind tries to take command. It follows that in physical dexterity we are more intelligent than the interference of the Mind may allow us to be. "Genius" is the harmonious development of both mental and physical intelligence, the one in designing, the other in executing. Nor is it only in our life of movement that physical intelligence assists us. The stomach must use intelligence in adapting itself to new dishes.

The existence of physical intelligence is also proved by the remarkable capacity that insects may display in adapting memorial, or instinctive, conduct to meet new strange circumstances through the analogical efforts that Biology terms "conditioned reflexes." These are illustrated with peculiar abundance in the natural history of the ant tribe.

By extending these conclusions we arrive at a solution of the great outstanding problem of Biology—the *origin* of the changes in organic structure that constitutes Evolution. These all involve the intensification of certain faculties by their local concentration. The skin, for instance, is in some degree sensitive to light, and is, indeed, the only apparatus for "seeing" possessed by earth-worms. Vision would be developed by the concentration of this vague susceptibility into eye-spots, effected by the analogical reproduction of tissue with special regard to its sensitiveness to light. So tactile sensibility would become intensified in the finger-tips and tongue; and feelers, or tentacles, gradually develop into prehensile limbs by concentration of their "clinging" capacities. Evolution may, then, be defined as the development of future activities by the adaptation of past experiences (which may have been quite accidental) to meet emergencies of the present. We are apt to attribute progress and decadence to the effect of "environment." They are really the effects of Intelligence, provoked, it may be, by changes of environment.

The evolution of the organs and faculties of plants and animals may, then, quite appropriately be compared with the development of man's civilized accomplishments and tastes. But, between the two, there is an essential difference. The one, with physical nature as its plastic material, works slowly but enduringly: the other, acting upon the Mind, is vastly more rapid, but is transient, because it is artificial. Its effects endure only in so far as they are conserved by education.

We can take a further step and trace to the "morbid" action of Intelligence the origin of some of the diseases—physical and mental—which afflict humanity. Certain of them—cancer, for instance—appear to result from the formation of the wrong kind of tissue in particular organs, and this may not unreasonably be attributed to a perverted use of analogy by physical intelligence. Insanity, again, commonly manifests itself in the extravagant mental use of fanciful analogies and comparisons, which overpowers memorial regularity. In both cases relief might be obtained could a remedy be discovered that would repress analogical reproduction, as alcohol and drugs seem to reinforce it. This would give repetitive reproduction a better chance of holding its own.

It may be concluded from the facts that I have marshalled that life is essentially a dualistic *reproductive* energy. In organs, vital energies and ideas—that is to say, in both the physical and the mental spheres—it is constantly producing things which are replicas of things that it has produced before, or are connected with these things by analogical resemblances. Memory is the repetitive reproduction of an organ, function, emotion, action, utterance or idea for familiar use in an established connection. Intelligence is their analogical and adaptive reproduction for use in new connections: it is, in fact, the *Evolution Créatrice* of Henri Bergson. Ancient Egyptian art might have visioned the Temple of Life as the gigantic pillared shrine of two heroic figures—a woman and a man, representing, the one Memory, the other Intelligence. *She* stands with downcast eyes, finger on lips, recalling things out of the past. *He* is more alert, and smilingly watches a flowery stream that falls from one hand to the other, undergoing evolutionary changes in the passage. These generalizations leave us, it is true, in ignorance of the real nature of the Energy that manifests itself in this fashion. But it is something to have simplified a vast number of diverse experiences and to have brought them under two general heads.

CHAPTER II

LIFE'S DUALITY AND ITS OUTCOMES IN MOTIVE AND MOVEMENT, EMOTION AND THOUGHT

Our pride shrinks from the idea that the body is not a Temple but a Home, in which a united couple of forces live together, generally in sympathy, but sometimes antagonized in a struggle for mastery. Yet we constantly admit that our nature is twofold. We speak of the "two sides of human character"—the practical and the emotional—of "self-esteem," "self-sacrifice," and of "self-control." It is obvious that "self-control" involves one that controls and another that is controlled, and that we are, in fact, endowed with a dual personality, the existence of which is obscured by the unity of consciousness.

One explanation of this duality is that, at man's birth, there is "breathed" into him an energy which is distinct from that of life—an animative "Soul" or "Spirit." Another explanation, which is more in accord with experience, is that man's nature is dual because he is the offspring of two parents, each source contributing a special character, or element, of its own. This dual generation is a peculiarity of all kinds of life—whether vegetable or animal—except in its lowest and most primitive forms. Each living thing springs from the union of two germs—which seem to be the ultimate elements of masculinity and femininity. It follows that every living thing is a compound of masculine and feminine attributes, and that the sex differences of *gender* result from an excess of one or other element which shows itself in appearance or character. Women are more feminine than men, and men are more masculine than women. But each of them contains something of the opposite sex. Have not men rudimentary mammary glands and their accessories? Do they not share with women the *practical* outlook which is called the "eternal feminine"?

It is very remarkable that the truth of this outstanding—if disillusioning—conclusion should be denied by psychologists, and be ignored by medical and physiological science. It is, nevertheless, the keynote of the Mendelist school of biology; this, indeed, insists upon individual duality, and regards individuals as "zygotes," or "yoked-fellows." There is in this matter a disconcerting inconsistency between schools of scientific thought.

Duality of origin implies duality of influence. And we are clearly subject to two contrary tendencies—the practical or "prudent," which regards the future, and the *emotional* which lives in the present. The former shows itself in purposeful motives or desires: it has in view a future *advantage*, or profit, of some kind, which is an object of *pursuit*. Our emotional tendency, on the other hand, is towards present pleasure or enjoyment. It is "playful," although it may indulge itself in politics, art and idealism as well as in "sport." We recognize its essential character in speaking of "play-houses," "playing the piano" and the "play of the fancy," or "of the intellect." Pleasure becomes an object of pursuit, as well as profit, because the two propensities join their forces. But the purposes in view are undeniably distinct. Profit-seeking and pleasure-seeking, as alternatives, are poles apart. Each morning's newspaper shows that the reasons, which may be employed to convince or persuade another, may either be practical considerations of future utility, or pleasures that appeal to purely emotional interest.

May we not reasonably conclude that our practical propensities spring from the feminine, and our emotional energies from the masculine side of our nature? For, taken generally, women are decidedly more practical than men—more impressed with the fundamental needs of the things which "common sense" shows to "really matter"—and less disposed to sacrifice them to emotional sensibilities and aspirations. How often is the wife busy with house and children whilst the husband is betting in the street or cheering at a football match? And it is fortunate for mankind that this is so. For women, as the educators of the young, are the guardians of civilization: if children are not civilized before they leave the nursery, any culture which they may subsequently acquire will be little more than skin deep. Their education—and home cares generally—are motived by a regard for *future* interests. We shall find that the most deeply seated of our *motives* are severely practical, and our experiences of human nature would accordingly class them as of feminine origin. Emotional activity would, on the other hand, be a masculine attribute. Motives become emotionalized because the two sides of our nature mutually interact. But the practical and the emotional are fundamentally distinct.

Practical feminine tendencies and capacities clearly include those of the body and its organs. It is obvious that life could not endure, or its reproductive continuance be secured, were we not amenable to impressions that are received by the sensory organs. Accordingly, these must also be feminine endowments. It is a very notable fact that they can automatically serve bodily needs during the emotional apathy of sleep: indeed we could not otherwise be awakened. Quite unconsciously we can shift our position in bed more comfortably, and throw back the bed-clothes, if over warm. And life would become extinct were it not insured by some peculiar sensibilities that arise in us—in some cases periodically. These are the discordant conditions that are felt in consciousness as pain, fear, hunger, thirst and lust, the anxiety of parents for their offspring and the craving for peace, security and protection of some kind. Life would not survive if undisturbed by these warnings. They generate urges, or "motives," that stir the depths of our nature—to *search* for the means of satisfying them or dispelling them, to *cling*[1] to the satisfying and protective and to *shrink*[2] from the unsatisfying or injurious. Search must be conducted through the external senses, and this is another reason for holding them to be feminine endowments.

The clingings and shrinkings of infant life develop into mental likes and dislikes. But they retain something of their material simplicity. "Attachments" are shown by spontaneous caresses. Our likings for others impel us to *touch* them in embraces, kisses or the contact of handshaking. During childhood this practical motive may be almost irresistible—the impulse to "pick" a flower, and to "pinch" anything that pleases. This is "kleptomania"—the involuntary childish origin of theft. Museums and picture galleries must safeguard their collections by warnings against touch. We "cleave" to our food when we swallow it, and to an odour when we sniff it. Attention is a mental phase of "clinging," we are physically drawn to its object. It is an effort of will only when it is given to the disagreeable—as by a child to its lessons.

The practical urge to search for, or pursue, the satisfying becomes mentalized as desire, or ambition, and is extended to the pleasurable as well as the useful. The unconscious craving for protection that is illustrated by the shells of molluscs, the cocoons of chrysalises and the nests of birds, becomes in man a conscious motive for the construction of houses and their furniture, and the acquisition of possessions that assure the future.

The functioning of our bodily organs is repetitive, and Memory must, therefore, be a feminine capacity, whereas Intelligence, we shall find, comes from the masculine side. The capacity for movement must also have its roots in

[1] Translated by us, egocentrically, as "having," "holding" or "possessing."

[2] Mentalized as of Fear.

feminine instinct. For, without it, feminine urges would be powerless. But, unless invigorated by emotion, movement is slow and feeble—is, in fact, "uninspired."

Masculine emotion, on the other hand, is extraordinarily elastic and variable. It endows us with resistant "strength": we are stronger when excited than in a mood of calm. Its elasticity provides us with a recuperative force which enables us to sustain the countless shocks, clashes, infections and injuries to which we are exposed. For life's stability is merely a condition of antagonistic equilibrium. The world of plants and animals displays this resistant strength, quite apart from purely functional activities. Indeed, to withstand the unceasing attack of gravity requires more resisting power than may be realized. Plants and animals of the land surface live, so to speak, under the constant downpour of a cataract. They possess an inherent elasticity comparable with that of the atmosphere; and accordingly words that describe the vagaries of the weather can be appropriately applied to the varying conditions of our spirits.

As a *condition*, emotion presents itself as a "mood," or "temper," of which we are conscious as pleasure or displeasure—joy or sorrow, exhilaration or depression—states of feeling which may be taken to correspond with "expansive" or "contractive" excitement. Emotion is, accordingly, two-phased. It can elastically recover itself from contractive depression. In good health we can maintain an even temper under a swarm of annoyances: grief tends to "wear itself out." Its recoveries may be sudden elastic "rebounds" as when bafflement is reversed into curiosity and fear into "physical" courage. Relief from apprehension or perturbation is commonly "revulsive." We laugh at fears that prove to be groundless, and when we escape from anxiety or perplexity. Popular fiction very largely consists in the resolving of imagined discords into harmonies. These revulsions are ludicrous, or comic, when the artificial claims of dignity are abruptly pushed aside by the vulgarly natural. There is nothing more ridiculous than the discomfited vanity of another. The mother in us seems to be laughing at the father's "airs."

Of particular evolutionary importance is the revulsion which follows the achievement of *success*. We have all experienced this as a glow of triumph. Failure, on the other hand, is accentuated by an emotional stress of disappointment or shame. The extraordinary development of ideas of these feelings is for later consideration; and it suffices to mention here that the mental glamour of success, actual social or "snobbish," is so attractive that it can almost outbid the most pressing of feminine urges.

The vehement intensity of emotional energy is shown by its need of bodily safety-valves or outlets. It must vent itself automatically in "expressions of emotion"—facial changes, gesticulations, laughter and tears, cries and torrents of language. What surges of energy burst forth in the roars of applause that accompany a race or a football match! They are automatic: the onlookers are scarcely conscious of the shouts that liberate their feelings, and can hardly control them. Indeed, emotion that is denied this safety-valve becomes unbearable: there are few who have not been relieved by an expletive. These emotional manifestations are the germs from which man's artistic accomplishments have evolved. But they are not peculiar to mankind. Young animals gambol; birds sing; there are beasts and birds that show their pleasure, or pride, in dancing. An excited dog cannot remain still.

The vehemence of emotional energy illustrates its remarkable instability. Our spirits do not maintain a uniform strength: one morning we are "in the pink," the next morning "off colour." These fluctuations account for the uncertainty that attends the performances of athletes and race-horses. Emotion becomes fatigued and needs rest, whereas the body can function unceasingly. But it remains a surprising fact that emotional energy should desert us entirely during our sleeping hours. It is evidently not a self-existing continuity, but a "potentiality"—a *capacity* for being excited by various *stimuli* and provocatives. These primarily come to it through feminine agency. It is to be noted that, in the process of impregnation, the male *spermatozoon* "imprisons" itself in the female *ovum,* so cutting itself off from independent communication with the outside world. Emotion must, then, rely for stimulation upon the body. It allies itself with the body to form our "physical" nature, and, by emotionalizing bodily conditions and functions, enters into sympathetic partnership with them.

Hence our emotional states are profoundly affected by our bodily conditions. Ill-health is commonly attended by the emotional feebleness of "neurasthenia." Emotional pain is caused by the discordant conditions of hunger, thirst and lust, and by bodily injuries and derangements. Emotional pleasure is aroused by the satisfaction of a meal, by the effects of alcohol and cocaine, and by bodily caresses. There is pleasure when we are physically attracted, displeasure when we are repelled.

Our sensory organs are, as we have seen, part of our feminine equipment. But emotion, as part of our "physical" nature, enters into the process of sensation. When unaccompanied by emotion, sensation is merely the reception of impressions from outside, and these in all probability are merely miniature repetitions, or *replicas* of their *causes.* Sound, for instance, would be merely a reproduction of its vibrations by the tissues of the ear. These impressions are transfigured, or "apparelled," by emotion: vibratory activities are presented as heat, light and sound. Sensation becomes a "duplex" process in which bodily and emotional faculties are combined. And it is by this infusion of emotion that the body becomes endowed with physical Intelligence. For this, as we shall find reason to infer, is a masculine, as Memory is a feminine, capacity. Sensory activity affects emotion very strongly. We are "bored" when our surroundings are uninteresting. Our spirits are invigorated by bracing weather, bright light, colours and music, as the life of a seed is by warmth and moisture. A warm, sunny climate increases emotional vivacity: to be sure of this we have only to call to mind the increase of gesticulation, as an accompaniment to conversation, as, in travelling, we approach the Mediterranean. A cold climate, on the other hand, is a steadying influence.

The emotional "transfigurations" of sensations and feelings can be isolated from their actualities, and then present themselves as "ideas." A mental sphere is evolved from the physical—an immaterial world, in which thoughts are inspiring stimuli. But ideas first arise as emotional "accompaniments." It is due to their presence that we are *conscious* of our bodily conditions, emotions and sensations. They are as essential an element of sensation and feeling as of thought. Their marvellous development is for consideration in the chapters that follow; and all that need be said here is that the ideas that haunt the "spirit-land" of thought excite emotion very acutely because they are its offspring; and words may be so exciting because they are the carriers of ideas.

Emotional energy can, then, be stirred by ideas and words on one side, or by bodily conditions and impressions on the other. Like the electricity of a piece of amber, it does not effectively exist until it is aroused, or "stimulated," whereas bodily life, although also subject to "stimulating" influences, runs continuously, as a timed "memorial" current. A stimulus is an experience which is pleasurably or displeasurably—enthusiastically or irritatingly—exciting *because it is harmonious or discordant*—a fact of which political speakers are very well aware. Harmony and discord are, then, conditions of vast importance. Our sensibilities to them are the regulators of our lives. Harmonies may be between two things that either run together or follow one another—that is to say, they may be in coincidence or sequence, distinguished in music as "symphonic" or "melodic." A further distinction is that they are objective or subjective according as they affect us physically or mentally. Objective harmonies are illustrated by the accord between a note of music and the third, fourth, fifth and octave above it, between a colour of the red, orange and yellow half of the spectrum and its opposite colour on the green, blue and violet half. There is objective harmony in rhythmic progress, in the procession of notes in a melody, in the cadences of literary style, in the alliterations and rhymes that add to the charm of poetry, in a landscape, a cathedral or a picture. Objective harmony is effectively exemplified by the correspondence that must be secured between a radio receiver and a broadcasting oscillator in order to render the receiver responsive.

Subjective harmonies are illustrated by the satisfaction of a want, the relief of a distress and the success of an effort. Of immense importance are the harmonies between our ideas of related successive events, as in the *just* sequences of reward and punishment upon goodness and badness, in the *honest* payment of what is due, and in *truthful* accord between facts and their expression. Hypocrisy, on the other hand, is so repellent because it is a violent discord between language, or manners, and feeling. The familiar is harmonious—as in the course of dishes at table. Hence, when we have become used to hypocritical politeness, we resent frankness. There can be subjective harmony between our sensations and our moods, between our impressions and our conditions. A compliment is so delightful because it harmonizes with our self-esteem. To one who is enraged, a storm is congenial. An uncouth or ill-drawn picture has charm if it harmonizes with an idealistic belief: to this much religious Art has owed its attraction. And emotion, through its revulsive elasticity, may use a discordant to generate a harmonious condition.

So pleasure is excited by the vicissitudes of gambling and of amusements in which apprehension alternates with relief. Hence comes the zest of danger.

Our emotional responses to harmony and discord are the pleasures and pains of conscious life—emotional states that, so to speak, reflect or echo them. But harmonies and discords only affect us through our *sensibilities* to them. Food and rest make no appeal to us if we have no appetite and are not fatigued. Music has no charm for one who lacks musical ear, and colours are vague to one who is colour-blind. We are, in these days, surrounded by "wireless waves." But they leave us untouched because we are not sensitive to them, whereas radiant light—their near relation—affects us very keenly indeed. We think too much of stimuli—or temptations—and too little of the sensibilities without which they are quite inoperative. And sensibilities are of great importance because they give such variety to life's enjoyments and pursuits. For they can be acquired, modified or lost under the influence of experience. It is, then, necessary to refer to them in some little detail.

They may be natural or artificial—that is to say, innate or acquired. We are *naturally* sensitive to the sweet, but *acquire* a taste for tobacco. Those that are innate may be born in us as actualities, or as potentialities that develop with growth. Of the first kind are those to injuries (felt as pain), to heat and cold, to the sweet and the bitter, to the satisfaction of feminine urges, and to satisfying relaxations from the strain of effort and the tension of surprise or suspense. A liking for rapid, or rhythmic, movement also seems to be innate—ministered to by the baby's cradle. Innate potentialities that develop with growth are illustrated by the arrival of the reproductive urge with puberty, and of sensibilities to the harmonies which are inherent in beauty and rhythm, are abstracted in our ideals, and are involved in the accord of success with purpose and of relief with comfort. The contraries of these harmonies are discordant afflictions. Theso innate sensibilities may be further distinguished according as they are constant, or recur in periods. We are at all times painfully sensitive to injuries. But our sensibilities to food, drink and sleep vary according as we are hungry, thirsty or fatigued. Other instances of periodic sensibilities are the "tropisms" of insect biology that have been mentioned in Chapter I.

To these innate sensibilities we add an immense number of acquired "tastes" in food, drink, intoxicants, dress, music and art that must be artificial since they vary, and have varied, from one country and period to another. New tastes can be adaptively grafted upon tastes already possessed—as, for instance, that for a new wine—through analogical kinships that are appreciated by intelligence. They are conserved by memorial familiarity—the force of habit. And, indeed, this force will enable one, by practice, to acquire tastes that have little affinity with existing ones—a taste for tobacco, for instance. Through habit we find harmony in the familiar. This is a point of importance. Briefly, then, we are harmoniously affected by the satisfaction of a sensibility, and this sensibility may be innate, may have become implanted by the memorial familiarity of habit, or may have been acquired through an intelligent adaptation of taste.

The difference between a temptation and a sensibility is that between the "objective" and the "subjective." The one—whether presented in sensation or in thought—originates outside us: the other is part of ourselves. Science is inclined to regard life as controlled by the objective because this is *measurable*, whereas the subjective eludes measurement. But the objective has no influence unless there is a subjective sensibility to it. This may be acquired through the familiarity of habit. But its independent existence is proved by the fact that it can come and go with time. An appetite for food, for instance, is periodic; so again is an inclination for sleep.

Both innate and acquired sensibilities vary in intensity from one individual to another. These differences can be detected when they affect appreciations of colour or music. In other cases they can only be inferred. Some persons are certainly less sensitive to pain than others. And the appreciation of moral harmonies is far from being uniform. The grip of an artificial taste—such as that for alcohol—varies in intensity. But in all cases the hold of a sensibility is so greatly dependent upon memorial familiarity—the force of habit—that it can be tightened or loosened by indulgence or restraint. That is to say, sensibilities are educable. They can be "reformed" if they are associated with the pain of punishment.

Harmony, objective or subjective, is, then, the mainspring of pleasure. But it is a striking fact—of much educational significance—that the most primitive and essential of our motives are the products of discords. The bodily urges, upon which the continuation and propagation of life depend, are all discordant. Their satisfaction is harmonious, and this leads us to pursue pleasure for its own sake. But there could be no satisfaction without the preceding discord of a *want*.

To return from this digression. We may, then, regard the feminine influence as a steady, driving pressure: masculine influence as a variable, elastic current. There may be the closest co-operation between these two forces. Emotional energy may reinforce bodily urges, converting passive attractedness into an active advance, shrinking into panic-stricken flight. But it may react[1] against these urges. Emotion may reverse apprehension into audacity, bewilderment into curiosity, the instinctive longing for peace into a fighting frenzy. The bafflement caused by a difficulty becomes a stimulus to effort, and a cringing acceptance of

[1] Emotional reactions and revulsions are the primary source of most of the ideas that are expressed by words beginning with the syllable "re." These ideas are enlarged by our experiences with things that are materially elastic—rubber, for instance. But their primary origin is within ourselves.

the injurious or the antagonistic is energized into angry irritation. The reaction which is primitively against our own fear, bewilderment or bafflement is externalized against the *causes* of these conditions. By confusing a cause with its consequence, the "subjective" becomes the "objective." The masculine element is, therefore, the source, not only of curiosity and effort, but of quarrelling and war. That these reactions proceed from emotional energy is proved by the fact that they commonly fail in conditions of ill-health or fatigue, and also under the passive conditions of sleep and hypnotism.

Emotional reaction underlies some of the processes which we attribute to the Will. Under this term we confuse three different activities. "Willing" may be simply compliance with the appeal of an attracted desire: it is in this sense that it is used, as an auxiliary verb, to express future happenings. It may be an emotional reaction against an obstructive difficulty that lies in the way of a desire or purpose. In this case it is an "effort" to overcome the near in order to attain the distant. And, thirdly, it may be a controlling power which *automatically* resists the effects of the torrent of impressions and feelings that falls upon us—which exclude those that are merely distracting—and preserves our "mental balance." This controlling power is necessary to the existence of complete consciousness. Our dreams are so eccentric and inconsequential because they are woven by Memory and Intelligence in freedom. One under hypnotic influence can receive impressions and can exercise thought. But he cannot reject suggestions however incongruous they may be. He is not, therefore, completely "conscious." The loss of this automatic control is one of the principal features of insanity. We need not wonder at the supreme importance that is attached to the Will.

The instruments of our bodily life—of our feminine aptitudes—are the organs of the body. Can we allocate to Emotion any organ of its own? We must not overstress the importance to life of its material instruments. During the chrysalis stage of butterfly life, the internal organs of the caterpillar—including its nervous system—dissolve into a featureless liquid from which is developed, without organic assistance, an entirely new set, suitable for an active winged life. A new machine comes into existence "out of the blank": a factory, so to speak, is reorganized without the use of a workshop. We possess, however, an organic peculiarity that certainly seems to coincide with our duality of nature. Our nervous system is dual—consisting of the sympathetic and the spinal systems. The former is undoubtedly charged with the service of bodily life—with the functioning of the internal organs. It is also intimately connected with the sensory organs. It will be objected that our sensory powers are centred in the brain, and that this appertains not to the sympathetic but to the spinal system. It is connected with the spinal system by a very elaborate "bridge." But it is linked more directly to the sympathetic system: and there are some very good reasons for holding that its primary affinities are with the sympathetic, and that it is, fundamentally, a *plexus* of the type that characterizes this system. For it shares with the sympathetic nerves a robustness which is lacking in the spinal cord and in its head, the cerebellum. It can be manipulated with astonishing immunity, whereas a touch upon the spinal cord or cerebellum threatens death. There can be recovery from the effects of removing part of the brain: indeed, dogs have survived for many months its total excision, eating, drinking and even getting angry. The spinal system, on the other hand, is shown by experiment to be associated with the development of energy in muscular movement, and may, not unreasonably, be regarded as the instrument of energy in general. It is an instructive fact that the construction of the cerebellum is peculiarly intricate in birds; and, by their flight and song, birds typically illustrate emotional energy in movement and in feeling.

There are, then, sound reasons for the conclusion that the cerebellum is the "broadcasting" origin of emotional energy. The apathy of sleep and anæsthesia would result from an interruption of communication between the cerebellum and the rest of the body. A switch, so to speak, is closed down, and dreaming is the consequence of its incomplete closure.

This table summarizes the capacities that may be ascribed respectively to feminine and masculine influences. It will be of assistance in digesting the chapters that follow:

Feminine	*Masculine*
Memory: Habit.	Intelligence: Imitation: Adaptation: Invention.
Protective motives.	Emotional spirits.
The bodily and sensory organs and their functionings.	The ideas that render us conscious of sensory impressions and physical conditions.
The reception of ideas.	The elaboration of ideas, and of thought.
The practical: Common Sense.	The sentimental: Idealism: Imagination.
The natural or vulgar.	The artificial or refined.
Care for the future: Prudence.	Present enjoyment: Play.
Common Sense reasoning from experience.	Reasoning from classes, rules and measurements.
Discipline.	Liberty.

CHAPTER III

THE NATURE OF IDEAS AND THEIR GENESIS

As to the nature of ideas, we can gather some clues from a tune which is "running in the head." It makes no *sound*: but we seem to "hear" it, and can "materialize" the notes at once by the voice or by whistling. The notes tend, indeed, to materialize themselves automatically. The whistling of boys, and the songs of the morning bath, are generally the spontaneous "sounding" of "note-ideas" that are passing in mind. The "note-ideas"[1] are not the notes, but have something in common with them, and can act upon us so as to generate them. What an extraordinarily close anology with the reception of a tune which is broadcasted! The notes that are brought by the wireless waves are immaterial and inaudible. Yet they can materialize themselves by affecting the electrical or magnetic conditions of a receiver.

Thought is obviously a current of ideas. But ideas are essential to a much simpler process than thought—to the *conscious* exercise of our senses. We have seen in the preceding chapter that every *conscious* sensation is accompanied, or "escorted," but an *idea* of it—an emotional "transfiguration" of its real character that may be likened to a broidered "vestment" in which a sensory impression must be "apparelled" in order to present itself in consciousness. These emotional "vestments," or "apparellings," also

[1] By listening to these "note-ideas" Beethoven could compose music that, owing to his deafness, he could never hear.

escort the internal experiences that we call our "feelings" —our motives, emotions and movements—and render us conscious of them. We can find in them the origin of the mysterious, immaterial "ideas" that present themselves in thought. An accompaniment evolves into an independent energy. This is one of the normal steps in evolutionary advances. Sound, for instance, begins as an accompaniment of material vibrations. But it reaches our ears as an independent stream of sonorous activity.

In the process of Thought, *replicas* of the ideas that serve as "escorts" to sensations and feelings evolve, so to speak, into a "flying squadron." Detached from their physical foundations they undergo some remarkable developments, and can present themselves in independent apartness. To employ another metaphor, they flow in a stream of their own, pouring from a spring-head of memorial or intelligent reproduction that may be spontaneous (as in "day-dreaming") or be controlled by a mental purpose. Ideas must, therefore, be distinguished according as they are *perceptive ideas* or *reflective ideas*. The latter are at their simplest in recollections.

There is an extraordinarily close parallel in electromagnetic conditions. It is indisputable that an electrified of magnetized body is surrounded (as with a "halo," or "aura") with an immaterial etheric energy, which extends beyond its surface, and has the power of electrifying, or magnetizing, any object which it can influence and is within its reach. Science terms this energy "electromagnetic force." It differs from electric or magnetic conditions in existing independently of matter: it will act in a vacuum. It ordinarily remains attached to the electrified or magnetized body which is its parent. But it may be thrown off into space by a sparking discharge, or by an oscillating current, and then becomes known to us as "wireless waves." Without forcing the analogy too closely, we may conclude that there is a similar connection between sensory impressions and the perceptive *ideas* that they generate—between physical stimulation and its mental offspring. And there is a curious resemblance in the fact that, as electro-magetism can be dissociated from the electricity or magnetism that generates it, so the ideas generated by sensation can exist and develop apart from sensory stimulation, so as to form reflective "thought-streams" which have a separate existence. Perceptive ideas and reflective ideas correspond in fact with electro-magnetism that remains attached to an electrified body and electro-magnetism that is broadcasted.

We can follow this analogy further. It is evident that we should become conscious, or "aware," of our experiences and thoughts if we "received" the ideas that accompany the one and constitute the other—as a radio-apparatus receives wireless waves. If different classes of ideas were received by different parts of the brain, there would be an explanation of the curious localization, in the brain, of its connections with particular faculties. And, since ideas might conceivably spread to, and be received by, another's brain that was sympathetically "in tune," there would be a clue to the understanding of the mysteries of telepathy.

It may seem impossible that we should act as the receivers of ideas that are generated by ourselves: it would be as if an electric oscillator, or broadcaster, received the waves that were broadcasted by itself. But this difficulty disappears if we recognize the essential duality of our nature, and connect ideas with the masculine, and the brain with the feminine, element. It may be objected, again, that ideas, being immaterial or etheric, could not affect us sensibly. But we are undoubtedly susceptible to certain kinds of immaterial stimuli. Radiant light, for instance, is immaterial. But it is "caught" by the eyes, and even by the skin.

A "duplex" combination of generative and receptive processes is illustrated with extraordinary aptness by the radio-gramophone. By the action of rotary momentum on a gramophone disc and needle, sounds are generated: they are communicated, as disturbances, to an electric current, and are, then, audibly uttered, or "broadcasted." The response of the gramophone diaphragm to the movements of the disc and needle corresponds to sensory impressions: the resulting sounds to ideas: the electric reception of the sounds to consciousness, and their utterance to speech.

A fact which it is difficult to realize is that our sensory perceptions as well as our "feelings" are perceptions of our own conditions—that is to say, of ourselves. Our physical states, such as hunger or thirst and their satisfaction, are obviously parts or phases of ourselves: they are, in fact, one with ourselves, and in becoming conscious of them we become "aware" of ourselves. So again with our motives, emotions and movements: if I move a finger it is myself that is the moving "strength." A little consideration will show that our sensory impressions of touch, taste, smell, hearing and sight are also phases of ourselves. They are impressed upon us by things that are outside us. But they are the *consequences* of these things upon ourselves that are not identical with their causal origins. A visual image that is formed on the retina is part of ourselves just as that formed on a photographic plate is part of the camera. The sight of a tree or the sound of a violin are really internal conditions of our own. This is proved by the persistence of visual sensations after their source has been withdrawn. This is only momentary. But it suffices to convert a succession of separate sparks into a connected line. The continuity of a light is not interrupted if we rapidly blink at it. We "externalize" our impressions—confuse them with their causes, and regard them as features of the outside world—because they are associated with the outside world by our *movements*—a point which will be explained later on. Sensations are, in fact, "feelings" of a sort. But they reveal conditions that are "objectively" forced upon us by our environment, through our sense-organs, whereas our *feelings* reveal conditions that "subjectively" arise within ourselves. Both are perceived by us introspectively, as conditions of ourselves that are attended by ideas. But, since they are of different origins, they must be distinguished in name. It will be convenient to limit the term "intuitive" (or "inward") "perception" to subjective feeling, characterizing objective sensation as "sensory perception."[1]

It is a point of great importance that, since our intuitive perceptions originate in ourselves and not in imprints from outside, their emotional presentments are nearer actuality. Our sensory perceptions are demonstrably untrustworthy. Those of touch are more reliable than those which are received through our ears and eyes. The evolution of these organs from sensibilities that were primitively located in the skin has added immensely to the *distances* at which things can be perceived. For touch—external and internal—and for taste, physical contact is required. The sense of smell extends perceptive power to furlongs, the sense of hearing to miles, the sense of sight to millions of miles. But as perception lengthens its range, it loses in direct instructiveness. Unless interpreted by recollections or inferences that are derived from *movements*, sounds and sights—and even touches—are quite meaningless. Vision, as the most refined of these developments, is liable to be the most misleading. But all our sensory perceptions need mental interpretation. The most poignant of our tactile sensations is that of *pain*. But it tells us little or nothing of the injury or derangement that actually causes it.

We rank sight so highly amongst our senses because its pleasures play so large a part in our lives. But, unless amplified by past experiences of movement, it tells us very little indeed. If ideas of distance, direction, shape, size and solidity were the products of vision, the blind would not possess their very accurate knowledge of them. Those

[1] In French the two are compared and distinguished as "sensations" and "sentiments."

who have been enabled, by a surgical operation, to use their eyes for the first time see at the outset nothing but a kaleidoscopic medley of forms and colours, the arrangement of which shifts with every movement of the head.[1] It is described by them as "pressing against their eyeballs"—being, in fact, inside not outside them. It is "externalized" by the *movements* that are involved in touching what they see, and little children spend much of their time in establishing this connection. And, by moving towards these externalized visions, inferential ideas of distances, direction, shape and size become memorially associated with visual ideas, and are reproduced by them as "perspective." Our senses of vision and hearing become sources of knowledge. But only as ancillary to ourselves. What wonders Helen Keller has done without them!

Visual perception is, indeed, absurdly deceptive. A train passing a view presents itself as a view passing the train—its details varying in velocity with their distance, the nearer moving more rapidly than the distant. And distance presents itself as a reduction in size.[2] Misrepresentation reaches its height if the view includes an object which is also moving: its motion is deceptively quickened if it meets the train, deceptively retarded if it is moving with the train. Such are the difficulties with which Astronomy contends in discovering the realities of apparent movements in the skies.

There are a multitude of facts to show that what we see depends very greatly upon the ideas that are before us. In fact we "receive impressions" through our eyes, but "see" with the Mind. One who is under hypnotic influence

[1] A well-known case in point is that of a young American clergyman named Hanna, who, after a long period of unconsciousness following a violent concussion, gradually recovered his sight in advance of the faculty of reproducing in thought the ideas that interpreted what his eyes presented. (*Multiple Personality*, by Sidar and Godhart. Appleton.)

[2] The optical angular measurement of an object indicates a certain ratio between the tangible measurements of its diameter and its distance, so that, if one is known, the other can be calculated. If the angular measurement is one degree, the ratio is 1 to 57.

will see a walking-stick as a snake if this idea is suggested to him. The unrealiability of sight is, indeed, established by the conflicts of evidence that occur in the Law Courts. Perfectly honest witnesses may disagree very materially upon what they have both seen. For we see for the most part, "what we expect to see" by inference, and there are legal authorities who would refuse to accept the statement of any eye-witness unless circumstantially corroborated. We must, therefore, suspect the evidence of those who take part in spiritualistic *séances*—especially when these are held in the dim light. How easily are our eyes deceived by a conjurer, and our ears by a ventriloquist!

From these uncertainties and errors, some philosophers have concluded that we have no means of knowing what things really are—that we live in a fantastic world of unreality that is made by ourselves. But this deduction—so disconcerting for scientific inquiry—goes far beyond the facts of experience. It results from the tendency to regard the senses of hearing and sight as the "windows" through which we look out upon our surroundings. They open the way—it is true—to an immense amount of pleasure. But—to carry on the metaphor—they are *painted* windows that transfigure the daylight; and it is fortunate, for the safety of our lives, that we have other more reliable means of enlightenment.

The most useful of our sensory perceptions are those of active touch. But in themselves they tell us little of the world around us. To be instructive, they must be assisted by intuitive perceptions, or *feelings*, of our various *movements* and their varying strengths—of the resistances that we encounter and the impacts that we receive. Moreover, our feelings give us ideas of *energies*, which can be extended to the outside world, and introduce us to our environment, not through passive submission to its effects, but by energetically acting against it. We use an extraordinarily large vocabulary in referring to them, since they differ with the point of view from which they are regarded, as well as in their phases. We refer to them as our "spirits," "temper" or animating "soul"—as our "passions," "moods," "emotions," "efforts" and "will." We metaphorically materialize them in thought as "our nerves," or as "our heart"—as in "heart-felt." They are all phases of the *emotional* energy which in the preceding chapter was brought home to the masculine element of our nature. Our intuitive perceptions are particularly illuminating when they inform us of the *movements* to which emotional energy gives strength. We feel a movement, not as the workings of the various muscles that serve it, but as a manifestation of "strength" exercised in a certain direction, over a certain distance and with a certain velocity. It is felt as something immaterial—as a phase of the "spirit of movement" rather than of material movement—as a vital not a muscular activity—capable of exerting not only a *pressure,* such as that of Gravity, but a *pull.*

Now these intuitive perceptions, or feelings, differ from sensory perceptions in that they introduce us to energies in themselves, not merely to the sensory *products* of external energies or stimuli. They are perceived directly—not through their consequences—and are therefore reliable. Our external senses can tell us of Sound, Light and Gravity only indirectly through their products in hearing, sight, weight and movement: but our own Strength we can feel in itself, as well as the movements that it produces. It will be shown that we owe to these intuitive perceptions the origins of some of our most important ideas—those of energy, of space, of time and of causality. But the points upon which I now wish to insist are that we owe to it our ideas of *movement* and its consequences, and that it is through movements that we are brought into true relations with the world outside us. It is through movements that we "externalize" sights and sounds that are actually within ourselves, and so convert the "subjective" into the "objective." We feel our movements in *themselves,* and know their strengths, directions and durations, quite apart from the things with which they bring us into tactile[1] contact. So long as we touch nothing there is emptiness or "space." When we touch something, there is resisting "substance." By the combination of movements with touches we gain ideas of *things*—of textures, solidities, shapes, sizes and weights—and of the *movements of things*, which must be in accordance with reality. For, if not, life would be quite unliveable. We should be in continual collision with the objects that surround us and be crushed by moving obstacles that crossed our path. It would be impossible to cross a street through moving traffic, or even to find passing room along its pavement. Our ideas of these external antagonisms must, therefore, be in accord with reality. The proof of their truth may be "pragmatic." But it is indubitable. Sensory *movement* is the fundamental source of our knowledge of the material world around us.

It is only natural that the energy, or "spirit" of movement, should be our clue to reality. For it is the typical activity of animal as growth is of vegetable life: its production seems, indeed, to be the primary achievement of animal energy. Amongst primitive creatures movement is incessant — if only in the vibration of *cilia*. It serves as an instrument for the venting of vital excitement. But it becomes *purposeful*, as movements of approach or avoidance, in response to stimuli that are harmonious or discordant. Higher up the animal scale it takes a change of phase—becomes disconnected from material movement—as *motive* and *emotion*. In ourselves, we can feel that motives and emotions possess some kinship with movement: this is, indeed, implied in their names. "Motives" imply movements as their consequences, and "emotions" move us physically as well as mentally.

[1] We generally think of tactile movements as of the *arms*. But those of the legs are, at least, as important. It is by walking that we gain ideas of other than short distances, and of the changes in visual perspective that accompany changes of distance.

As a further development, Thought appears. It possesses some curious *liaisons* with movement. Both can be initiated and swayed by an effort of will, whereas no will-power can generate or extinguish an emotional motive. We cannot rid ourselves of fear, anger or love by an effort: we can do no more than control their manifestations. There is, also, the illuminating fact that movement and thought are alike in their effects. Both establish new connections, or relations, between two things. A movement, however objectless, connects the place of its start with that of its finish: it generally has the effect of giving some external object a new relationship in space. A thought similarly establishes a new connection between two ideas by "ascribing" one to the other, if it is merely the ascription of a "feeling" to oneself. The ascription may be complicated by a host of descriptive details. But it is the motive of every thought, and therefore of every sentence. And, finally, it is in common experience that thought can *take the place* of movement. We can find relief in thinking of an action without proceeding to it.

These facts seem to indicate that the moving current of thought has gradually evolved from the emotional spirit of movement, and attends it as electro-magnetism attends electricity. The current is "figured" by ideas as wireless waves are "figured" by the various peculiarities that convert themselves into sounds in the receiver. The energetic current of thought would be evolved from the energy of movement. This conclusion gives the doctrine of Evolution a far profounder significance than when it is limited to the development of material organs. For these are, after all, only *instruments* which are employed by life's energies in order to adapt themselves to various environments. There is more depth and completeness in a law which traces life's growing complexity to a growing sublimation of life's energies in themselves.

It is, then, to be concluded that our acquaintance with realities comes to us, in most part, through the process of internal, intuitive, perception that is commonly called "feeling." This gives us first-hand information of ourselves and of our material surroundings. Its neglect by psychology is the reason why this science has remained so superficial and unsatisfying. Volumes have been written on the sensibility of our faculties of touch, sight, hearing, smell and taste, and on the results of attempts to measure its degrees. But the revelations that come to us through intuitive perception have been most imperfectly explored. They are incapable of measurement, and are, therefore, scientifically uninteresting. But we owe to them, not only our perception of movements, and of the *space* that affords room for them, but our fundamental ideas of *time*. It is true that the source of external Nature abounds in timed successions—the rising and setting of the sun, for instance. But the successions of changes and intervals which affect us most intimately are those of our own lives—the periodic insistencies of hunger, thirst, fatigue and other physical urges, and the periods of "waiting" which from time to time delay their satisfaction.

Moreover, it is from experiences of ourselves that we receive our primary lessons in the pressure of *necessity*, the chances of *possibility*, the incalculability of *accident*, the contrast between activity and passivity, and the achievement of *possession*. We owe to them, again, our most primitive ideas of *causality*—of the relief of hunger and thirst by food and drink and of fatigue by sleep, of injury as the cause of pain, and of injury as the consequence of rashness and folly, and of scolding words and blows as the consequence of anger. And still more important is the information which we gather from ourselves as to the existence of *energies*. By the external senses these can only be detected indirectly—by inference: the sight of one running gives one no idea of his energy unless we collide with him. But within ourselves we are conscious at first hand of energies which, we can feel, exist independently of their material consequences because these can be suppressed whilst the energies are irrepressible. They do not conserve their characters or intensities: they come and go, rise and fall. They are in direct contradiction to the self-conserving Energy of science, that is of such great mathematical utility.

By external perceptions through the "five senses" these impressions of self are extended to the outside world and vastly elaborated. Our own energies warrant us in attributing energies to Nature. Ideas of substantial form and texture are completed by ideas of the colours, sounds, odours and tastes of things, that are perceived as their "qualities." Space is visually partitioned off into places, distances and directions, and movement is appreciated as a succession of changes of place, as well as an energy. Ideas of time are extended by our observation of the course of Nature, of birth, growth and death, of changes of season and weather; and we obtain a wider view of timed successions in development—not merely of those of cause and effect, but those of derivation, as of origin and outcome, of material and product. These combine with our intuitive perceptions of movement to teach us the changing character of the world in which we live, and its products in points, periods and directions of time—towards the past or towards the future. Our relations with our fellows bring home to us that life consists of passivities as well as of activities, of hinderings as well as helpings, and demonstrate the close dependence of our happiness and unhappiness upon the conduct and language of others.

But these observations would leave our understanding quite incomplete were they not supplemented by the *analogical extension* of conditions of our own to other persons and objects. It is, indeed, by this process that we distinguish them as "individuals." They are presented to us in sensation as impressions of various and varying shapes. We invest them with separate existences by analogically extending ideas of our own individuality to them. And we go further, we endow them with the various conditions that are signified by verbs—vitalities or phases of existence—

that are analogically derived from our own. When we notice a tree as "standing" or "waving" or "being tall," we are investing it with activities that are analogous to our own. That is to say, we interpret the outside world through ourselves. Clearly, it is only by associating feelings of our own with external appearances that we "understand" the personalities that are presented to us in pictures by a cinema film and on the stage. It is obvious that this process contributes essentially to our comprehension of things. It will be considered in more detail in the chapter following.

There is a third—very distinct—phase of perception which may be termed "comparative." In this process perceptions are not merely received and appreciated, they are *compared* either with other perceptions, or with ideas that are mentally presented by being analogically reproduced through connecting resemblances. The immense importance of comparative perception is very imperfectly realized. Comparison is initiated by the unifying force of a resemblance between two things, and brings out differences in other respects, including those of "more" or "less." We owe to it our ideas of equality, of differences in quantity or amount, and some of the most abstruse of our conceptions. "Value" is the result of comparing two things in respect of the pleasure or advantage that they offer. Comparison reveals likenesses, as when we perceive that a stream is "running," or that another's disposition is "asinine": also distinguishing differences and those which show the occurrence of changes. The likeness may be that of a ratio between two pairs of numbers or quantities which render the "rule of three" so useful an instrument of calculation —or that between correlative contraries, neither of which can exist without the other. There can be, for instance, no victory without defeat, no superiority without inferiority, no father without a son, no external activity without a passivity; and it is the likeness between these correlatives that enables one to suggest the other.

Comparison also reveals *degrees* of difference—shows differences to be, not only of more or less, but of *amounts* of more or less. These degrees of differences may be in the particularity or generality of things in space, of occurrences in time, or of mental identifications and classifications. Such ideas as those of "all," "some," "few" express degrees of generality in space: those of "always," "often," "seldom" degrees of generality in time: surnames and proper names, generic and specific names, the definite article, possessives and demonstratives express degrees of particularity in identification and classification.

The standard of comparison may be the *idea* of a normal: adjectives and adverbs expressing intensity, in size, weight, amount ("large," "heavy") or in the velocity of movement ("rapid"), always involve comparison with "class normals." What would be "large" for a dog would be "small" for a donkey: what would be "rapidly" for a horse would be "slowly" for a motor-car. It may be an idea of number, abstracted from the comparison of different *numbers of things*—of the fingers, for instance—with one another. It may be an artificial unit of measurement, as when we perceive that a thing is "a foot long." Our fingers and arms, as well as our feet, provide us with simple ideas of such units. A double handful[1] is probably the origin of the pound. And still more suggestive is *pacing*, for this involves the rhythmic repetition of a unit. We assuredly owe to it the minutes and seconds into which the hour is divided. For a processional march of two miles an hour takes approximately 3,600 paces, and 60 is the square root of this number. Rhythmic movement can be translated into the graduation of a measuring scale, precisely as spoken language can be reduced to writing. The evolution of measurement from the pace has had an extraordinary effect on modern thought. In pacing, space is measured by rhythmic movement. Time can also be measured by rhythmic movement, as by a clock. And,

[1] Cf. "a good pounding."

by contrasting units of space with a unit of time, movement itself is measured as *velocity*. Time and Space are, accordingly, both measured by movement, and movement is measured by a combination of time and space. This *liaison* between the two underlies, beyond doubt, the relativist idea that one may be a function of the other. But this notion is in cloudland. It is the fruit of an ingenious elaboration of hypothetical thought. Space and Time are, in fact, contraries: the one is a series of places and distances that exist in coincidence: the other a series of happenings and intervals in succession.

Now it is obvious that the process of comparative perception is closely akin to that of inferential reasoning. If, for instance, we feel that it is "unusually hot" for the time of year, we are drawing an inference, or deduction, from the comparison of the heat that we are experiencing with an *idea* of the usual temperature. If, again, we notice that a boy "has grown" since we last saw him, we are inferring this conclusion from a comparison of his present appearance with a *recollection* of his appearance in the past. In both cases we are going upon the results of a comparison. This process develops into the "reasoning faculty" through which we derive assistance in divining the unknown, or in forecasting the future, by drawing inferences from mental "standards" that are offered us by our knowledge, doctrines, beliefs or units of quantity. Their pronouncements are in terms of possibility, probability or certainty, of necessity or obligation, and so provide us with ideas of immense importance. They may be used as qualifying distinctions; or they may enter into a verb as phases of existence—as "can," "may," "will," "must," "ought."

And since we are conscious of the passage of thought, we can form ideas of its processes—of Memory, and of Intelligence with its instruments in Identification, Comparison and Inference.

To conclude with a general reflection. It is sometimes

said that man, in his conduct, is the "creature of his environment." This is true only if we understand by his "environment" the *ideas* that are emotionally derived from his physical self and his surroundings, are elaborated by his intelligence and are transmitted to him by the words of others.

CHAPTER IV

THE DEVELOPMENT OF THOUGHT FROM FEELING, SENSATION AND INFERENCE

WE are accustomed to regard the ideas which occur in thought as essentially different from those which give "consciousness" to feelings and sensations. They differ, it is true, in the degree of their elaboration: the ideas which are the subjects of thought are commonly "generals," "indefinites" or "abstracts," whereas those which come to us in perception are "definite" or "particular." But the one, as we shall see, is evolved from the other. And the process of *inference*, which is the principal instrument of thought, commences in perception. We "recognize" a familiar object or experience by identifying it with an *idea* of it which has been formed on a previous occasion and is reproduced when the object again presents itself to the senses. That is to say, we *infer* that it is the same because it is identical in appearance. If the object is not familiar, there occurs the thought, "What is it?" We endeavour to solve the question by identifying the object with a class, or kind. This again involves inference. For we deduce from the class the object's general character and name.

The process of inference, therefore, is a feature of perception, whether this be intuitive (as, for instance, in regard to the origin of a pain) or sensory: indeed, we not uncommonly identify it with perception in its consequence of "knowing." We "know" that there are matches in a box by shaking it. It is, as we have seen in Chapter I, the process by which we connect sensory and intuitive perceptions with reality—that is to say, we convert the "subjective" into the "objective" by externalizing it. It serves to connect feelings with their causes and consequences—irritation with the person who excites it, and a man's manners towards us with his feelings towards us, for instance—and movements with their origin in energy, or "strength." We have seen that it is by inference that we invest our visual impressions with substantiality by associating them with experiences of movement, and appreciate distance through the comparative sizes of perspective. It is inferentially that we connect our experiences with what must have preceded, or will follow them, and "know" that if corn-crops are heavily laid, there *has been* heavy rain and there *will be* difficulty in harvesting them. In all these cases we mentally link an incident with a "standard" that is derived from experience, and infer that what preceded or followed the standard has preceded or will follow the incident that has been analogically connected with it. This method of reasoning is appropriately called "common sense."

The perception of an object is generally followed by a *thought* which "ascribes" some distinguishing attribute to it through the use of a verb. This ascription is always some idea of vitality, or of some phase of vitality, if it be only bare existence ("is"). We comprehend other persons by inferentially uniting them with some vital conditions or activities of our own, through analogies between their appearance and our own when under the influence of these conditions or activities. We have no immediate perception of their internal conditions, and "invest" them with such vitalities as our own by intelligent metaphor. We extend this process to all things, whether inanimate or animate. If we pass in review the conditions which we ascribe to the various things on a tea-table, we shall find that they are represented—more or less nearly—in ourselves. There is little that can be said of a milk-jug that cannot be said of a man. It may be "transparent." But a man is this when his features betray his emotions. We can invest things with shapes and colours that are not our own by considering these attributes to be phases of existence, and with activities that are not our own—"flying," for instance—by regarding them as phases of the animate energy which we ourselves possess. Moreover, since phases of vitality come and go, ascriptions must always be "timed." The grammatical instrument of ascription is the verb, and the meaning of a verb always includes that of a point or period of time.

Accordingly, a verb ascribes to its object[1] the possession of some attribute or other in present, past or future time. Nevertheless the ascription is always in the present. It "presents" itself so that a series of thoughts is a series of "presentments" like the changing pictures of a cinema. Perception and thought are out of relation to the sequences of time. This explains the curious fact that we lose count of time when we are engrossed with observation, or are immersed in thought, whether this be our own, or is prompted by listening to the speech of another, or by the words of a newspaper or book. We are aware of the passage of time, not through perception or thought, but through the changing current of our own conditions, or "feelings." It is, then, necessary to use a special contrivance for the mental introduction of time into perception and thought. This is the investment of past and future conditions, or happenings, with the *qualities* of being looked back upon, or looked forward to—of being behind us or in front. This is, however, a link in *space*, not in time, and consequently perception and thought deal with time in terms of space. "He came" means that "coming" is ascribed to him, looking backwards. Most of the prepositions that express "timings" are the same as those used for points and distances in space. In like fashion we use *qualifying*

[1] In reflective thought termed "subject."

adjectives and particles to express situations in past or future time. A participle, such as "departed," *qualifies* a verbal condition by its timing. "Frictional" heat represents friction as a coincident quality of heat, whereas, actually, it *produces* heat in causal succession. In "painful news," again, the news is "qualified" by its consequence. We call clothes "warm" because they are "warmth-giving." This confusion of cause, or consequence, with quality is very evident in some scientific conceptions —as that, for instance, the *product* of a force is its "coefficient."

The simplest of perceptive thoughts consists, then, of an individualized *object*, and a "vital" condition of some sort that is ascribed to it by being mentally unified with it. Both object and ascriptive union may be greatly elaborated by descriptive detail: this may be drawn from inference, as that "the blackbird's nest is one of last year's." The ideas that "present themselves" in the course of a perception may, therefore, be classed—according to the rôles which they play in perceptive thought—firstly, as individuals that are the objects of perception; secondly, as timed ascriptions of vitality, with which objects are united; thirdly, as descriptive particulars which amplify, define or qualify either the object of perception or the ascriptive union; and, fourthly, as links in relationship which bring these particulars into connection with the object or the ascriptive union. The first are represented in language by nouns and pronouns: the second by verbs: the third by adjectives, possessives, demonstratives, participles and adverbs; and the fourth by grammatical unions, by prepositions, and by conjunctive and comparative particles. In analysing the process of perception we are, then, dissecting the grammatical constitution of sentences: we are investigating the foundations of grammar—the most primitive of mental "arts." This is a laborious and tedious undertaking, which is, moreover, complicated by the fact that, by undergoing small modifications, ideas can change the rôles that they play in the composition of a thought. It is for this reason that a thought can express itself in such different fashions. One may think of a view, for instance, that "it is *pleasing*," "it *pleases* me," "I am *pleased* with it," or that "it gives me *pleasure*."

First, now, of our ideas of *individuals*. The perceptible world around us seems to consist of persons and objects, living or lifeless—that is to say, of "individualities," possessing a "substantive" existence, apart from their surroundings. But, strange though it may appear, these individualities, while actually in accordance with reality, are figures created by the Mind, and are not directly perceived, as such, by us. The outside world presents itself to our sense-organs as a congeries of various and changing "conditions." We are, however, acutely conscious of our own separate individuality. Our "apartness" is forced upon us by the fact that we perceive ourselves inwardly or intuitively, whereas our perception of other persons and things is external. Our intuitive perceptions, or "feeling," establish a continuing identity: we are the same persons to-day as we were years ago. This is what is called our "personality." We inferentially extend this notion of continuing separate identity to anything which can be held to exist apart, and even to parts of things that seem to be detachable. That the Mind is capable of this process of "individualization" is evident from the fact that it individualizes things which have in reality no "substantive" existence—numbers and quantities, for instance, which have only a mental existence apart from the things that they specify. "Fragility" cannot exist in reality apart from a fragile object. Yet the Mind individualizes it. And, indeed, it is only by mental individualization that persons and objects *can* exist as continuous individuals. For they change their appearances, attitudes and situations so frequently that very little *particular* continuity is preserved. The conclusion is unavoidable that the individuality with which we invest the objects of perception is of mental creation, although it is in general accord with actuality. There are, moreover, curious facts to indicate that we mentally individualize external persons and things by likening them to ourselves. One is the "animism" of savages and young children, which attributes to their toys and to inanimate objects generally such feelings as their own. Being individualized through one similarity to ourselves, it is assumed that they possess other similarities. Another remarkable illustration of this "animism" is the attribution of *gender* to inanimate things. There is again the curious notion that, by eating the flesh of an animal, man can be infected with its peculiar quality—with the courage of a tiger, the timidity of a hare, the uncleanness of a pig. Growing intelligence shakes off these fantasies. But man owes his capacity for creating the imaginary, fictitious personalities of Art to the fact that he individualizes others by a mental, not a sensory, power.

This process of individualization, it may be remarked, brings together into combination a vast number of different conditions, qualities and attributes. Our ideas of most individuals are, in fact, highly complex "idea-combines." What a number of different qualities are, for instance, brought into combination in our idea of a motor-car—or even in that of a chair. Its *purpose* is, perhaps, the most distinctive of them.

In this fashion we endow with individuality not only our external perceptions, but our internal feelings—our energies of motive and emotion and their material consequences in movement—anger and a blow, love and a kiss. So again are individualized the transient harmonies and discords of pleasure and pain. Arguing from our own energies, we individualize those which must exist in the outside world—light, heat and gravity, for instance.

In the next place, of the *ascriptive* ideas that are signified by verbs. The vitalities which we may ascribe to an object may be those of acting or being passively acted upon, of internal conditions of excitement or energy, or of appearance ("seeming"). They are very commonly phases of existence—that is to say, existence that is qualified by descriptive particulars, as, for instance, of shape, or colour, of situation in place or time, of origin or outcome. They may be comparative conditions, as of "resembling," of being "more" or "less," or of differing in measured degrees. They may be inferential conditions of possibility, probability, certainty, obligation or necessity which is coupled with an idea of existence in the verbs "may," "can," "will," "ought" and "must." They may be negative conditions.

It is by a mental process that these ascriptive conditions are united with their objects. We use reasoning inference in uniting other persons with emotions and motives such as our own, for the appearances which serve us as analogies are identical with our own. But our inferences become more and more imaginative as we endow with vitalities other animals, plants and things which are really lifeless. When we see that a tree "is fresher" than it was, "waves" its branches, or "sheds" its leaves, we are attributing to it vitalities of our own which are certainly not possessed by it but resemble those which are manifested by it, although proceeding from very different causes. That is to say, we "perceive" our surroundings by mentally animating them. We can "think" of them in the same artificial manner—animating them reflectively instead of perceptively; and, by a further development, can think in this fashion of purely abstract subjects.

The ascription made by a verb, being drawn from life, must be *timed*. This, as already explained, is effected by regarding situations in time as a *spatial* quality; traces of this process can be detected in vulgar language. By the use of participles, in combination with timed phases of existence (auxiliary verbs), time can be spatially described apart from the timing of the ascription. The verb "having" is employed to connect an object with a past condition because one can be figured as "possessing" his past. Hence "it has withered" means that it is connected in the present with a past condition, the effects of which continue. The ascription of a future (or "forward") condition is effected by the use of the verbal *purposive*—commonly called the "infinitive"—omitting the preposition "to" and employing "will" or "shall," since purpose is ordinarily the consequence of a wish, an intention or an obligation. Or we may employ "going to" as expressing a future condition, using the analogy between the march of movement and of time. In the Romance languages a future condition is ascribed as the *possession* of a present intention—as in parler*ai*—I *have* to speak. Other successions than those of time are also statically expressed in this fashion. "Becoming," "moving," "retreating" and "reasoning" are all *progressions*. But they are expressed as static conditions with implications of "direction."

Thirdly, of the *descriptive* details that are used to particularize, or qualify, the object of perception, and its ascriptive union. These qualifications are very various and complicated. They may be distinguished accordingly as they are directly perceived, or arise from *comparison*. To these must be added distinctions that are contributed by memory or by inference.

Distinctions that mark the course of our own motives, emotions and movements (as, for instance, an *angry* movement) are directly perceived by intuition, and may, by analogy, be attributed, as distinctions, to other persons and objects. Our perceptions of being pleased or vexed, of purpose, of activities and passivities, are obvious in themselves, as also those of the object, method and instrument of an activity. So, again, are perceptions of simple "sensory" qualities—of textures, shapes, colours, sounds, scents and tastes. And it is by direct perception that we distinguish an object, or occurrence, as being associated with, or conjoined to, something else.

Distinctions arising from situation, direction and

distance in Space, or from position, direction (past or future) and periods of Time, are also obvious in themselves when they are detected by the intuitive perception of our movements and our feelings. There is nothing comparative in our experiences of distance and direction in touching things, or in the appetite which tells us that it is lunch-time. But they become comparative, or "relative," when their perception is assisted by vision: "perspective" results from comparison. And they are plainly "relative" when they are appreciated by comparison with a standard of measurement—whether in yards and miles, or in minutes or hours. This introduces us to the use of *comparison* in perception. Its importance has already been stressed. It is the origin of our capacity for estimating and measuring. The standard with which a thing may be compared may be another thing (a "rival"), a total, a normal or a scale of measurement. In all these cases the comparison is reflective, not perceptive, unless it is made by the actual juxtaposition of the things compared.

The subject of comparison is a *quality* or *quantity* that is possessed by the things that are compared. When we conclude that one flower is brighter than another we refer to the flower's *colour*. Our appreciation of differences enables us to perceive comparative distinctions of "more" or "less" between a quality or quantity and another with which it is contrasted, and the excess or deficit is graduated by estimate as "rather," "much," or "little," strengthened in the case of the two latter, by "very." Or it may be estimated in terms of one or other of the things compared, as when we conclude that one is "twice as large" as the other. Superlative degrees result from comparisons with totals that may either be perceived or exist in idea.

We consciously use a *normal* as a standard of comparison, when we perceive that a man is "taller than ordinary." But our unconscious use of normals is much more extensive than would appear. For distinctive attributes may be relative—that is to say, comparative—although they are expressed in absolute terms. Some of the adjectives in commonest use—those of size, weight, velocity, or intensity—express degrees of comparison with mental normals or units. These normals vary with the class of things to which they apply. What would be "large" for a shrub would be "small" for a tree: what would be "fast" for a horse would be "slow" for a motor-car: what would be "long" for a call would be "short" for a sermon.

Attributes signifying degrees of multiplicity or quantity in space, and of frequency in time, are also derived from comparison with ideas of totals, continuities, or normals that are mentally elaborated. They may be expressed by adjectives or adverbs. There is a comparison with totality in *space* in "all," "most," "some," or "none," and with continuity in *time* in "always," "generally," "sometimes" and "never." "Many" and "few," "often" and "seldom," on the other hand, are deduced from comparisons with normals, which vary with particular circumstances or periods. "Many" in church would be "few" at a football match: "often" in a week would be "seldom" in a year.

Degrees of quality or quantity are measured when they are compared with units of *measurement*. These may be multiplied by *numerical* units—or numbers—used either successively, as in counting, or in numerical groups. The use of both kinds of units has been suggested by experience. But their development has been due to mental elaborations which will be discussed in the chapter following. Inches or numbers have no real existence apart from the particular object which they qualify. They are mental "abstractions" that are materialized by being embodied in scales, counters, or figures.

A distinction which is more important than it may seem is that between the particular and the indefinite—that is to say, between a thing as a definite object, and as the indefinite representative of a general class—between *the* tree and *a* tree. All perceptions are "particulars": they are of *the* things which we are perceiving. The attribute of being "a" tree cannot come to us by simple perception, for it owes its existence to a mental process of elaboration that occurs independently of perception. Hence the indefinite article simply means "one," and in some languages is altogether lacking. Particularity[1] is signified by names or pronouns, by demonstratives and possessives and by defining adjectives and ascriptions, as well as by the definite article.

Memory aids perception by suggesting distinctions that arise from the connection of an object, or an occurrence, with a particular possessor, antecedent or origin, consequence or outcome. These connections in succession are, as we have seen, viewed as "qualities." And it is to inference from experiences that we owe—amidst much else—our appreciation of the possible, probable, certain, the obligatory and the necessary, signified in the verb by the auxiliaries "may," "can," "should," "ought" and "must."

It is to be added that a tentative perception may be reversed into a negative if it is contradicted by another source of information.

In the *fourth place*, of the links in relationship which bring these various particulars and qualities into connection with the things to which they apply. The simplest of them is union by "adherence." In this manner the object of an action is connected with it as its "accusative"—that is to say, as its "causative." Some primitive people have been unable in all cases to differentiate object from action: in Cherokee, for instance, there are separate verbs to signify washing oneself, and washing one's clothes. Adjectives, participles, adverbs, the definite and indefinite articles, demonstratives and possessives are all united adherently to the ideas that they qualify. The union may be tightened by imaginative assimilation in gender.

[1] "All" is definitely particularized as "every" and "some" as "certain." "Any" is the *indefinite* particularization of "all."

There are, however, many other devices for connecting a thing with that which it particularizes. Particularization may be by possession (or "having") or by being possessed ("mine") by situation "in" the quality, if it is an emotion or a mood, or being conjoined to it ("with"). A thing may be defined either by that from which it springs—its class, or kind, origin, cause, material, or beginning ("some of my friends," "pieces of timber," "the son of Charles"), or by that which springs from it—its particularity, possessions, consequence, outcome or end ("a flock of pigeons," "the owner of the motor-car," "the father of Charles," "a war of disaster"). The genitive preposition "of" (for "off") is commonly employed as the connective, with extraordinarily multifarious implications: as a forward link to a cause or origin, it means "coming off" ("the scent of lavender," "the handle of the jug"): as a forward link to a consequence or outcome, it means "giving off" ("the object of his visit," "a test of purity"). It is, therefore, like many adjectives, a qualificative or static expression of successions. But it can also be used to define a thing by its coincident qualities, as "a man of means," "a work of art"—meaning, it seems, in this case, "showing off." Prepositions are attachments for the connection of one idea with another in various relationships. These may also be signified by postpositions, or case endings, as in "John's umbrella." Our ideas of these relationships are clearest when they are spatial, and consequently spatial prepositions are largely used to signify relationships of other kinds. Purpose, for instance, is signified by "to" or "for," meaning "towards" or "fronted by": method, as in associative conjunction, by "with": instrument by means of "by" meaning "juxtaposed." The prepositions used to signify times ("at," "in," "before," "during") are for the most part spatial.

Simple conjunctive association is signified by "and": "or" implies comparison with an alternative that is connected by a resemblance. One can take an umbrella *or* a walking-stick, but not a walking-stick *or* a coat. Identity is expressed by "as" or "the same as," also by relative pronouns and conjunctions that are used to identify something in an explanatory thought with something expressed or implied in another thought. The demonstrative "that" is also used in this identifying sense. "Yes" identifies one's own condition or conclusion with the suggestion of another. When an object that is compared with a standard of any kind, exceeds or falls short of the latter in a quality, the standard may be brought into conjunction in either of three methods that illustrate very strikingly the ingenuity of mankind. One may turn one's eyes from the standard to the object that is compared with it, from the object to the standard, or may identify the two, and these three methods are used, respectively, in Latin by the ablative, in English by "than," meaning "then," and in French by "que," meaning "as." The conjunction "if" introduces supposed or hypothetical conditions; "although" and "but" emphasize a reflection by stressing the incompatibility of its predecessor, or its own inconsequentiality.

Perceptive thought may be *interrogative*. We often ask ourselves a question when in doubt as to what we see or hear. A doubt may arise as to the attribute—or some particularity of the attribute—which is ascriptively united to a known subject, or *vice versa*. "What is that noise?" "Where does it come from?" for instance. In this case a question is put by the interrogative use of a relative conjunction. It may arise as to the existence of an ascriptive union between a known object and a known attribute. We express this by putting the ascriptive link in the forefront—"Is it an insect?" The solution must be searched for through a clue—"Has it six legs?"

CHAPTER V

THE ELABORATION OF IDEAS

The term "abstract" is generally limited to such highly sublimated ideas as those of "Time" and "Space." We shall find, however, that—recollections apart—all the ideas that feed reflective, as contrasted with perceptive and imaginative thought, are the products of a mental process of "abstraction" by which the accidental or peculiar is eliminated, leaving the essential as a remainder. Recollections of various feelings, sensations and deductions that have an element in common are refined by the elimination of their individual peculiarities, leaving their "subsisting" common element—or "essence"—outstanding. This process of refinement is what is meant by the terms "conception." New ideas are "brought to birth."

However improbable this may appear at first sight, the materials of the ideas thus elaborated can all be traced to intuitive or sensory perceptive experiences, or to inferences that are drawn from them. The evolutionary process of refining abstraction, or elimination, by which perceptive ideas give birth to reflective ideas, or "concepts," eludes consciousness as completely as the workings of purely physical intelligence or of digestion. But we are conscious of its results, and can infer its nature from them. It is as though we could only learn of the generation and growth of the creatures in an aquarium by observing those which rise to its surface. If, however, we realize the action of Intelligence in initiating comparisons, we can follow the steps by which this refinement comes about. Two ideas (one of which may be analogically reproduced by the other) are drawn into comparison by an identity which exists between them. The effect of the comparison is to "disintegrate" them. Differences between them are "brought out," or isolated, as their respective distinctive *qualities*: the identity that unites them remains as something which is characteristic of both, or common (or "generic") to both. Below the differences which distinguish a horse from a dog there is the subsisting resemblance that both are quadrupeds. This process of comparison leads by progressive steps to the evolution of ideas of increasing subtlety. From a multitude of particular perceptions of an individual, there is formed a *definite idea* of the individual as a continuity. Perceptions of a multitude of individuals give rise to ideas of *classes*. From a class emerges the idea of an *indefinite* individual as representative of the class. And the evolutionary process culminates in the production of the quintessences that are termed "abstract ideas."

Ideas are *definite* when they represent particular individualities or personalities, including our own. Ideas of individualities differ widely from recollections. For we may have many various recollections of the same object or person—including ourselves—differing in accidental or passing details. Recollections of ourselves vary with our moods and activities. And on each occasion that we meet a friend, we receive a different impression of him—conveying different details of his manners and dress, attitude and situation, and our idea of him would be a confused multiplicity of recollections were they not refined by the elimination of features that are transient, or accidental, and the concentration of essentials. Through the action of Intelligence one recollection of him analogically reproduces another: various recollections are then brought together and compared; and, by their comparison, such features as they all possess are assimilatively unified and their differences eliminated. By this process their "essence" is extracted as a consistent idea of him, which is *definite* in representing a particular person, and is accordingly distinguished by the person's name, by the definite article "the," or by a description ("a man whom I met yesterday"). It is not the result of "generalization," for this means the grouping of individuals into a *genus* or class. Nor is it an *average*, for it is the product of addition and subtraction, not of addition and division. It is the idea by which we identify or recognize a person or thing in perception. For it is analogically reproduced by the perception, and the two are united, since the more detailed is included in the less detailed: the perception is "absorbed" by the idea. It is by a similar process of elimination and assimilation that one forms an idea of "oneself."

The next stage is the process of *generalization* properly so called. Through their similarities, ideas of particular persons or things are brought together into classes which are signified in language by the use of plurals, or of the word "kind"—as in "mankind," for example. Differences between them are eliminated, as in the case of definite ideas; and there results an idea of *class*—a "generic essence"—representing the features that are held in common by all the members of the class. We use these ideas in *classifying* objects. Qualities are classified like objects, their classes being expressed by adjectives. "Red," for instance, includes a large number of different shades of the colour.

From the class is further evolved an *indefinite* idea of a unit-individual of the class—that is to say, a representative of the class is individualized. From the general class "mankind" is derived the indefinite idea of "a man": from the general class "red," an indefinite idea of "a red colour." This is commonly termed a "general" idea. Here again there is a misapprehension—a confusion of an outcome with its origin. An indefinite idea is evolved from a general idea. But the two are quite distinct. If "a man" signified "mankind" the indefinite article—meaning "one"—could clearly not be applied to it. The word "general" is, in fact, confusedly employed in two senses —to contrast the indefinite with the definite, as well as the general with the particular.

The vagueness of our ideas depends in degree upon the variety of the perceptive ideas and recollections that contribute to its formation. Our idea of a "giraffe" is fairly distinct. On the other hand, our idea of the "tree-kind," or of "a tree," is nebulous in the extreme. Apart from size, it includes little but a notion of "growing." The idea of "a dog" is, in the main, that of its character, the idea of a chair one of its function or purpose. "Something" and "anything" illustrate extreme refinement: both are indefinite ideas, the former representing the individualized essence of all things of a certain class; the latter representing the individualized essence of all things. So indeterminate, indeed, are the ideas used in thought that they may seem to consist of nothing beyond the words that express them. Not so. The word for "dog" in an unknown tongue means nothing to us. Behind the word there must be a "meaning" of some sort, however subtle.

Definite ideas are "real" in that they correspond with actual sensory experiences. General ideas—those of classes—are so far connected with reality in that they originate from actual similarities between things or between qualities. Indefinite ideas are unreal mental figments. "A man" does not exist except in the Mind. It is owing to their unreality that general and indefinite ideas are so useful in thought. For since they are not linked to particular individuals, objects, or experiences, they can be used detachedly in thinking. This is a point of immense importance. An idea of one's own dog, for instance, would not enable us to think of another person's dog, if it had never been perceived by us, or to wonder whether he has "a dog." A general idea of "dogs" would, no doubt, carry our thoughts farther afield. But it would not enable us to individualize what was outside our experience. On the other hand, the indefinite idea of "a dog," being detached from any particular experience, can be used in any connection. And it can, reflectively, be converted into a definite idea by a name or description of some kind ("Ponto," or "an Alsatian dog," for instance)—a particularizing "trick" which imaginative thought turns to much purpose.

So far as we can judge from their behaviour, the lower animals—however intelligent they may appear—possess very imperfect power of generalization, and lack the more advanced faculty of forming indefinite ideas. Their ideas, when not simple recollections, are mostly definite, and are attached to particular experiences. A dog that has learnt by experience, in the course of random efforts, that he can open a gate by lifting a latch with his nose, can only apply the knowledge to the particular gate, or to a gate that closely resembles it. He cannot use his knowledge to open a latch of a different pattern because he cannot see that the latter is of the same *kind* as the former—is, in fact, a latch which can be opened by a process analogous to that by which he can open *the* gate. He cannot be denied the possession of a mind. But if his faculties are described as "mental," those of man are certainly "hypermental." Man's birthright is a capacity for gradually refining ideas into "idea-essences" of increasing subtlety. Abstracts are very imperfectly grasped during childhood. And in some backward peoples, the capacity of refinement has been imperfectly developed. They cannot, for instance, think of a number apart from a number of *things*.

The formation of ideas of definite and indefinite individualities, and of general classes, involves the progressive isolation of all attributes but the essential. In conceiving of our own individuality, for instance, we eliminate from it our transient vital conditions of motive and emotion, activity and thought, of age and appearance. These become detached *attributes* of ourselves. Similarly, in forming ideas of the individualities of other persons and things we exclude the transient in concentrating the essential, and isolate, as attributes, their accidental features of appearance, of situation in place and time, and their connecting relationships. General and indefinite ideas are then formed of these attributes, as they are of individualities, by progressive steps of refinement. The indefinite idea of "going" is a refinement from a vast number of experiences, and can, therefore, be used in a variety of different senses: the indefinite idea of "red" is an extract from many different shades of this colour, and that of "in" an extract from many different phases of inclusion. These attributive essences are, then, individualized: "going" as a verb becomes "going" as a noun, "vain" becomes "vanity," "solid" becomes "solidity," "red" becomes "redness,"[1] "more" becomes "excess," "towards" becomes "direction," "of" becomes "origin" or "offspring." An attribute may, indeed, be individualized as a "substantive," immediately it is isolated, so that its adjectival form is derived from its individuality. "Vicious," for instance, is derived from "vice" and is subsequently individualized as "viciousness." The vocabularies of different languages show that the use of this line of development has been irregular and inconsistent.

In this fashion the varying conditions of existence, as disclosed by perception, become individualized in mind as indefinite existences. Indefinite ideas are formed of directions, distances and areas in space, and of points and periods of time. "Life" is isolated from the things that are endowed with it. The essences of mental faculties are indefinitely individualized as "memory," "intelligence" and "comparison." So again are the mental results of comparison. "Analogy" is the essence of the effects of all samenesses between two things in bringing them into comparison: "justice" the essence of all harmonies

[1] The termination "ness" signifies something more than the individualized essence of a quality. It has an implication of *possession*. "Solidness" is not quite the same thing as "solidity." It implies the existness of something that *is solid*.

between what precedes and what follows; "humour" and "wit" the essences of contrasts between the dignity of the mental, or the *pretended*, and the vulgarity of the real, and between the obvious meaning of a word and a meaning that can be put upon it.

This mental process of sublimating refinement culminates in the development of the individualized ideas called "abstracts." These may be described as the quintessences of certain branches of experience from which all qualifying, incongruous, or discordant, features have been eliminated. Indications of their evolutionary origin are almost completely distilled away, and they stand forth as absolute and eternal continuities, or verities. In words they are distinguished by capital initial letters. There is more dignity in Space than in a "a space," or "the space," in Truth than in "a truth," or "the truth," in Liberty than in "a liberty," or "the liberty."

Certain of these abstracts are of strong emotional interest and are exceedingly stimulating, inspiriting, or "elevating." They are called "ideals": they are also "idols," for they can inspire feelings that lead to fervent self-disciplinary, loyal, aggressive and missionary endeavour in political and private life. They may present themselves as visions of excellences or as qualities that are attached to ourselves, to other—it may be imaginary—personalities, or to objects and experiences, as "beauty" is to a landscape. In all these cases they excite the enthusiastic liking and pursuit that are distinguished as "admiration" and "ambition."

Ideals evoke this emotional enthusiasm because they are essentially *harmonious*: they represent phases of harmony—sharply distinguished from corresponding phases of discord—which from time to time capture the feelings of mankind—as do the various actors in a drama—and lead masses of them in very diverse, and often contrary, directions. To classify them is difficult and indeed impossible unless one probes into their evolutionary origin, and this seems to involve some degree of disrespect. They will be illustrated in some detail in the chapters following, and here a brief notice will suffice.

Harmonies, as we have seen in Chapter II, are *objective* when they are between two outside experiences, *subjective* when they are betwen an outside experience and ourselves. Subjective harmony is illustrated by success: also by the accord of familiarity, which is so potent that habit may actually impart a charm to the discordant in music and to the ugly in art.

The mental identification of others with ourselves is subjectively harmonious. It leads to sympathetic fellowship—that is to say, to Unity as contrasted with alienating discordances. It is illustrated by the Golden Rule—to do to others what we would they should do unto us. It manifests itself in Loving-kindness, Generosity, Charity and Pity—also in the narrower feelings of party, or secretarian, spirit and Patriotism. The ideal of Peace is also subjective: it is harmonious with the deeply seated longings of our feminine nature, since it bears with it an assurance of *future* security. Hence Custom is idealized as a conservative force. Under a conservative policy we know what to expect. This is the origin of our respect for the laws of our country, for its conventional morality, for the manners and dress of our class, and for the observances that constitute "Good Form."

To be sharply distinguished from this conventional morality is that which is idealized as Ethical principles. These are *fundamental* harmonies that occur between successions of events—in the following of one thing by another that accords with it. These appeal to all mankind, irrespective of custom. Truth is a harmony between the mental—or artificial—and the real: Honesty, one between word and deed, and between what is received and what is repaid: Virtue is a harmony between behaviour and the obligations of morality: Justice a harmony between conduct and its reward or retribution: Gratitude a harmony between favours and their acknowledgement: Loyalty and Constancy are in harmonious accord with affection and respect. There is also a harmony in Revenge which renders it so attractive. The "æsthetic" ideals of Beauty and Elegance are objective when they represent harmonies between various elements of sensation. These are subjective when the harmony is between our sensations and our feelings. And, since harmony may be merely a subjective accord with the familiar, standards of Beauty may vary with the fashion of the day.

The most stirring and influential of ideals are, however, those that are derived from experiences of success and failure. Success is harmonious both in the glow of triumph that follows it and in its accordance with the desire that preceded it. As a feeling of shame, the humiliation of failure is, on the other hand, one of the most discordant of sufferings. From the evolutionary point of view, success and failure are of immense importance. For, in the lack of instinctive aptitudes, man must rely upon them in making the experimental discoveries that have progressively developed material civilization. He must also rely upon them in learning the discoveries that have been made by others. But it is an irony of Evolution that the fruits of Success may be poisonous as well as nourishing. Pride inspires: but it also misleads. Ambition opens out the future: but it may also wreck it.

The glow of pride that follows a success is one of the most delightful of experiences. To realize this one has only to listen to the conversation in a golf-club house. One can be proud of small, as of great successes. Indeed, some of us may remember the pride of first buttoning our own clothes. To one who "takes a pride in it" the daily round of work may be as inspiring as a glass of whisky or a football match. The solving of a problem may be as exhilarating as the establishment of an athletic record. Nor must it be forgotten that a great success is won by subduing oneself—by self-control and self-abnegation.

By its "static" view of "current" changes the Mind drifts very easily into the confusion of things with those that precede and follow them. Hence the glamour of success is extended to ideas of its causes and consequences. Its causes are all phases of Power—such as courage, strength, skill, eloquence and numerical preponderance. Power may be over oneself—that of Self-control—the indispensable instrument of Duty, and of the enduring resistance of Patience. These causes are idealized, for they are as emotionally stimulating as the success from which they spring. As our own possessions they arouse the self-admiration of pride, or self-complacency: as the possessions of others, they provoke admiration and respect. The *consequences* of success are still more complicated. They are typified by Superiority, Dignity and Worth. Decency is an ideal because it harmonizes with human dignity, and the same harmony, from a different point of view, raises the self-expression of Liberty, Equality and Democracy to ideal rank. These, again, may be possessed by ourselves, or by others, exciting, respectively, pride and admiration. There are other remote consequences, in the attitude of others, from which our success can be *inferred*. Such are Honour, Glory, Fame and Notoriety—all phases of *succès d'estime.* And success can be won by being mentally associated with the successful—the success which is pilloried as "snobbish."

Estimation and measurement are amongst the most distinctive of human capacities. Estimation begins with the elaboration of *normals*—as standards of comparison—and develops into measurement by the elaboration of *units* of measuring, counting and reckoning. Normals are in constant use for the estimation of degrees, as when we think that "the heat is greater than usual for the time of year," or that a dog is "large for its kind." In the preceding chapter we have seen how important is the part played by these normals in comparative perception: they underlie the meanings, not only of adjectives that are employed in terms of comparison, but of a number (such as "large") which take the appearance of "absolutes." Ideas of them are formed, it seems, by the use of successive experiences in amplifying or reducing vague ideas of intensities in feeling and sensation (varying with the kind of object or experience to which they apply) and vague ideas of durations in space and time—and of multiplicity in the one and of frequency in the other—that are connected with occasions of different kinds. A normal, accordingly, differs from an arithmetical *average*.

Measurement takes the place of estimation when comparison is with units instead of normals. Ideas of measuring units probably sprung from coincidences, or trials, in experience. There are natural units in the pace, the foot, the finger-span, the last joint of the thumb, and in single or double handfuls. Ideas of their qualities as measuring units could be isolated from them, since, *as things*, they varied with the persons who employed them, whereas their *utilities* in measurement remained unchanged. There followed the mental conception of standard units which could be embodied in artificial scales and measures. That is to say, experience suggested thought, and thought suggested experience. Measures are used by the application to them of numbers which may be successively counted, or used in groups. These appear to have first presented themselves in the fingers and thumb—the primitive origin of the decimal system. The joints of the four fingers would suggest the standard of 12, their joints and ends the Indian standard of 16. Ideas of numbers, like ideas of measures, were isolated from these material symbols by comparisons. "Oneness" or "fiveness" may be common to a number of objects and can, therefore, be dissociated from them. The material origin of this evolution is indicated by the fact that the divorce between numbers and things is still incomplete: we still speak, for instance, of six "head" of cattle.

Once isolated, numbers could be conceived as existing in groups, like the fingers, or as following one another in rhythmic succession like the steps in pacing. Their conception introduced man into a new world, peopled by units and groups of units, which afforded scope for interesting exercises in calculation, and was at the same time of assistance in the practical concerns of life. Ideas could be formed of ratios, of quantities that existed merely in relation to other quantities, and of the various complexities that are the materials and instruments of the science of Mathematics. But these are not realities: they only exist as shadow-shapes in the Mind.

A remarkable faculty of Thought—possessing a superficial resemblance to electrical activities—is that of changing ideas into their negatives or contraries. These are sometimes confused. But they are really quite distinct. "Dissatisfied" means something more than "unsatisfied." A negative may be likened to a "stop": a contrary to a "retreat" which takes the place of an "advance." We negative by nullifying an ascription or attribution: we contrarify by converting it into its opposite. Contraries are illustrated by the minus quantities of algebra. These are not "lacks" but "owings."

Experience involves the process of negativing when a tentative ascription or attribution is arrested by further observation or inference. The suggestions of another are similarly arrested when they are out of accord with our conclusions, beliefs or states of temper: a naughty child negatives everything. Contrarification, on the other hand, is the conversion of one element of a contrast into the other. There are contrasts—termed "correlative"—in relationships of space and time ("in" or "out," "before" or "after"), in succession (cause and consequence, father and son), in the result of antagonisms (victory and defeat, superiority and inferiority), in commercial exchange (selling and buying, credit and debit, profit and loss), and in feelings and motives (pleasure and displeasure, clinging to and shrinking from). Collaterals automatically suggest one another in mind, since the existence of one depends upon that of the other.

The processes of negativing and contrarifying are primarily involuntary, but become voluntary in accordance with a rule of momentous importance—that, in conscious life, the spontaneous may be repeated by a purposeful effort. A smile is an involuntary manifestation of pleasure. But we can smile at will, if we please.

So far of the elaboration of ideas from materials that are supplied by perceptive experiences. The process extends to inferential deductions, made in the course of perception, which give us knowledge of things that we cannot directly perceive. Some of the most influential of our ideas are drawn from this source—amongst them our conception of the Future, the Probable and the Possible. As we have seen in Chapter II, we are *physically* compelled by the feminine element of our nature to pay some regards to future interests, and this instinctive urge contributes to the formation of prospective ideas of future occurrences. But our *idea* of the future is elaborated by the Mind. We are assured by Memory that the past was once the present—that the past has given way to the present—and, by intelligently identifying the present with the past, we infer that present experiences will in their turn be succeeded by others that are in the unperceived beyond. By the abstraction of these expectations, definite and indefinite ideas of a Future are formed as "subsisting remainders," which enable us to live in prospect as well as in the present. Man becomes subject to a mental environment—quite distinct

CHAPTER VI

THE INFLUENCE OF THOUGHT UPON EMOTION, MOTIVE AND MOVEMENT

WE are conscious of the existence of ideas when we are *thinking* under the promptings of Memory or Intelligence. But ideas, as we have seen, also enter into the process of conscious perception, although in this case they merge themselves in their material background. We are also influenced by a current of ideas when we are listening to, or reading, the words of another. Our thoughts are dictated instead of self-presented. But they are by no means the less stimulating on this account. Words are received by us sensorily: they impress us through hearing or sight. But they affect us only as "idea-carriers." If they are in an unknown tongue, they leave us unmoved. We are, then, under the influence of ideas when *consciously* perceiving, thinking, listening, or reading. But when thinking, listening, or reading we are confronted with an "artificial," immaterial, and, maybe, very fantastic environment: we become subject to an influence resembling that of "wireless waves," which may move us quite independently of our actual experiences, or bodily conditions. So, when racked by pain, we may think, or read, of Paradise.

Since ideas are immaterial, we hardly realize their stimulating power. They may affect our physical nature by generating either (1) their physical *replicas*, or (2) their *consequences* in feeling or action. The first of these processes is popularly called "auto-suggestion." In very sensitive persons the idea of a sensory impression or physical condition may generate it in actuality—may convert the "subjective" into the "objective." Persons of a certain temperament can "visualize" their ideas—if they think of an exciting object, can actually "see" it—can even conjure up a physical pain or illness, by thinking of it. This is, indeed (as we shall see), the process by which ideas of *movement* automatically reproduce themselves in conduct or speech.

The effect of an idea is, however, very different when it generates, not a physical replica of itself, but a consequential effect, as when, for instance, the idea of a motor drive pleases us or prompts us to take one. In this case its influence may be conveniently termed "provocative." In common speech this is confused with autosuggestive influence in the word "stimulation." But this obscures a distinction of essential importance.

The provocative effect of an idea is, in the first place, to excite an emotion of pleasure or displeasure—sometimes called "pain." This is on the masculine side of our nature, and may be figured as a state of expansive or contractive energy. It becomes *impulsive* by drawing into action a feminine motive. This may be one of "clinging" or "shrinking" in the present, or of "searching" or "avoiding" in the future. In either case there is a sequence of two causal successions.

The provocative ideas are of *causes*. For emotions can hardly be excited by ideas of themselves: we cannot throw ourselves into love, grief or triumph by simply thinking of these feelings. Pleasures and displeasures are therefore associated in mind with their causes, and are regarded as of different *kinds*. But the pleasures that are given by a meal, a concert, a game of bridge, or an appealing sermon, are all alike in being emotional "upsprings"; and we recognize this in applying the same word—"pleasure"—to all of them, distinguishing it as "of the table," "of music," "of amusement," or "of inspiring uplift." The pleasure that comes from the satisfaction of a *want* primarily appeals to the feminine side of our nature and is less emotional than the pleasure that "inspires." But we should not *feel* a satisfaction unless it was accompanied by emotion.

Physical pleasures that arise from harmonious bodily conditions or sensory impressions are shared by us, in great measure with the lower animals. But the Mind improves upon them by adaptively elaborating from experience a vast number of different tastes or sensibilities. It also provides us with more artificial pleasures of a purely mental origin. These may be distinguished as Revulsive, Idealistic and Imaginative. Those of the *Revulsive* kind are the products of harmonious emotional "rebounds" that follow the sudden relaxation of a strain, the dissipation of an anxiety, or the disappearance of a bafflement. They include the pleasures of amusement, in their myriads of phases, and those given by humour and wit. But by far the most notable of them is the glow of success, which, as we shall see, is of vast evolutionary importance. *Idealistic* pleasures are aroused by ideals—harmonious mental abstracts which may be so exciting as to intoxicate. Amongst them is that of Sympathy—springing from the analogical identification of ourselves with others, which, as we have seen in Chapter III, plays a necessary part in perceptive life. It makes us sharers of their joys and sorrows. *Imaginative* pleasures are peculiar in that their primary origin is not in the effect of thought upon emotion, but in the effect of emotion upon thought. They will be separately discussed in Chapter VIII.

Pleasure-giving, or pain-giving ideas (as already mentioned) affect motives as well as emotions—the feminine as well as the masculine side of our nature. They provoke a succession and an after-succession; masculine emotion is kindled by a sensation or thought, and feminine motive is aroused by masculine emotion. Motive gives their effects a *practical* bent. They become "impulsive"; their exciting causes become "objects" of present attachment or repulsion, or of pursuit or avoidance in the future.[1] The two impulses differ in the *timing* of their outlook.

A *present* attachment is one of *liking*, or "loving"—an impulse that manifests itself in such "tactile" ways as by kissing, caressing, embracing or hand-shaking, or by such kind treatment as we would show ourselves. If the liking is for things, it prompts us to possess, or appropriate, them. Should this emotional attachment be not very strong, we call it "sentimental." A sentimental affection lacks force: it is more an inclination than an impulse. If the emotional pleasure is of an "idealistic" kind, a like becomes enthusiastic as *admiration*. This also takes a practical turn. It manifests itself by the earnest attention of adoration and by decorating or glorifying its object—that is to say, by imitatively fulfilling what must be its wishes.

A liking that affects *future* conduct is a wish, or desire. The pleasure that is provoked by its object becomes "prospective," or anticipated. This again manifests feminine influence. For masculine emotion is in the present: an urge to "search for," or pursue, its cause—as an "object"—is a development of practical foresight that comes from the feminine side of our nature. We are impelled to "realize" the prospective pleasure by converting the idea of it into a perceptive experience through seeking it, or pursuing it—a motive that we feel as a *purpose*, and very commonly confuse with the process of "willing." If the prospective idea is idealistic, or imaginative, desire takes the enthusiastic form of *ambition*. This again presses for realization, and may achieve it not only by acquisition, but

[1] Ideas of *physical* pleasure which do not merely accompany actual perceptions can only move us *in the present* as recollections or imaginings. But they can urge pursuit in the future, like ideas of mental pleasures. We can "look forward" to a good dinner.

by "serving" the ideal—as by conforming with that for which it stands, or by extending its influence—or by expressing it artistically in painting, sculpture or music.

It is ideas of prospective pleasures and pains that excite the emotions of Hope and Fear—the former if realization is pleasing and probable, or displeasing but improbable—the latter if it is displeasing and probable, or pleasing but improbable. Probability is an expectation based upon inferential reasoning from the past—unless it is merely the offspring of irrational optimism.

Future prospects may be of a more substantial character than mere thrills of joy or distress: they may be of *material* gains or losses. Through the satisfaction or dissatisfaction that follow them, these become pleasurable or painful. But they influence us fundamentally as mental counterparts of practical feminine urges. The appreciation of "empty" pleasures—present or prospective—is, on the contrary, predominantly masculine; and it is a remarkable fact that these two different tendencies should alternate so markedly in controlling the lives of individuals and nations. Under the influence of mere pleasure, life is that of a butterfly, fluttering in sunshine over a flower-bed. But the butterfly's careless *insouciance* was preceded by the practical activities of its caterpillar life. In man this sequence is reversed. It is the young that lead a butterfly life: with maturity comes the serious outlook of the caterpillar—often, however, interrupted by reversions to the butterfly stage. These remarkable changes testify to periodic and occasional fluctuations in the relative strength of masculine and feminine proclivities. Judging from experience, we may infer that the feminine motive of practical purpose is strengthened when the present is dull, and the future is secure—that is to say, offers trustworthy expectations of a continuing advantage. The effect of these circumstances may be prolonged by habit. On the other hand, masculine emotions take command when the present is gay or when the future is uncertain or obscure. These emotions can, however, be excited through the body by alcohol. And the development of sensibilities that accompanies the spread of sophistication is a powerful impetus to the invention of new pleasures, their enjoyment and pursuit.

Under the lure of pleasure life becomes so extrordinarily varied because pleasure varies so greatly in its phases and in its power of appeal. Its origin is a harmonious accord between a physical or mental *experience* and a physical or mental *sensibility*, or a revulsion from a discord between the two. Its character being determined by its cause, it is constantly evolving into new phases with the invention of new causes—new dishes, new dresses, new music, new games and entertainments, new objects of ambition and new ideals. These are harmonious, because, with the development of cultured life, sensibilities multiply themselves as their provocatives increase.

In this comparison pleasure has been contrasted with "business." But since business satisfactions are mentally pleasurable, we are led by visions of pleasure whether our aims are practical or merely enjoyable. There follows a momentous effect upon the object of life. Except during such catastrophes as famine and war, or under the pressure of dire poverty, man is drawn by harmonious ideas instead of being driven by discordant urges. His mind offers him such a relief from these painful constraints as is not enjoyed by most of the lower animals. He seeks food, for instance, not to satisfy hunger but to gratify tastes of the palate. Life changes its outlook: pleasure is its lure instead of pain being its warning. It is even by the pursuit of pleasure that one is "good"—by the pursuit of the pleasure that is provoked by moral harmony, and of the self-congratulation that follows its achievement. A pleasure is so attractive that, in the absence of discipline from outside, or the obstacle of a countervailing inconvenience, man cannot be drawn from its pursuit except by the eclipsing prospect of another pleasure. Fortunately, this may be the triumph of self-control. This may enable him to cultivate a new sensibility which may conquer an enslaving obsession. "Willing" as opposed to desire, or ambition, is simply a reactive effort, which enables him to confront and overcome an unpleasant obstacle that stands in the way of a pleasure —as, for instance, the payment of a price for a purchase— or to subject himself to a pain that is less threatening than another that looms ahead—to face danger, for example, in preference to cowardice. As a result life becomes optimistic. In business, sport and war we think of victory, not of defeat; and, when confronted with trouble or difficulty, are apt to turn our eyes aside from it to discover an excuse for its occurrence, or a means of escaping from its effects. This feeling has now banished from religion ideas of the devil, of hell, and even of repentance.

The chains by which prospective pleasures draw us are riveted on the Mind by the persistent recurrence of ideas of them. This gives continuity to the feelings that they excite—may, indeed, render them obsessions. Love is fed by visions of the beloved object, as is revenge by those of an injury. Sexual appetite is converted from a periodic into a perennial obsession. Our self-esteem is constantly reinforced, until it becomes, if not the strongest, at least the most durable of our feelings. It is by the persistency of thought that joy is prolonged into happiness, grief into misery.

Leaving these generalities, let us now trace in rather more detail the influence which ideas of present and prospective pleasures have had on man's achievements and conduct, and on his relations with other men.

To begin with physical pleasures. Ideas of prospective physical comfort have been the lode-stars which have drawn men from cave life to the construction of houses and furniture. It is a prospective idea of avoiding cold that led to the invention of warm clothing. Associated with points of time—such as meal-time and bed-time—ideas of prospective satisfaction take the place of hunger, thirst and fatigue in regulating the routine of life. It is to ideas of prospective punishment and its avoidance that the State owes its powers of repressing crime. Ideas of future sensory pleasures have urged the development, not only of cookery, but of the various forms of industry and commerce, as well as of amusement, from dancing and music to dog-racing and the cinema. A reference suffices to the far-reaching consequences of the passion for alcohol.

In the next place of pleasures that are of Revulsive origin. In its primitive phase, revulsion is an automatic emotional—or " nervous "—rebound, such as, in mindless creatures—and in our physical selves—converts fear into courage and bafflement into curiosity. The current of thought—whether spontaneous or suggested—may bring depressing or disconcerting ideas in its train, that are followed by others which immediately relieve them; and relief is followed by an elastic expansion that is much more energetic than the preceding contraction. This provides life with the diversion of *amusement*, which can thrill dullness into smiling gaiety, and can actually make use of confusion or anxiety as " fuses " for the firing of explosions of laughter. It relieves the boredom of monotonous regularity. By these revulsions of feeling, tragedies, comedies and farces can keep the spirits pleasantly tingling: the most tragic of dramatic incidents is, after all, only " make-believe," while the essence of the comic is contrast. *Humour* is a revulsion from the impressive effect of the dignified or artificial which is caused by the abrupt intrusion of the vulgar or natural, as when an impassioned speech is suddenly interrupted by a hiccough. This is a descent from the sublime to the ridiculous—ridiculous because our own self-esteem or credit is not involved. A sense of humour is a " saving grace " because it detects the artificiality of ideals that seem to be overwhelmingly impressive. In *wit* a revulsion follows the dispersal of disconcertment or confusion by the sudden comprehension of a word's double meaning.

When the incongruity is between the success of ourselves—or our "side"—and failure in a prolonged struggle for victory, the oscillations of feeling are too sustained to be catastrophic, and the outcome too personal to be laughable. But they render games of all kinds absorbingly exciting: we are thrilled by successes—and by hopes of successes—when contrasted with the chances of failure. The frenzied shouts of a football crowd testify to the emotional violence of its ecstasies. In solving puzzles constraint is similarly relieved by hopes of success. In racing and gambling we pit ourselves against the ups and downs of chance; our spirits blench under losses; but thoughts of past wins, and hopes of repeating them, restore, and indeed increase, their elastic tension. One who makes a bet buys hope at a price which is generally below its emotional value to him. It is revulsion that gives spice to adventure.

The passion for amusement grows with civilization as a protest against its mechanical artificialities. It stamps itself on the country in theatres, cinemas, gambling clubs, race-courses and playgrounds. In England, at the present day, the amount annually spent upon cinema tickets reaches forty million pounds. Man thinks much less of the inventors whose intelligence has benefited him so materially than of those who beguile him by providing amusement or kindling enthusiasm.

From Revulsive we pass to Idealistic pleasures. The exhilarating uplift of Idealism is one of the strongest of human motives. For an ideal excites admiration in the present, and pursuit in future. In the preceding chapter it has been defined as a harmonious quintessence from which all discordant or incongruous elements have been distilled. The truth of this description is established by a very familiar experience. The ultimate foundations of sexual and maternal love are instinctive: but a lover "idealizes" the mistress of his heart, and a mother the children of her womb, and, consequently, neither of them are conscious of any defects in the objects of their affection. They see them through a halo of excellencies. For ideals are not only exhilarating in themselves. They may be attached, as qualities, to persons or things—including ourselves—and in each case they " adorn " their possessors. They stimulate an admiring love, which becomes a practical motive. It leads, in the present, to the " adherences " of admiration, glorification and decoration—an urge which no one can deny who has given the girl of his heart presents of jewellery. And, in the future, it impels us to the ideal's " imitative " service. An artist is imitative when he expresses idealized qualities in painting, sculpture or music; the moral enthusiast is obediently imitative when his behaviour is influenced by his ideals. Pride is the admiration of oneself: it produces similar consequences. Ideals which remain abstract visions also move us in these ways. Their admiring votaries serve them by extending their influence through missionary endeavour, and conforming, so far as is possible, with the excellences that they represent. But ideals (as we have seen) may be attached to persons or things *as their qualities*, and this is a materializing development which greatly complicates the description of their influence upon the aspirations of mankind, and upon the behaviour of individuals.

There is frequently a conflict between an ideal provocative and a temptation of a more " natural," or selfish, character. This involves a mental contest—a condition of tension—which we figure as a struggle between our " higher " and " lower " nature. The ideal competes with the more " natural " inducement for being energized by a feminine like or desire, and this entails the deflection of this motive from that which automatically, or naturally, attracts it. A " victory " is won, for instance, when kindness overcomes selfishness, justice or truth overrides self-interest, and idealistic Art prevails over " bread and butter " interests. In this contest the more natural has the seductive advantage of familiarity, and, very commonly, of utility. The ideal, on the other hand, is attractive as a quintessence of the harmonious. The victory of the idealistic is commonly ascribed to an "effort of will." But, in reality, it is won by the superior attractiveness of the idealistic, which is greatly increased if it can ally itself with an idea of Success. Since it is gained by the deflection of a motive, it is the conquest of the feminine element by a challenging idea that is of masculine origin.

"Conscience" is the protesting urge of an ideal, and the glow or chill that follows its success or failure. We "conscientiously" obey our country's laws and observe our duties. An artist is "conscientious" when he adheres to æsthetic ideals. Selfish success dispenses with this safeguard. It is natural, not conscientious, to be wholehearted in the pursuit of pleasure, power, riches, fame or popularity. Conscience is, in fact, an incitement to struggle with oneself.

All men are acutely sensitive to ideals of Success, since it is only by unceasing successes that man rises and maintains himself above a brutish level. Of this, more hereafter. But it is clear that sensibilities to the various other ideals vary in delicacy from one person to another. Collectively, they constitute individual "character." As, however, we have seen in Chapter II, sensibilities can be sharpened by the familiarity that is gained by practice—under the disciplining control of others, of public opinion and of oneself—as they can be blunted by their habitual neglect or violation.

We will now concern ourselves, in more detail, with these immensely important idealistic provocatives. They may, as already stated, be distinguished as ideals of Peace, of Unity, of Morality, of Beauty and of Success. The ideal of Peace, with its attendant comfort and security, appeals, more or less, to all men, since its roots are firmly seated in feminine instinct. But it cannot maintain itself against stresses of masculine excitement that stimulate either covetous or ambitious aggressiveness, or the angry resentment of injustice, insults, threats, or injuries. For aggression and injustice naturally provoke anger: a feminine "shrink" is spurred to retaliation by a masculine reaction. Peace can, then, only be preserved by the strict repression of these provocatives. Within the State they are restrained by the law. It is assisted by public opinion, good feeling and the customary rules of considerate behaviour. But experience shows that these are ineffective unless supported by penalties. This is sufficiently illustrated by the criminality of some American cities and by the recklessness of motorists. There are no such authoritative safeguards for the maintenance of international peace, unless nations can unite in repressing the aggressive activity or injustice of any of their number.

The ideal of Unity in fellowship (with its outcome in loving-kindness) has quite a different foundation. It springs from the mental identification of others with ourselves, that is accentuated by the possession of a quality, or interest, in common. Unity with others in idea analogically impels us to *share* things with them. It is the primitive fountain-head of hospitality and generosity. Union naturally begins with that of the family, which, in China and elsewhere, endures after death. A sense of unity consolidates the affection of friendship, quite apart from the influence of admiration, habitude or a sense of favours to come. Those to whom we are "attached" are, indeed, idealized by their union with ourselves as being "on our side." As a social ideal, Unity is extended, naturally, from the family to the tribe, and, artificially, to the caste, profession, club or society, religion and nation. It is promoted by distinctiveness in dress and peculiarity of ceremonies—as those of Free Masonry, for example. Nationality has now become the most impressive of social *liaisons*. But it rests upon an arbitrary conception that has been nursed by political propaganda. Its origin can in most cases be traced to the glory or humiliation of a military conquest. Identity in place of residence is not *naturally* unifying. Such closely related birds as blackbirds and thrushes do not become allied by living in the same garden. Nationality is then easily overridden by more intimate ties. Patriotism is no protection against strikes.

Sexual love has a unitying influence: so has admiration for another, since it draws us to imitate him. A sense of Unity is strongly enforced by a common danger or need. This is proved very strikingly by the comradeship of war. Trades Unions are consolidated by the antagonism of Labour and Capital. A common grievance has drawn the people of Germany into one. Union is also promoted by community in hate. Hence a war may be a most effective means of restoring patriotic solidarity, and of quieting revolutionary unrest. The effect of the mental identification of oneself with others is illustrated very clearly by Sympathy. If we are quite indifferent to another person, a fortunate or unfortunate experience that has occurred to him merely excites our "interest," since it might have occurred to ourselves. If our attitude towards him is antipathetic, we simply regret his good fortune, or rejoice in his bad luck. But, if we are mentally unified with him, the idea of his experience autosuggestively produces in us a *replica* of his *feelings*—in however small a miniature. We "feel with him" and experience his pleasure, or pain, with its consequential motive.

Sympathy is, then, an *emotional* development of the mental process by which we "understand" the behaviour of others. We do this by attaching to them *ideas* of such feelings as we should be experiencing, if our appearance and our circumstances were such as theirs. When they are identified with ourselves, these ideas become emotional actualities. This sympathetic sensibility appears to be a distinctively human capacity and to depend very greatly upon mental culture. Beasts and birds show little trace of it: they persecute the helpless or injured of their own kind. Man does this only under the influence of anger, jealousy or religious zeal. But uncultured man is disposed to be contemptuously cruel—a disposition which in the cultured is called "sadistic." Children are by no means as sympathetic as one would like them to be. It is with advancing mental culture that a sympathetic sensibility is acquired. Its power over us depends greatly upon the degree of our affection for its object. But we can sympathize with strangers, and even with the admired personalities of fiction and the drama. It is this that holds us "enthralled," and not merely amused. Without sympathy, gossip would lose much of its piquancy. It would only stimulate the praise or blame of others, and their comparison with ourselves to their disadvantage.

It requires some mental refinement to be sympathetic, since the process entirely depends upon our appreciation of "indefinite" as contracted with *definite* ideas. We could not attach to ourselves, for instance, a definite idea of a particular motor crash that had injured someone else. But an indefinite idea of "a" motor crash can be attached to oneself. So it becomes "particularized" and gains it a definitely stimulating application.

Sympathy is the source of unassuming Charity. For, if we feel the hardships of others, we are pressed, by our appreciation of correlative analogy, to give the relief for which, in their place, we should be seeking. Widespread charity is one of the most distinctive features of the present day. The Romans distributed bread to the workless, but, it seems, more with the object of quieting them than out of kind-heartedness. This motive also enters into the State charitable relief of the present day. And it must be admitted that charity has become a fashionable pretext for social entertainments, and is degraded by the sloppy sentimentality with which journalism sugars over disconcerting misbehaviour. But, when all this is said, there remains enough to warrant present-day civilization in congratulating itself. Sympathy has extended to beasts and birds a fellow-feeling which they do not have for one another, and interests itself warmly in protecting them from cruelty—so long as this does not interfere with sport.

The ideals that are called "Moral," or "Ethical," may be fundamental or conventional. Fundamental moral harmonies are those which link together experiences that occur in successions, and accordantly assimilate them, rendering a consequence similar to its cause in goodness or badness. They exist, therefore, independently of "subjective" familiarity, and possess an attraction which lies deeper than that of "use and wont." Honesty is an accord between what is due and what is paid: Justice an accord between desert and its requital in reward or punishment. Other illustrations have been given in the preceding chapter: they comprise Truth, Sincerity, Virtue, Gratitude, Loyalty, Constancy—and also Revenge. These are the origins of our conceptions of eternal Right and Wrong. And they are obviously of immense practical value in securing the future. For they give some assurance of the future conduct of others as well as of ourselves: they ensure, for instance, that goods supplied on credit will be paid for. Their appeal is universal and independent of law, custom, public opinion or education. It is felt by children and savages as well as by the cultured—indeed it may be held that their influence is weakened by civilized sophistication. They are all comprised in the notion of "fair play" and mark the "gentleman," whether cultivated or savage.

To this fundamental morality feminine prudence and masculine imaginative enthusiasm have added an immense number of legal or customary rules—in regard to conduct, beliefs, manners, food and dress—which gain their force from convention, and are "subjectively" harmonious because they are in accord with law, custom, or public opinion. They are fantastically elaborate in the Indian caste scruples. They may be of practical use in safeguarding the future or of sentimental interest in conserving distinctive peculiarities or in satisfying emotional aspirations. The protective force of law is idealized as Legality, the observance of sexual restrictions as Chastity and Modesty, and beliefs in the supernatural as Religion—all differing greatly in interpretative detail at various periods and in various countries. We idealize, as Fashion, rules concerning manners and dress which in these days are extraordinarily ephemeral. Being artificial, conventional may command greater respect than fundamental morality: "good form" may count for more than "goodness." But it is a slander upon human nature to hold that morality is purely conventional. Its fundamental prescriptions rest upon sensibilities that are innate—in an appreciation of harmonies that exist independently of conventional rules. Their breach is a sin against human nature, not merely a law-made crime.

Behaviour that conforms to these moral ideals is admired and affords through its harmony a glow of gratification: their violation by others excites indignation (the consequence of "unworthiness") and may arouse remorse, if by ourselves. These feelings manifest themselves in praise and blame. It may be remarked that the observance of *conventional* morality is not so effective in evoking praise as in provoking blame. Hence it is safeguarded by a desire for "respectability," as well as by the fear of punishment.

CHAPTER VII

THE INFLUENCE OF THOUGHT UPON EMOTION, MOTIVE AND MOVEMENT—*Continued*

We pass from Moral to Æsthetic ideals. They are summarized in our notion of "Beauty." This is a quintessence of harmony between different qualities of simultaneous or successive sensations, between successive feelings, and between sensations and feelings. There is, for instance, Beauty in the elegant and congruent lines of the human figure or a building, between the successive notes of a melody, between charity and forgiveness, and between love and the flowers of spring, or anger and a thunderstorm. It is, then, to be found in inanimate and animate Nature, may be personified by ourselves or others, and may be enshrined in works of Art.

Beauty is admittedly very difficult to define, since our sensibility to its harmonious quality may be influenced by our feelings or by our habitudes. To a lover his beloved is beautiful. To one who has become habituated to them, a skyscraper ranks with a Gothic cathedral, and jazz has more charm than classical music. For they possess the harmony of the familiar. Beauty is, or should be, the inspiration of Art. But its attractions have varied in their phases with the changing sensibilities of mankind. How great is the difference, for instance, between ancient Egyptian, Greek and Gothic architecture! Yet it is possible to find a real harmony in all three. The Egyptians felt it between design and the mysterious, the Greeks between design and phases of elegance in Nature and man, and the

Gothic builders between upward aspirations in construction and in faith. Modern architecture seems to aim at a more practical harmony—that between construction and room-space.

Art is *inspired* only when it is æsthetically idealistic. But skill (as we shall see) is also idealized as a phase of Success, and our admiration for the "cleverness" that is displayed in originality of design and eccentricity of execution may blind our appreciation of the beautiful. So men may at one time admire the works of Michelangelo, and at another time those of Jacob Epstein.

From the evolutionary point of view the most interesting, and fruitful, of idealistic conceptions has been Success—man's indispensable passport to each little stage of his progress in civilization. It has arisen from both physical and mental experiences. In physical life success is a condition which, by its harmony with instinctive or conscious motives or sensibilities, relaxes the strain of an effort, or the tension of suspense or surprise. An effort may be incited by the opposition of an adversary as well as by a difficulty. In this case success involves the superiority which is given by victory. The relaxation of strain, or tension, is followed by an expansive *emotional* revulsion. The success, which produces it, is at the same time exceedingly harmonious, since it is in accord with self-interest or purpose. The result is a glow of masculine excitement—of satisfaction or gladness—which acts attractively upon feminine motive, and consequently provokes self-admiration, or pride, in the present, and prospective desire, if an idea of it occurs as a future possibility. Failure, on the other hand, is a discordant condition which generates self-repellent feelings of shame or humiliation. These pleasing and displeasing feelings can be provoked by recollections, or ideas, of success and failure. There is no one who is not pleased by thoughts of past successes, or by compliments,

In physical life, therefore, success is a harmony which relaxes tension. In mental life there is a like sequence. An ideal is "successful" with us through the tension and subsequent relaxation which its attractive harmony produces. For tension is involved in the deflection of feminine motive from the temptation of a selfish or "lower" idea. There is relaxation when this deflection is achieved; and the relaxation is followed by a glow of self-satisfaction. Consequently, a triumph is won by this mental victory as by a physical effort or a lucky surprise. In this mental conflict again success involves *superiority*. For there can be no victory on one side without a defeat on the other.

By our experiences of objective life, the notion of superiority is extended to conditions which are mentally assimilated with success, either as causes or consequences from which success is to be inferred, or as identifying ourselves with the successful and rendering ourselves successful by this association. The most obvious of the causes of success are strength, size, courage, skill, education, industry, perseverance, intelligence, prudence and eloquence. These are idealized as phases of Power—one of the most exciting of ideal provocatives. Other sources of Power are authority, rank, possessions, riches (giving purchasing instead of commanding power), and luck. The consequences of successful superiority are Dignity or Worth in ourselves: also the admiring attitude of others from which our success is irresistibly inferred—that is to say, *succès d'estime.* This takes the form of Honour, Fame, Respectability, Popularity and Notoriety. Ideas of them are as exhilarating as ideas of Success: ideas of their contraries are depressing.

To other causal implications of success can also be traced our respect for numerical majorities, for age and for the mysterious. Preponderating numbers are successful in conflict, and we accept them as a determining factor in public opinion and in democratic government. A respect for age—testified to by the institution of "Senates"—is an inheritance from the days of childhood, which remains with us—in greater or less strength—throughout life. It is the source of our curious relish for "the antique." It is from its implications of *power* that the mysterious is reverenced. For it has unknown potentialities.

This remarkable mental extension of successful superiority to its causes and consequences results from the static character of thought. It resembles sensation in presenting a changing succession of causes and consequences as a series of "spatial" pictures. A thing's "dynamic" relationships are, therefore, taken to be its static qualities, as in mathematical physics the effect of a cause is taken to be its "co-efficient." It is successful to be skilled because skill is a cause of success; to be learned, because learning is the consequence of success; and to be admired or popular, because these are consequential conditions from which success is to be inferred. As thus diversified by the Mind, Success ranks with food, lust and sleep amongst the greatest of human needs and pleasures.

These phases of success may influence us as abstract ideals. But they take an objective, or material, form when they are attached, as qualities, to persons, things, or lines of conduct. Thus impersonated or embodied, our admiration is attracted to their possessors, whether ourselves or others.

Ideas of success are extraordinarily powerful. For we must succeed in order to be civilized. Civilization is a non-heritable artificiality that can only be achieved by the individual through an unending series of conscious successes. There is no conscious success in digestion or respiration. But one must succeed in order to learn to speak, and even to stand upright. Trial, or endeavour, followed by success, is the fountain-head from which have sprung the artificialities of civilization. Accordingly ideas of success evolve into becoming masterful provocatives in themselves. The emulative spirit of games, the pursuit of popularity, have nothing but "empty" successes before them, and there may be nothing beyond this in the excitement of gambling and of war. But the most valuable function of ideals of Success is to reinforce the influence of other motives. We are urged by our feminine nature to have a prudent regard for future well-being, and to take thought for its increase. But the accumulation of capital has been in great part urged by a desire for *triumph*. This has been, in the main, the lure which has tempted man to make the efforts of trial that has led to his discoveries and inventions—to acquire the "accomplishments" that supply the place of the directive instincts with which he is so poorly equipped—accomplishments which, being unstereotyped by heredity, are capable of such marvellous variety. The learning which transmits them from one generation to another is stimulated, in very great measure, by the pride of learning in itself. Success in prospect has, then, been the creator and preserver of material civilization. It can, indeed, claim to have been more than this. By reinforcing the influence of social, moral and æsthetic ideals, it assists, very materially, in raising the standard of man's conduct above merely selfish or impulsive levels, and endows him with the capacity of self-control. For we are "successful" when unselfish, just, honest or artistic, as when we are prudent, and fail when we do not follow the dictates of conscience. Nor is it only as a spur to individual effort that success affects our motives and behaviour. When ideas of any of its phases are attached to others, our lives are profoundly affected by the admiration, respect, or faith with which we regard them.

Amidst these evolutionary ramifications, it is difficult to find a scheme for the intelligible classification of the various influences of ideas of Success. The simplest primary distinction is that between their egotistic and altruistic effects, between their effects in attracting us to ourselves and to others. Their attractive effect can then be distinguished according as it provokes present *admiration* or prospective *pursuit*, and these, again, according as they influence our subjective or our objective life.

Egotism is the feeling of self-satisfaction, self-admiration, or pride with which we are infused by a conviction of our own successful superiority. This attracts a feminine motive of "liking" towards ourselves. It is, therefore, "self-love," and is one of the strongest and most durable of feelings, naturally impelling us to decorate ourselves with clothes and jewellery. It is a spark ever ready to kindle the flame of a quarrel or the furnace of war. The universality of its possession—even by those who have no apparent claim to it — is an outstanding peculiarity of human character. But this is explicable if we realize that the least successful of mankind would hardly have risen above the level of the brutes had not his successes outnumbered his failures. These continued triumphs introduce a note of active, personal, self-assertion into thought: "it was said by me," becomes "I said": feminine "clingings" become "havings" and "possessings." Pride endows us with a serviceable self-respect. But in the form of vanity, it inclines us to boastfulness and "swank": it renders us unwilling to admit past errors, and to draw profitable lessons from them, and it lays us disastrously open to the influence of compliments. A "charming" personality is one that radiates compliments in speech and manners. Pride flowers in ideas of Equality—that is to say, of non-inferiority—of Liberty and of Democracy, and impels the votaries of these ideals to become their active missionaries.

The contrary of Success, in failure, generates a feeling of disappointment that is motived against oneself as Shame. This is one of life's greatest miseries—the most frequent motive of suicide. We resent blame or censure except from a respected authority: prophets are stoned because their revelations are uncomplimentary. We are even depressed by the suggestion of inferiority—the "inferiority complex" —that is implied in the superiority of another. Appreciating this feeling in others, we soften it by deprecating any compliments that they pay us. But the humiliation of Shame, like other discords, may bear most wholesome fruit. For it is the idea of Shame, in the guise of Conscience, that frowningly guards the influences of the social and moral ideals that are our "duties." It is commonly more effective than the hope of self-approval.

Prospective ideas of success—to be gained by ourselves—generate an Ambition to win them either subjectively or objectively—a distinction that involves some complicated analysis. Subjective ambition may be practical or emotional. It is *practical* when it presses us to self-control in the following of an ideal or in a prudent adherence to the Golden Mean between idealism and a selfish prudence. It becomes *emotional* when an instrument evolves into an object—when it is practised merely to gain the self-satisfaction of self-conquest. This is the asceticism of "Saintliness." The victory at which it aims may seem barren. But its practice may be useful in developing a "reserve" of power for the exercise of self-control in practical directions. In either case, the call of self-mastering Success is the "Voice of Conscience."

Objective Ambition may take no less than four distinct phases: it may be practical, emotional, inferential or identificative. In its practical form it has been the mainspring of civilizing evolution, spurring mankind to the tryings, doings, makings, gettings and savings that have developed the comforts and luxuries of life, and have endowed it with artistic treasures. Society stagnates if ambition is stifled by custom or convention as by the Indian caste rules, or by such restrictions as those upon which Trades Unions rely for their influence. So the pursuit of an emotional pleasure, of masculine origin, contributes to the material well-being which it is the object of our feminine nature to secure. Ambition affects us *emotionally* when its object is merely victory—to be won in emulative games, in gambling and in war. An instrument of civilizing Evolution becomes an urge to emotional extravagance. Ambition becomes *inferential* when its object is to acquire conditions from which the possession of successful superiority can be inferred—the admiration of others, honour, fame or notoriety. Titles and decorations are instruments for attracting this admiration, as are also manners and dress. And Ambition is *identificative* when it seeks success through the society of the superior —that is, in being unified with them.

Egotism and Ambition take an altruistic tinge when they admire the success of one's leader, family, "side," friends, party, union or nation, and desire to increase it. These are all mentally identified with ourselves through an important identity of interest, and our enthusiasm for them is really self-admiring, or self-seeking, although, under the names of loyalty, family feeling, social solidarity or patriotism, it may claim to be disinterested.

The influence of ideals of Success becomes completely altruistic when they are attached, as qualities, to other personalities, objects, or lines of conduct, with which we have no identifying connection. The course of our admiration follows the possession of these qualities as a compass-needle follows a magnet, and is consequently attracted to their possessors. The personalities that are thus admired may be those of Religion, of Politics, of History or of Romance, as well as those within our own experience. This altruistic admiration begins in the family: from the home it is extended to the master, the chief and the king. It shifts to the artist, the athlete and film star. Admiration becomes Respect when it is inspired by Power with its potentialities of punishment. The Omnipotence of God makes a strong religious appeal. Faith is added when the admired Power is protective and assures the future. These feelings provoke the obedient imitation of the revered personality's wishes, as well as its glorification, and the spread of its influence by missionary propaganda. But Respect cannot be won by caresses, chocolates or compliments. What a difference there is between the behaviour of children before their capable nurse and their incapable mother! And Respect and Faith are the strongest consolidating bonds of society. For the votaries of a creed are mentally unified by it.

It is, as we have seen, through an *idea* of another's Power that we are drawn in respect to him, and, unless his power has been actually experienced, this idea is one of his "prestige." This idea must be cultivated by its object through a certain aloofness of manner—by "dignified" behaviour which is the reverse of *camaraderie*. The captain of a merchant ship must always dine alone. For prestige is easily undermined by suspicions of equality and, once lost, can hardly be recovered. For there are few things more contemptible than faded dignity begging for its lost respect.

There may be a conflict between our admiration for another and the distasteful feeling of inferiority—the "inferiority complex"—that is aroused by his superiority. This is the source of Jealousy. But Jealousy does not arise if our admiration is "whole-hearted." In other cases we are apt to be jealously disquieted by the successes of others, and to be pleasantly reassured by their failures. Rivalry in distinction of dress and appearance is a fertile source of petty jealousy, and men have done wisely to abandon it. Gossip owes much of its savour to the sense of superiority which the discredit of others correlatively reflects upon ourselves.

We may altruistically admire things, or lines of conduct, as well as persons; in this case we are touched more nearly by artificial than by natural excellences, since the Mind wins success by the "artfulness" of its conceptions. Artificiality in manners, dress and language is a social passport as "politeness." Language is more artificial than observation and inference, and we are more impressed by eloquence than by experience. Mathematics, as the most artificial branch of science, are in high esteem. The extension of education is a watchword with all political parties without much regard for its practical utility in providing the young with abiding interests, or in enabling them to fit themselves into the complicated mechanism of economic life.

Our primary attitude towards another's failure—as

towards our own—is one of Contempt. This may be supplanted by the Pity that is generated by the effects of thought in arousing feelings of Sympathy. But sympathy may be blunted by jealousy—as when one, who seems to be pitiable, denies his inferiority by self-assertion, or even by aping our manners.

So far of the effect upon our sensibilities, emotions and motives of the ideas that are presented in Thought. But ideas also accompany conscious perception, and it is, therefore, difficult to decide how far—in perceptive as opposed to reflective life—our emotional and impulsive responses are provoked by these ideas and how far by physical "realities" that underlie them. Purely physical life, as we have seen, includes sensory impressions, emotions and impulses, but not ideas that would bring them into consciousness. Ideals may very possibly exist—electro-magnetism is the inseparable attendant of electricity—but they are not "received"; and life's driving forces are therefore inherited sensibilities, and inherited responses that are adaptively "conditioned" by physical intelligence. The life of an insect runs in this fashion and also the functioning of our bodily organs.

The course of evolution has clearly progressed from this unconscious physical level by two outgrowing developments —*firstly* by the reception of ideas that are primarily natural accompaniments of perception, but are of assistance in appreciating it, and in drawing inferences from it, and, *secondly*, by the elaboration of these ideas into an artificial mental environment. In the first stage, Mind is *helpful*; in the other it is *predominant*. The life of an ant is purely physical. That of a dog is *helpfully* mental. In man the Mind *assists* the Body in eating, endeavouring, loving, helping and fighting: it takes *command* when its thoughts are sentimentally inspired by abstract ideas or are intellectually interested in such a subject as algebra. A serviceable instrument has evolved into a dominant obsession. Hence, in natural life, it is deeds, not words, that count, whereas, in the artificial life of the Mind, words are the more impressive. In its desire for self-approval, a sophisticated mind pins its faith to "principles," and ignores the realities of human nature. Yet, in matters affecting the future, they are the facts best worth consideration. Hence mental artificialities have been, in great measure, the evolutionary causes of the ups and downs that mark human history. This gives some support to the theory that civilization runs in cycles. From the simplicities of physical life, the Mind gradually develops refinements of thought, speech and conduct which are "elevating" in that they tend to lift man into an empyrean atmosphere. But, on attaining a certain altitude, he falls back into the simple life. Civilization reverts into barbarism.

But with all its ramifying complications Evolution conserves the preceding stages of its progress. Man's bodily organs function physically. And he is strongly moved by urges which, although attended by ideas, are not originated by them but are caused by physical provocatives. Such are pain, hunger, thirst and lust, followed by feminine shrinkings, clingings and searchings, or by the masculine emotional reactions that convert alarm into "physical" courage, bafflement into curiosity, resent injury by anger, vent anger by a blow, and retaliate a blow by imitating it. These physical urges are governing forces during early infancy, and also during adult life when it is stirred by such stresses as love, rage, war or famine. But, ordinarily, they submit themselves to the guiding reins, the whip and the spurs of the Mind.

Amongst our physical capacities is the elastic strength of emotional energy—a capacity that is confusedly identified with conscious "willing." It has already been noticed in Chapter II. It makes us automatically "spring to attention" towards provocative sensations and ideas, and unconsciously enables us to maintain our equilibrium against the innumerable distractions that assail our senses, and intrude discursively into thought. There is insanity if it is altogether lost. It is the source of the "independence" which protects us against the seductive influence of propagandist oratory: lacking it, we should be as amenable to suggestion as is one under hypnotic influence. It endows us with continuity of attention and intention—or purpose. We take these to be phases of effortful "volitions." But no "willing" is involved in *present* enjoyment; and when we are in pursuit of a *prospective* pleasure, our "will" merely expresses our intention of pursuit—a motive that is a feminine urge. An effort appears to involve "volition" when it is directed towards the overcoming of an obstacle that lies in the way of an inducement—whether physical or ideal—or of a threat that is less painful than its alternative. But our "choice" in this case is merely the outfacing of the unpleasant in order to secure the pleasant that lies behind it. So the advantages offered by "work" provoke strength to endure its tiresomeness.

An effort may take the form of a prospective "resolution." This is commonly formed after the struggle of some hesitation. In looking forward, we are influenced by a feminine propensity: it is the *attraction* of an ideal, or an idea of success, that brings us to a decision. We may choose a pain in order to gain a pleasure, or to avoid a greater pain: we may renounce a pleasure in order to avoid a pain. Our choice in thus "making up our minds" rests upon the sensibility of the moment to their relative "values"; and, accordingly, resolutions are broken, if when the time comes for their fulfilment, our sensibility has changed, or our prospective valuation has been misleading. We may regard a resolution as a "self-conquest." But the conquest has been secured by the prospective joy of a victory.

Finally, of the influence of thought upon our external

movements—that is to say, upon the bodily activities which combine to fashion our conduct, manners, or behaviour, and become utterances, articulations, or speech, when they are those of the chest, throat and mouth. They are obviously *instruments* for the execution of motives or for the relief of emotion. But they are of such invaluable service that they become objects in themselves, and are held in respect as artificial "accomplishments."

Amongst mindless creatures these movements must be of purely physical origin, guided and controlled by physical memories—inherited or acquired—and by physical adaptive intelligence. In the behaviour of ants and bees there is much that strikes one as stupid—reflex actions that are repeated "by rote" without regard to novel difficulties that present themselves. But, on the other hand, illustrations abound of the intelligent adaptation of instinctive conduct to new conditions—adaptations that are styled "conditional reflexes," but certainly manifest an intelligence that exists apart from a mind. It is quite possible, as already noted, that an "idea-stream" may be attached to their physical conduct and to the sensory impressions and motives that urge it. But the ideas are not "received," and are therefore a surplus product, like "wireless waves" that pass uncaught. Higher up the animal scale, ideas are "received" and life becomes *conscious*. There is an evolution of mental as contrasted with physical activity. But it seems doubtful whether *ideas* of conduct are commanding in the detailed direction of conduct, until the human level is reached.

The instinctive behaviour of an animal may, it is true, be varied by the learning of artificial modes of behaviour, or "tricks." Their acquirement and performance generally result from the memorial repetition of conduct which is imposed by constraint and followed by a satisfaction. It is illustrated in man by the rapid finger-movements of a pianist who is playing "by heart": each movement memorially generates the one that follows it—a process which is miscalled "associative" by taking a static view of a dynamic succession. "Tricks" can also be learnt by the imitation of an example through such physical intelligence as "infects" an audience with coughing. Repetition and imitation may be unconscious as well as conscious. Unconscious repetition is illustrated by the accomplishments of "performing fleas." They learn to repeat, unconsciously and "mechanically," constrained tasks under the inducement of a physical satisfaction—their physical remembrances running backwards from the offered inducement to the task. That recollection may proceed backwards is in everyone's experience. Higher up the scale, with the development of consciousness, the learning of artificial modes of behaviour is illustrated by the accomplishments of dogs and chimpanzees. Under a mental inducement—the *idea* of reward or praise, of punishment or blame—the animal repeats, by physical memory, conduct to which it has been constrained and is memorially connected with the hearing of certain words of command. Apparently, it may also learn, through physical intelligence, by imitating an example. But we may doubt whether its actions, although conscious, are directed by ideas of them—whether its knowledge of what it is doing actually prompts it to do what it does, and is not merely an accompaniment of merely physical promptings. And since its artificial accomplishments conflict with its natural behaviour, no inspiriting idea of "success" is gained by the performance. They are not spontaneously practised, and are easily interrupted by relapses into instinctive conduct.

In the case of man there is no such conflict, since his hereditary movements of practical utility are of the very simplest—to hold tight, to suck, to cling, to shrink, and, vaguely, to search. He offers, then, a blank page for the generation of movements of conduct and speech by imitatively converting ideas of movements into actions—that is to say, by the process of autosuggestion. Hence his capacity for learning comes to him from a loss of "automatic" natural aptitudes. For emotional expression, he has a more generous physical endowment of smiles and frowns, ejaculations, gesticulations, laughter and cries. But since they are attended by ideas, they can be *auto-suggestively* produced by ideas of them: we can force ourselves to smile or frown by means of ideas of smiling or frowning. There is apparently, as we have seen, a connection of origin between movement and thought, and hence ideas of movements can easily set movements into action.

The process of autosuggestion involves the "reversal of parentage," which, although unrecognized by Science, is one of the most important processes of both inanimate and animate Nature. A current of electricity generates a stream of electro-magnetism, and this again generates electricity. Radio broadcasting is entirely dependent upon these alternations. Radiant heat gives rise to material heatedness and this gives rise to radiant heat. Vibration generates sound and sound gives rise to vibration. So the ideas of a speaker generate words, and these words generate ideas in one who hears them. The autosuggestive effect of an idea is clearly reproductive, not provocative, and it is unfortunate for understanding that the same word—"stimulation"—should be used for both these very different processes.

In man this mental process develops with the growth of his mental faculties. During infancy, speech and manners are apparently learnt through such physical repetitions and imitations as endow an animal with its "tricks" of accomplishment. But as mental faculties develop, they become learnt autosuggestively—that is to say, through their production by ideas of them. So the natural is lost in the artificial. The artificiality of human manners and speech is proved by the extraordinary differences that distinguish and have distinguished those of different countries and of different epochs.

Our comprehension of this evolutionary advance is distorted because speech and behaviour that have been autosuggestively learnt, revert to a lower plane of activity. *Physical* memory and intelligence take charge of these autosuggestive acquirements. We may be faintly conscious or altogether unconscious of these workings. We are generally vaguely aware of what we do "under the force of habit" which connects certain movements or lines of conduct with the execution of the motive of the moment—in reminiscent but "conditioned" detail. But we are quite unaware of the complicated movements that are involved in using the acquired dexterities of walking, eating, speaking, writing and playing lawn-tennis. In exercising them, we have reverted entirely to the physical plane. By an effort of attention, under the influence of a motive, we can capture ideas of them and bring them into consciousness. And a child is very conscious of them when painfully learning them. But, when they "run of themselves," they are on a par with the "conditional reflexes" of insect life, although they have their origin in mental autosuggestion and are not inherited.

Apart, then, from his meagre physical endowments, man's speech and behaviour are elaborated artificial instruments of his Mind; and, if we take them to be determining elements in his life, we are appraising the tools on a carpenter's bench without regard to the energy and skill of the carpenter. This conclusion is directly contrary to the views held by most psychologists, and in particular by those of the "Behaviourist" school. In their view, behaviour is a crucial feature of life, and consciousness hardly more than an incidental "epiphenomenon." The cart is, in fact, put before the horse. This remarkable inversion of understanding has proceeded from two causes. In the first place, the material seems to be more important than the immaterial because it can be directly perceived and measured. So Biology localizes life in the *cell*, whereas this obviously presents only one side of it. And, secondly, the observation of our actions and utterances gives some ground for the flattering notion that we possess the ennobling faculty of Free Will. We can autosuggestively move our limbs, and our tongues and lips if we "choose" to do so. But in fact there must be a *motive* in the background—provoked by an idea of a successful trial or demonstration—and our action is "voluntary" only in so far as it involves the "taking of trouble" in order to win the gratification of a success. Over emotions and motives the Will has no power whatever. Who can will himself out of love?

It may be remarked here that the "reversal of parentage" which is involved in speaking and hearing, and in the generation of a movement by an idea of it, may appear to offer us a means of using thought and speech to influence our motives and emotions, and even our sensory and bodily conditions. A toothache generates an idea of it, and the idea generates words of complaint. An asseveration of its cure should then produce, not only an idea of its cure, but its actual disappearance. This process is obviously far more complicated than the generation of a movement by an idea of it. There are persons of such acute autosuggestive sensibility as to derive exceptional powers from it—persons who can *see* an object that is suggested to them, or can produce a pain by thinking of it. But this is—fortunately—beyond the powers of the ordinary man. It is impossible to calm a fit of anger by declaring that one is not angry. It is true, however, that movements which instinctively express emotions are so closely connected with them that one can undoubtedly induce a mood of cheerfulness by purposely smiling, and a feeling of reverence by revential behaviour—that is to say, by reversing the connection between the two. But this falls very far short of the curative powers that have been claimed for autosuggestion by some enthusiasts.

[On page 249 the evolution of our Impulses from provocative ideas —realistic and idealistic—is traced in tabular form.]

CHAPTER VIII

THE INFLUENCE OF EMOTION UPON THOUGHT

The Mind is a blend of Emotion and Thought, and these two currents energetically interact upon one another. Thought, as we have seen in the last two chapters, is a powerful stimulus of Emotion. On its part, Emotion masterfully affects the character of Thought—driving it into the channels that are called "imaginative." In this figurative shape Thought reacts by powerfully stimulating emotion, or "sentiment," as we term it in its milder forms. Emotion and Thought, in fact, interplay like the alternate oscillations of a shuttle.

The most obvious effect of Emotion upon Thought is to drive indefinite ideas back to their origin in the definite, particular ideas of sensation: it converts the abstract into the concrete. It works in this fashion quite unconsciously; and it is not easy to appreciate its action, since its course is part of ourselves, and the observed is lost in the observer. It presses its way into mental life in a series of evolutionary developments. The most primitive of them—observable in birds and quadrupeds as well as in man—is the automatic conversion of its energy into muscular "expressions of emotion"—gesticulations, cries and changes of facial expression—which vary with changes of emotion as a landscape under passing sunlight and clouds. It affects the tension of the muscles: pride automatically braces them as shame relaxes them. When angry, nervous, or delighted, it is almost impossible to remain still. Emotion gives violence to language: praise becomes enthusiastic, blame becomes a curse. These manifestations originate as safety-valves: energy vents itself in movement. If they are repressed, the feelings that they should relieve grow in intensity and may become overpowering. There is truth in the line, "She must weep or she will die." But evolution can put roots to life's tendrils and use them as cuttings for the growth of new developments. Automatic expressions of emotion are the origin of purposeful dramatic Art.

By these muscular expressions Emotion manifests itself "objectively" or "concretely." Its effect upon Thought is similar: it renders ideas figurative or picturesque—that is to say, it assimilates them to those of sensation. Vague ideas of danger present themselves as fearful images of possible causes; thoughts of prospective happiness are fore-shadowings of definite pleasures; love bestows imaginary excellencies upon its object, which increase its passion. These images are all analogically connected with the emotions from which they spring. For they are of possible causes that are connected with the emotions as *qualifying* them—as, for instance, the pleasure of a meal is qualified by its dishes. In its use of analogies Imagination is, then, *intelligent*: it is, indeed, intelligence pushed to an extreme, for the likenesses through which it works may be very far-fetched—far more superficial than those that are used by sober common sense. Imagination is also intelligent in its *inventive* powers. But it invents the exciting or amusing instead of the useful—games and fairies instead of pins and needles.

It may be remarked here, in passing, that, since Emotion stimulates so markedly the intelligent appreciation of analogies, and Emotion is of masculine origin, we may safely conclude that Intelligence comes to us from the masculine—as Memory does from the feminine—side of our nature.

Imagination, moreover, exaggerates the mental faculty of "understanding" our surroundings by investing them with vitalities such as our own. It goes farther and *personifies* them. To the lively imaginations of children and savages the wonders of nature possess living personalities, and can, therefore, very easily be deified. So, on a higher mental plane, the poet animates the inanimate. To Shelley dark clouds were "angels of rain and lightning," Wordsworth could hear cataracts "blow their trumpets." and Keats could see, in a Grecian urn, a "still unravished bride of quietness."

And there is a further development. Emotion alters the basis of the judgments that are formed in thought. In the process of reasoning, emotional assumptions are substituted for "common sense" conclusions that are derived from the lessons of experience—emotional assumptions that are dictated by like or dislike, hope or fear, desire or aversion, admiration, contempt or pity, and, above all, by the esteem that we feel for ourselves, our country and our class. These assumptions are commonly called "beliefs"—a word which testifies to its original signification. For it primitively means "by like." "Belief" is a feminine attachment to an attractive masculine suggestion. Amongst the strongest is that one's own judgment cannot be wrong. Hence the expression "I cannot bring myself to believe" is used as an absolute refutation of another's arguments.

The degree in which emotional energy automatically affects Thought in these fashions depends upon its excitability. This varies very greatly in exuberance from one person to another. Two general conclusions can, however, be formed. Excitability is far greater during childhood than in maturer years; and it is increased very notably by the action of light. For children "the earth and every common sight" is "apparelled in celestial light." Their feelings become pictorial: anger is a "black dog." They are not only passionately fond of story-telling: they spend most of their time in acting little stories of their own. For most men this excitable sensibility fades as years advance. The artist retains it.

The effect of light upon emotion is also undeniable. Are we not set into good spirits by a fine day and sunny weather? This invigorating effect of sunlight is ascribed to the ultra-violet rays; and it has been found that its artificial application increased very greatly the licentious gaiety of the Zoo monkey-house. We can, then, understand why Southerners are so much more emotional than peoples of the North. There is a well-known contrast in France between the Norman and the "meridional" temperament. The enforcement of speech by gesticulation becomes more and more pronounced as one travels southward in Europe. This connection between climate and emotion has very important political consequences. Democratic rule by majority is only possible if there is a readiness to compromise over distracting issues —"to give and take"—which recognizes that the possession of power does not warrant the persecution, enslavement, or extirpation of rival political parties—can see, in fact, that politics are, after all, a kind of game. Those of highly emotional temperament cannot suffer such a "brake" upon their feelings. They are, so to speak, "out for blood"; and political life becomes a clash of enmities that is incompatible with order or justice. It is an historical fact that the people of southern Europe and America have never been able to maintain democratic institutions; and our own experiments in extending them to warmer regions of the Empire have been the reverse of encouraging.

Now, it will be objected that this discussion of the *automatic* effects of emotional excitement is out of all connection with imaginative talents — as we ordinarily think of them—that is to say, with the achievement of imaginative Art. But there is a law of immense evolutionary importance which brings the two together. It is that a muscular, vocal or mental activity which is the spontaneous product of emotion can be brought under conscious command by the energy of a motiving *purpose*—by the control of what is confusedly called the "Will." That is to say, demonstrations of masculine emotion can be turned to practical purpose by feminine *motive*, as childish exuberance is controlled by a nurse. Laughing, coughing and winking are primitively automatic "reflexes." But they can be deliberately imitated. The art of dramatic "acting," whether on the stage or for the cinema, involves the imitation of facial expressions and gestures that are originally automatic or reflex. Paintings and sculptures are obviously "imitations" of their subjects. Imitation, as we have seen in Chapter I, is a manifestation of intelligence. For mimicry is the representation of a thing by an *analogical* replica of it. By a further step imitation develops into invention—the analogical *adaptation* of one thing to serve the purpose of another. So, through intelligence, purposeful ingenuity evolves out of automatism.

When stirred by Emotion, invention is not practical but "playful": it devotes itself to the designing of new amusements, new sources of æsthetic pleasure, new reassuring or comforting beliefs. These novelties are the fruit of special artistic aptitudes. Children all enjoy a "new game." But it is one of their number who invents it—one who possesses the germ of the creative or artistic talent that gives some persons such immense influence over the emotions of others. Men differ very greatly in the variety and clearness of the emotional images, or fancies, that the Mind presents to them, and in their physical ability to express them—that is to say, in the degree of their imaginative and executive intelligence. All men appreciate the pleasure that is given by romance, by beliefs and by amusement. Most men have "inspired moments" when they are visited by exciting visions or fancies. This occurs particularly when they are in love. But something more than this is required for imaginative "authorship." The visions or fancies must be "produced" or "executed," that is to say, *imitated* in material expressions: they must be given a sensory actuality by which they can be communicated to others through perception of movement, through sight or through hearing. And their execution must be "skilful"—that is to say, "artistic." For this adds to their charm by exciting admiration. Ideas, however "poetic," do not move us unless they are expressed in poetic language: on the other hand, poetic language may suffice to please us although it may be impossible to discover its meaning. An imaginative "creator" must, then, also be a skilful "artist." The methods of his execution vary with the character of his fancies. If they are of rhythmic harmonies, they are executed by drumming or dancing: if of musical harmonies, by singing or playing: of aspects of Life or Nature, by dramatic "playing," by delineating or carving, by declaiming or by descriptive writing. And there is a further complication. The execution of an author's ideas may be effected through an interpretative artist. In painting, sculpture, fiction, rhetoric and poetry, the author is his own interpreter. In the drama, interpretative "actors" are employed. In architecture, interpretation is committed to masons. When one is dancing, singing and playing, he is himself interpreting the harmonies which are inspiring him.

This creativeness may employ itself in the invention of new forms of amusement—the cinema and dog-racing, for example. On a higher plane it sees visions of the beautiful, the powerful, the heroic or the terrible and gives material form to them: it also conceives beliefs that are impressive by reason of their mystery, of their threats, or of the comfort that they offer. It is reassuring to believe that the world is under beneficent governance, although this can only be held by disregarding the testimony of earthquakes, famines, pestilences and wars, and the fact that myriads of living creatures can only live by destroying and consuming their living fellows. It is encouraging to believe that man possesses Free Will, although this is negatived by a scrutiny of the origin of his motives. Such imaginings and beliefs are the fountain and channels of the very diverse religions of mankind. The originators of a religion are its prophets: priests are its interpreters. All religions rest upon the belief that the successions of events which constitute "experience" can only be explained on the assumption of supernatural control or interference. This relieves us from the disagreeable idea that we are the puppets of Chance. The Powers of Nature—and even our own transient passions—whether they are imaginatively personified, or are more or less symbolically imagined as deities—excite feelings of admiration, respect and faith which impel us to imitate—that is to obey—their supposed wishes, to adore them, glorify them, and even to spread their influence through missionary endeavour. And, at the same time, the prudential side of our nature urges us to seek future benefits from these Powers, to win their favour by propitiatory ceremonies and prayers, and even to exact it by magic incantations that can bring the deity within the influence of man's desires.

Religious beliefs have given hope and comfort to millions of mankind. Religious ceremonies have brightened life by contributing—*salva reverentia*—to its amusements. This can be realized without resentment if one thinks of the miracle plays of mediæval times. And is not church-going, in these days, something of a "distraction"? By their terrors, religions have assisted to consolidate social morality: they have also strengthened moral rules and obligations by crediting them with inspiration. But their claim to be an indispensable mainstay of good conduct is not supported by experience. Sceptics may be amongst the most virtuous of men. Indeed, were the claim true, morality would have been lost by the mass of the working classes, for whom religion exists but in name. Man has, in fact, an inclination towards "righteousness" implanted in him by his appreciation of moral harmonies. A stronger claim that religions may advance is that they have been a powerful factor in welding masses of mankind into peaceful union by the exercise of an authority that is far more enduring than that of kings or dictators, and more respectable than that of democratic assemblies. It is now being realized that the decline of this centralizing control may have serious consequences. On the other hand, differences of creed have caused so much misery, in war and persecution, as to lead some philosophers to wonder whether religious enthusiasm has not been more of a curse than a blessing.

Art is generally accepted as the typical manifestation of imaginative creativeness. It "imitates" its various "particular" mental images by expressing them in many and various ways—in rhythm, in music, in dramatic action, in descriptive fiction and poetry, in delineation, sculpture and architecture. The growth of artistic talents and methods can be traced. It is stimulated by the *refinement of taste* which is gained by the intellectual exercise of the senses; it is extended by efforts of trial that have given rise to *artistic combinations*—of various musical instruments, for instance—and it is developed by the intelligent appreciation of analogies, suggesting *substitutions*, as of a musical instrument for the voice, of oil for water colours, of stone for wood, and bronze for stone. Art, like religion, has its "beliefs"—the tenets of its various "schools." And it not uncommonly adds to its attractions by being amusing.

It is at its simplest in the imaginative development of rhythm. We are, as has been explained, rhythmic animals in that our methods of progression—by walking or running—are rhythmic. The unit of a "pace" can be imaginatively subdivided, and the subdivisions can be expressed, or "interpreted," by drumming or dancing. The drum sounds throughout the world, and dancing is as primitive, as it is general, in its use for at once relieving and gaining excitement. Rhythm is an almost indispensable ornament of poetry, and is introduced into decorative art by repeating the unit of a pattern. It has become an essential element of music. But a stream of sounds can be melodious although unrhythmic. There is no rhythm in the song of a bird.

Music—the succession or combination of "ringing" sounds—apparently has its origin in the fact that man is gifted with a singing, as well as with a speaking, voice—the first distinguished from the second by its combining of *undulation* round the cavity of the throat and mouth with the *vibration* of the vocal cords. Since undulation consists of waves that traverse a surface and can extend to any depth below the surface, it can reinforce any note that vibration can produce. Man's first musical essays were, not improbably, the crooning of a lullaby, yodelling, or the shouting of a war song. These would mentally reproduce themselves by "running in the head," and could therefore be elaborated by mental images of changes or variations. These could be "imitatively" expressed by the voice, or by the various instruments that have been substituted for the voice by intelligent experiment. But the composition of new music is a *mental* process: the artist is conscious of it before he expresses it.

Music has real harmonies of its own. In a melodic progression of notes, there are intervals that are more harmonious than others because the two notes are more "akin" to one anoher; and this, of course, is also true of combinations, or chords, of notes. It can be demonstrated that there is a real "objective" accord between a note and the octave, fifth, fourth and third above it. A vast number of musical phrases are in themselves unsatisfying: standing alone, they produce an uncomfortable sense of incompleteness which is dispelled by the notes which follow them. Discords are disconcerting until they are resolved. There follows the pleasure of a revulsion. But these acoustic relations are far from explaining all the intervals and combinations that are used in musical composition, and it is clear that the harmonious relation of one note to another depends very greatly upon the acquired sensibility of familiarity. Musical harmony is in fact a *liaison* between two notes, causing one to *suggest* the other, that arises not only from an acoustic kinship between the two, but also from an acquired taste. The effect of familiarity in "generating" harmony is shown by the fact that most people welcome music that they know—that is to say, successions and chords that are *expected*. And, since sensibilities are acquired by efforts of trial, they may vary greatly from one people, or period, to another. We can understand why Europeans and Asiatics are each incapable of appreciating the other's music, and why, to ears that have become used to Beethoven and Mozart, much modern music is painfully repellent.

When the imagination plays with the appearances or incidents of life and nature, it may express its fancies by describing them, by acting (or dramatizing) them, or by portraying them in miniature, using for this purpose the arts of drawing and painting and sculpture. Story-telling and acting are the earliest imaginative expressions of childhood, and are probably of about equal antiquity. The various personalities of a drama present their imagined emotions and motives through their conduct and words, but can disclose their unexpressed thoughts only through the awkward means of soliloquies. In descriptive fiction, the author, in the rôle of interpreter, can present the inner thoughts of his characters; and some modern novels contain little but the mental experiences of their personalities. Poetry is dramatic, epic or lyric according as it leaves its characters to express themselves, describes their emotions, motives, actions and thoughts, or presents the poet's own feelings and thoughts as excited by various provocatives. Its language is decorated by rhythm, by the harmonies of rhyme, alliteration and accentuation, and by the dignity and picturesqueness of its language—that is to say, by the "particularity" of the poet's images. And, since the poet's feelings and thoughts are imaginative, they may be a very untruthful expression of his real character. It is as unreasonable to judge of the one by the other as to assume that a comedian is happy at home because he keeps an audience in roars of laughter.

When subjects that are emotionally or imaginatively derived from life or nature are represented by drawing, painting or sculpture, they are obviously imitated through movements of the hand guided by the faculty of *comparison*. There is, as we have seen, an identity between form and movement: a circular movement of the hand is identical with a circular *shape*. Manual imitation is, however, more difficult than descriptive or dramatic, and has been evolved by slower steps. In all time the excellence of the Homeric poems will hardly be surpassed: but, when they were composed, Greek painting and modelling were in their infancy.

Architecture is an imaginative expression when it serves no material purpose. The uses for which a tomb, a temple or a cathedral is designed are immaterial, and these buildings are amongst the flowers of Art; indeed, a Gothic cathedral is perhaps its finest flower. Their construction was inspired by admiration for the lives which they commemorated, or the spiritual Powers whom they housed: exalted by this feeling—at periods when dwelling-houses were generally mean and inconspicuous — men reared religious edifices which surpass the most spectacular structures of the present day. Modern civilization is "economic," and its ambitions are represented by the useful, but monotonous, outline and arrangement of the skyscraper.

Let us now turn from Art to other pursuits which are not ordinarily held to be imaginative but are more or less influenced by imaginative beliefs. And first of Politics. It is obvious that the government of a country will only be conducted with a prudential regard for future prospects when it is committed to men of experience, who have outgrown the emotional impulses and fancies of youth—that is to say, to a *Senate*. It was under a Senate that Rome rose to be mistress of a new civilization in the Mediterranean; and it was when the House of Lords was a power that this country extended its influence so widely in Victorian days. Democratic politics, on the other hand, must be very largely emotional. Masses of men may be persuaded by the offer of pecuniary advantages. But imaginative appeals to idealism or self-esteem are more effective. The "beliefs" of democratic politicians are, therefore, of the nature of imaginative assumptions. Each party has its own emotional "slogans." Amongst the most misleading is that "one cannot put the clock back." If this were true, there could be no repentance. Experience counts for little. It teaches, for instance, that industry is blunted by uniformity of wages. Yet democratic politicians dare not oppose the levelling wage-rules of Trade Union fellowships.

Nor are scientific doctrines free from imaginative influence. They rest very greatly indeed upon hypothetical assumptions which are "imaginary," although, for the most part, not inspired by emotion, but suggested by the needs of mathematics. This is, then, not the place to refer to them. But one of these doctrines certainly possesses a sentimental flavour—the conception that movement is only a change of relative place, and that Time and Space combine to form a mysterious Entity. So far from being "relative," movement appears to be the origin of, and to underlie, all the energies with which we are acquainted. And Time and Space are essentially different: the one is a *succession* of happenings and intervals, the other a *coincidence* of places and distances. Professor Einstein, indeed, confesses to the imaginative character of Relativity when he maintains that geometrical speculation should free itself from experiences of reality in order to give to its structures the "fullest possible logical unity."[1] But an extravaganza may develop logically and still be quite farcical. There is significance in the fact that *Alice's Adventures in Wonderland* was written by a distinguished mathematician. Imaginative theories concerning the stellar universe can hold the field because they cannot be checked by experience.

[1] *The Theory of Relativity*, page 2.

A bridge which was precisely constructed upon mathematical *data* would convict its engineer by collapsing.

So again the science of Logic has little in common with practical reasoning. For it would have the general lead to the particular, instead of the particular leading to the general; and it uses the complimentary assumption that the words we have invented are "things in themselves," and not merely irregularly fashioned signs for the expression of ideas. Political Economy is of such little practical utility because it develops the fanciful assumption that man acts prudently and not also emotionally. The practical business of economic life oscillates under the disturbance of an emotional—or, as it is called, a "psychological"—factor. For this leads to the over-estimation and anticipation of future possibilities, and this again to extravagant borrowing for expenditure and to financial speculation. Speculative borrowing and lending, buying and selling, swell the credit-assets of the commercial world, and greatly augment purchasing power. Prices rise, and there is a period of optimistic activity, followed by a commercial collapse when credit-assets disappear in bankruptcies, and it is realized that the future does not contain the possibilities that have been attributed to it. This seems to be the true explanation of the "booms" and "slumps" which periodically derange economic life.

History, again, is misled by the influence of the "dignity" of its subject: it is sentimentally—that is to say, self-complacently—expurgated and decorated, and assumes that important consequences must have important causes. But this is contrary to experience. "Behold how great a matter a little fire kindleth." That Helen should have kindled the Trojan war may be an artistic invention. But it is typical of much that has seriously influenced international politics.

Accordingly, Emotion brightens and dignifies life by mentally transfiguring it, so that it transcends the sober limitations of "common sense." It is the source of most of the joys that delight the present. But it misrepresents the future, for it is out of accord with some of our most imperative motives, and with the natural forces by which we are surrounded. It is no safe foundation for prudent forecasting. Marriages, full of hope, turn out unhappily. National achievements crumble and fall. Man loses touch with the future if emotional soarings drag his feet off the ground.

CHAPTER IX

REASON AND ITS ACCOMPLISHMENTS

WE contrast Reason sharply with Imagination. And justly; for Imagination creates, whereas Reason explores. Imagination is the typical product of masculine emotion. The ultimate origin of Reason is a protective feminine shrinking from the unknown, which, by a masculine reaction, is reversed into Curiosity, or a desire for discovery. Intelligence and Memory co-operate as its instruments. Its object is to discover the unknown from the known. It is, therefore, an indispensable guide to the gain of understanding. But it is infected by the depressing air of its origin, and its exercise gives no such pleasure as attends the use of the imagination. It must be tempted by the prospect of a definite success. Otherwise it is pleasanter to take refuge from doubt under the shelter of a belief.

Reason is constantly invoked as a High Court of Appeal. But attempts are rarely made to define it, and its jurisdiction is that of a very nebulous authority. Nor is this surprising. For "reasoning" may take one or other of three very distinct phases. They are developments of a very rapid process of inference, which eludes consciousness when it follows familiar lines and is not impeded by a doubt. We have seen that it plays an important part in everyday perceptions. When, for instance, we see that the pavement is wet, we know that it has been raining, although we have not seen the rain. The process has been described in Chapters I and IV. Its course may be likened to that of a shuttle which runs backwards in order to grip a thread and draw it forwards. Its backward course is guided by the intelligent appreciation of an analogy of some kind. This may be a connection in time as well as in space—in causality as well as in quality. In our illustration, the perceptive idea of a *particular* wet pavement analogically reproduces a reflective idea of a similar wet pavement in the past—or of a wet pavement in the indefinite—and this memorially reproduces an idea of rain, as its cause, since the two have been connected, as cause and consequence, in experience. A perceptive idea has thus led to the intelligent regeneration of one reflective idea, and this to the memorial reproduction of another. The latter is ascriptively united with the perceptive idea as its cause, forming the "conclusion" of the inference. Intelligence has opened a spring of memory which has supplied knowledge that would otherwise be missing.

The essential feature of the process of inference is the "identification" of one idea with another that brings recollections in its train. The more detailed is included in the less detailed and becomes one with it. It is by this identification that we recognize familiar objects.

When inference is impeded by a doubt, it runs slowly and deliberately, and presents itself more clearly. In this case a connecting clue, or "piece of evidence," is required in order to start the process. In reasoning about the weather, our clue is generally the barometer: in judging the merits of an apple, it is the name of its kind: in calculating the cost of a material, its price-rate. It is this clue—the "minor premiss" of scholastic Logic—that is commonly cited as "because," since the "generality" to which it leads is too obvious to need mention. There will be more to say on this point when we deal more generally with the process of thinking.

Conscious deliberate inference has evolved into three very distinct reasoning processes, differing in the source—or "reel," so to speak—from which the shuttle draws the needed thread. This may be either (1) experiences of the successions in which events occur as cause and consequence, origin and product, (2) generalized classes or rules, which classify and specify things or occurrences by their qualities or properties, or (3) standards of measurement which, through comparison, bring out equalities or differences of more or less between two qualities or properties. In the *first* case the idea of a mental or perceptive experience analogically reproduces an idea of a similar experience that has occurred in the past—or an indefinite idea of the experience—and this is succeeded by the memorial reproduction of and idea of what preceded or followed it. In the *second* case, the idea that is analogically reproduced is that of a general class, or ascriptive rule, which memorially supplies an idea of a quality or property that was previously unknown. In the *third* case the analogical reproduction is of a measuring standard, with which the initiating idea is compared in intensity, amount or degree. Degrees may be *quantitatively* defined by units of measurement, which are computed by numbers. The three processes may, accordingly, be distinguished as Consequential (or "Empirical"), Classificative and Quantitative. Consequential reasoning is that ordinarily appealed to as "Common Sense." It is "practical" in that it is based upon experience; and we shall find grounds for inferring that it is the reasoning process in which feminine influence predominates. For its standards are suggested by the *memory* of actual experiences.

In the first place of reasoning, in Common Sense fashion, from experience. Its object is to discover what has preceded, accompanied or followed a particular occurrence, or what will precede, accompany or follow it. So we reason, for instance, when we conclude that we have caught cold *because* we have been sitting in a draught, or that, as we are sitting in a draught, we shall *therefore* catch cold. These inferences from experience can, of course, be used negatively as well as positively—to contradict incorrect connections that have been drawn between incidents and their causes, accompaniments or consequences. Their trustworthiness depends upon the invariability, or generality, of the experiences from which they are inferred. If based upon casual or accidental successions, they may be very erroneous, confusing "post hoc" with "propter hoc." Nevertheless, Common Sense has been the lever by which man has raised his material position above that of the brutes. It is the reasoning instrument of *practical* science. For it suggests experiment as the means of discovering successions. It is strictly "logical." For Logic (akin to "ligament") implies *linking*, and Common Sense links the past and the present.

Classificative reasoning is the instrument of Logic and Philosophy, and is largely employed by Science. Its ultimate foundation is the instinctive faculty of the Mind to generalize ideas and ascriptions, thus producing classes and rules. We reason classificatively in deciding, for instance, that a plant is poisonous because it belongs to a poisonous species. The syllogistic form of scholastic Logic reverses the natural process. Its "classical" illustration is "All men are mortal: Socrates is a man: therefore Socrates is mortal." But in the natural course of inference, we think of Socrates as a man before we recall that "all men are mortal." It is only in scholastic Logic that the major precedes the minor premiss—that a general rule comes to mind before a particular call for it.

Classificative reasoning takes a "static" view of life. But it can widen its scope by treating the causes and consequences of things as their *qualities*, and in this fashion can be used as an instrument for reasoning from successions that occur in experience. From the general rule that "heat is expansive," for instance, we can infer that hot water cleanses more effectively than cold because it loosens particles of dirt by expanding them. But this rule involves the confusion of a precedent cause with a coincident quality, for expansion is not a characteristic *possession* but a *conse-*

quence of heat. This confusion of the dynamic with the static may lead to very incorrect conclusions. And there is another fertile cause of error. A class may be incorrectly generalized—including, for example, an Araucaria amongst Pines. Rules are often quite fanciful, being the offsprings of imagination, speculation or sentiment. A law that is often quoted is that "there is purpose in everything." But of what use are its wattles to a hen, its colours to a peacock butterfly or a cold in the head to any one of us?

In this process of reasoning there is an *appearance* of causal succession. For it runs inductively from the particular to the general—its "reason"—and deductively from the general to the particular—its "conclusion." It is, therefore, logical in that it involves *linking,* although its conclusions differ essentially from those arrived at by Common Sense. For they are irrespective of time: the *present* time in which they are expressed means no more than substantive existence. They are, however, drawn in terms of causality: their general grounds are introduced by a "because," and their particular conclusions by a "therefore," as if one was the *cause* of the other. The phases—positive or negative—that Classificative reasoning may assume have been elaborated with immense ingenuity by formal, or scholastic, Logic. But this cannot claim to have added materially to human understanding.

Quantitative reasoning is in relation to a unitary *standard* of measurement. An appropriate, but unfamiliar, title for it would be "Mensurative." The standard may be either perceived, or supplied, by the Mind as an idea. The process begins with the analogical comparison of two substantially similar qualities that are possessed by two objects, by an object and an idea, or by two ideas, one of which is used as a standard for determining the equality or difference, more or less, of the other in intensity, amount or degree. The standard may be the idea of a normal: a "large dog" is one that is larger than the normal size of dogs. Degrees of more or less are defined approximately by adverbs, quantitatively by numbers—that is to say, by arithmetical units that are derived from measurement, but evolve into a mental, or abstract existence. Arithmetic works with groups of these numbers, used in accordance with memorized rules. A further step leads to the evolution of Mathematics. The material worked upon may consist, not of groups of numbers, but of quantities that are defined by the ratios in which they stand to other quantities. The simplest of ratios is that between two numbers which if extended to another number discloses a fourth by "rule of three." Ratios are the wheels of mathematical science; they also serve as pegs on which to hang tissues of calculation, and the advance of mathematics has been pushed by discoveries—or assumptions—of their existence—as, for instance, of those between gravitationally attractive mass and distance, between optical angle, measured distance and actual size, between orbital velocity and distance from the orbit's centre, and between the expansive force of a gas and the volume to which it is reduced by pressure. They are generalized as "laws," but are by no means in all cases indisputably reliable.

Quantitive reasoning is also "logical": it draws deductions from contrasts. But the facts upon which it works, and the conclusions drawn from them, are, like those of Classificative reasoning, out of time. The multiplication table is a catalogue of timeless identities. Two and 3 do not *produce* 5, but *are* 5: equality is not a result but a self-existent fact: minus 4 does not contrarify 4, but is its contrary: 20 is not produced by 14 in the ratio of 7: 10, but *is* its complement. Quantitative, like Classificative, reasoning endeavours to extend its scope to successions. But it does so by treating an effect as existing simultaneously with its cause—as its "function," of "capability." Hence mathematical calculations are fundamentally "static" and may be out of accord with the actual results of the "dynamic" successions which are the realities of Life and Nature.

There is, then, a sharp contrast between Common Sense

and the processes of Classificative and Quantitative reasoning. The former depends upon actual experiences of successions in time, whereas the two latter are "spatial" mental processes. From the higher degree of their mentality they are inclined to lay exclusive claim to the title of "Reason." Hence Dr. Bridge's paradoxical line—"Reason will repudiate thee if thou thinkest to ask—why?"[1] This is a question which is always on the lips of Common Sense, and its disregard is an abounding source of error and unhappiness.

This fundamental difference between Common Sense and purely mental (or "intellectual") reasoning is in curious accordance with the fact that we have two distinct means of acquiring knowledge—that we draw our knowledge from two kinds of experiences—those that occur in time, and those that occur in space. The most intimate of the first kind are those revealed by our *intuitive* perceptions or feelings: they *follow* one another: pain follows injury, satisfaction food, shrinking fear, shame failure. Life is a series of successions; and this is borne out by the successions that we observe and remember in the world outside us. *Sensory* perceptions, on the other hand, "present" themselves as a series of standing pictures into which past or future changes are introduced as past or future *qualities* of the things that they affect. So we speak of "coming foliage" and "outworn fertility." Sensory perception involves, as it were, the sorting out of a collection of motor-cars in a parking place by comparing and identifying them, not the observation of a stream of cars in procession. And it is *material*—since our senses can only perceive immaterial energies through their material, or physical, effects.

It is a notable fact that the influence of these two worlds—of ourselves and of our environment—varies with the progress of civilization. The former loses and the latter gains in impressiveness, as man becomes sophisticated by the refinement of his sensory tastes. The Homeric poems

[1] *The Testament of Beauty*, I, 129.

and the Hebrew scriptures illustrate the earlier of these phases. They are concerned, for the most part, with human emotions, motives and conduct: the harmonies of justice, loyalty and gratitude, the successes of courage, skill and endurance are vividly appreciated and closely linked to the consequences that follow them: the "ups and downs" of life are keenly realized and ascribed to their causes in Fate or Divine Judgment. Impressed with his own vitalities, man extended them—literally, not figuratively—to the world around him. He "animated" Nature with human feeling, and deified its powers; and was led by fanciful analogies into attempts to control its action by magical contrivances. This tendency is illustrated in every page of Sir James Frazer's *Golden Bough*. With advancing sophistication man becomes more influenced by his sensory than by his intuitive perceptions; and, since his sensations present his surroundings as material, his outlook upon life becomes materialized. The influences which control him are *circumstances* that affect his senses—climate, food, riches, comforts, locomotion, education and hygiene. The Middle Ages were "spiritually-minded" and dirty: we are "materially-minded" and clean. War is regarded as the result, not of quarrels, but of armaments. On the other hand, there is a loss of introspective acumen—of insight into human nature. This is freely illustrated by the current of modern politics—by the grant of universal suffrage, for example. This mental blindness culminates in the theory of "behaviourism," which regards causal emotions and motives as merely the adjuncts of the conduct that they produce. It is the precise contrary of "animism."

Let us now consider the developments of Consequential (or Empirical) "Common Sense" reasoning, and what we owe to it. The simplest view that can be taken of two events in succession is that one is the leader, the other the follower: the Mind distinguishes particular successions as of stimulation and response, origin and offspring, source and product, energy and movement, action and result. From these there emerges an abstract idea of "causality." Causes are distinguished as generating, stimulating, developing, impelling, disturbing, resisting and transmitting. And it is discovered that causal energies are immaterial, their consequences material, and that these consequences develop into causal energies. Anger leads to violence, and violence to regret. Radiant heat engenders material heat, and this again radiates the immaterial.

These mental discernments are, however, of little practical importance compared with the knowledge that has been gained by the artificial experience of trial experiment—that is to say, of "arranged accident"—often initiated and guided by purely accidental discoveries. Judging from the inventions of recent years, man owes to experiment all the comforts and amenities of civilization—the use of fire in cooking, of various food-stuffs and intoxicants, of methods of cultivation and the development of staples, of weaving, moulding, carving and building. It is intelligent experiment that discovered the expansive energy of steam and of gas explosion, the action of propellers in driving steam vessels and aeroplanes, the mutual regeneration of electricity and of electro-magnetism—and has brought these forces into harness through the ingenious elaboration of mechanical contrivances. Faraday and Edison—pre-eminent amongst inventors—were experimenters, not mathematicians; and the brothers Wright—the pioneers of aviation—have expressly disowned any obligations to mathematical theory.

Wireless telephony, is, perhaps, the most notable of recent inventions. It was a lucky accident that set Hertz on the path to discovering that electro-magnetic (or "electrogenic") energy could be detached from the electric conditions that generate it, and could be broadcasted across space, to re-electrify suitably tuned metallic receivers. Accident is a feature of immense importance in our experience. How many men owe to it the wives that they marry, the careers that they choose, and their success or failure!

It dignifies us to attribute good or bad luck to Fate or Providence. But accidents can be reasonably explained. They are commonly due to clashes between the courses of different successions. We are surrounded with incalculable myriads of successions: each blade of grass, each pebble, has a succession of its own. If I tread on the cat's tail, it is because the course of my activities has clashed with the behaviour of the cat. There is such a clash between the shuffling of a pack of cards and its regular distribution in fours. An accident may also result from irregularity in the strength of one force which is competing with another. This leads to the accidental dropping of a teacup. It is utilized in roulette and the tossing of a coin. In both cases the steady force of gravity is met by muscular efforts which are never of exactly the same strength.

With all its victories, however, Common Sense reasoning must admit many serious defeats. For the preservation of health it has discovered such reliable remedies as castor-oil, opium, chloroform, quinine and zinc ointment. But its shortcomings, in this respect, are proved by the multitude of nostrums that are advertised in the papers. The origin and course of the common cold remain as mysterious as those of cancer; and, if the spread of malaria has been traced to a mosquito bite, the ultimate source of the mosquito's *virus* remains undiscovered. Surgical skill has attained marvellous efficiency. But medical science concerns itself too exclusively with *organs*, ignoring the physical effects of excess or deficiency in Memory, Intelligence and Emotional excitability. It is true that a tree cannot be felled with an axe that is broken: but the axe is useless without the vital energy of the man behind it. In predicting the weather, common sense is notoriously untrustworthy. It has been baffled by the facts that weather conditions result from the interaction of no less than four forces—gravity, heat, atmospheric elasticity and the earth's movement—that heat varies in intensity, and that these forces may act antagonistically as well as in co-operation.

In the sphere of politics, again, common sense has been of little avail. For its lessons are antagonized by idealism on the one hand, and by egotism on the other, and the effect of these motives varies very greatly with the influence of language as a persuasive "flux."

Turning now to the accomplishments of Classificative reasoning. Working upon the results of observation, this has given us—in the "ologies"—a vast amount of systematized knowledge, and has enlarged our vocabulary with many thousands of scientific names. But its material predisposition has blinded it to the causal influence of the immaterial, and, consequently, its researches lead very frequently to "dead-ends." It offers no explanation of the wonders which it systematizes. Geology shows that revolutionary changes have occurred in the climate of the earth's various regions: fossils of plants that required warmth and sunshine are found, for instance, under the glaciers of the Antarctic. Common sense would suggest that those shifts must have resulted from drastic changes in the inclination of the earth's axis. Science ignores this inference: it is disconcerting to admit that the earth can have "wobbled" so greatly. The curious variations of the compass are similarly left unexplained, although experience would attribute them to changes in the earth's shape. For a change in the direction of a magnet's north and south poles follows a change of form that shifts the line of its longest diameter.

Arguing from the discovery of primitive skulls in various parts of the world, man's original habitat is located in places where he would have starved, before he learnt to produce and store food, or have been frozen, before he had learnt to warm and clothe himself. The Mind is identified with the brain, in disregard of the experience that masses of the brain can be excised without loss of mental powers. Vital activities are narrowly identified with organs in spite of the illuminating facts that the organs of a caterpillar, or a fly grub, are dissolved into a featureless fluid as it passes into the chrysalis stage, and that from this unorganized mass there develops an entirely new set of organs, suitable for a winged life. The doctrine of Evolution is accepted. But evolution is entirely dependent upon the occurrence of variations, for which the only logical explanation lies in the initiatory energy of *physical* Intelligence. But the existence of intelligence apart from the Mind seems to belittle the Mind, and science has shrunk from accepting it.

Quantitative (or Mensurative) reasoning can also, of course, pride itself upon its triumphs. It has elaborated the indispensable art of spatial surveying. In the domain of Astronomy, its calculations have weighed the earth, and the heavenly bodies, and have reduced the Universe to a spaced and timed system of rotations and revolutions. In its highest flights it has elaborated cosmic hypotheses which stir the imagination with the spirit of Romance. But these hypotheses are privileged in that they cannot be subjected to a practical test. Engineers must multiply by five[1] (the Factor of Safety) the mathematical bases of their projects. We can understand how the Romans built so securely before the cipher was invented, and how Gothic cathedrals were constructed by "rule of thumb." The brothers Wright—the pioneers of aviation—found that mathematical *data* (or ratios) were of no service to them in their experiments, and have expressly declared so. The mathematics of sound do not protect an architect from building a hall which is acoustically deplorable.

The truth is that, in its unremitting search for quantitative *data*, or ratios, mathematical science attempts to measure the immeasurable. Solids and liquids can be gauged easily enough. But a gas can only be measured when it is *confined*—when, that is to say, it is deprived of the expansive buoyancy which characterizes the gaseous condition. Consequently weighments of air greatly overstate the weight of the atmosphere, and understate its volume. This is, however, only one of a series of difficulties. Movement

[1] In the case of the unfortunate airship R101 the factor was only 3.

cannot be measured *quantitatively*, since it possesses no volume: hence mathematical physics can ignore its energy, and regard it as simply a change of place. Natural conditions are entirely dependent upon such immaterial forces as gravitational pressure, elasticity, heat, light, electricity and electro-magnetism. These vary in intensity, but not in quantity, and can no more be quantitatively measured than a headache or a fit of ill-temper. Endeavours are made to measure them through the amounts of the material effects that they produce—as heat, for instance, is measured by the expansion of mercury. But these material consequences are by no means in regular proportionate accord with the intensity of the forces that produce them. The material expansion produced by heat is not quite regular in the case of mercury, and with water is extraordinarily uneven. Water actually *expands* on freezing, and, when melting ice or evaporating steam, its responses change their character and become transformative instead of expansive. Heat is also measured in "calories." But these are units, not of heat but of water-volume, that are raised a degree in temperature. The measurement of energy is, again, attempted by measuring the material consequences of the resistance it meets and overcomes. But the relation between an energy and a resistance is not constant: it varies, not only with the character of a material, but with the abruptness of the onset and at different stages of the conflict. Measuring an energy by its material effects may, indeed, be likened to the measurement of a father by his son. The distinction between an energy and its product may be disguised by regarding the product as a "function" or "co-efficient" of the energy. But this is an evasion that may easily become deceptive. For instance, the "Second law of Thermodynamics"—the source of so much speculation—confuses the energy of heat with the gaseous expansive energy which is its product.

There are other illogical conventions that are employed to meet these difficulties. It is assumed that all energies are merely phases of one all-pervading self-conserving Energy which can be regarded as a mathematical "constant." But this is contradicted by experience. Movement cannot be identified with heat, although it can produce it. Nor can heat be unified with gravity: indeed, changes of weather are in great measure due to an enduring conflict between the two. In experience, inanimate, like living, energies rise and fall, come and go. Energy may remain "latent," as a "potentiality." But it is in this case merely a "sensibility," since it can only be aroused by a stimulus—that is to say, by the action of another energy.

Gravitational pressure is the most tremendous of the forces that assail us. The tenets of science in regard to it are out of date as well as inadequate. The doctrine that defines it as an attraction that draws material bodies together has been discredited by the discovery that it deflects light. In actual experience—electrical action apart—things do not attract one another, and instances that can be cited to the contrary can be otherwise explained. In generating the tides, the sun and moon do not attract masses of water. For it can be proved that the tidal impulse, or "throb," spreads itself at hundreds of miles an hour, and if there was a shifting of water at this rate, navigation would be impossible. There is no material rise and fall until the sea-water nears coast-lines, and loses the resistant support of its own mass-continuity. Gravity is held to be the moving force of the solar system. But experience would ascribe these rotations and revolutions to a "gearing" of enormous vortices, or whirls, that are immaterial but as real as are radiant heat and light. Gravitational pressure would be a vortical product. The solar system would be a combination of material substance with immaterial movement; and, if the protons and electrons of matter also revolve in immaterial vortices, the extraordinary fact can be explained that the material can be affected through the immaterial and the immaterial through the material—that we can warm our hands by exposing them to radiant heat or by the material friction of rubbing them. The atoms and molecules of chemistry would not be "substantial" but "materio-etheric" systems of various complexities. The combination of immaterial movement with material substance would, moreover, explain two striking facts. One is the *elasticity* of matter, which is incompatible with substantiality. The other is the curious "alternate reversals of parentage" that occur not only in the inanimate world but in ourselves. Radiant heat kindles material heat and is radiotively kindled by it: our own energy generates movement and is regenerated by it.

In fine, quantitative calculation is of indispensable assistance in dealing with the material world, but its invasions of the immaterial world are hopeless, however heroic. Science would gain closer contact with Nature if it kept closer touch with experience. The study of acoustics affords an illustration in point. More attention should be given to the dimensions and shapes of halls that have proved to be satisfactory. This might disclose a relation between dimensions and sounding, such as that between length and frequency in radio reception. And it would at least provide exemplars for copy. Similarly with the uncertainties that attend radio transmission. The vagaries of "wireless waves" might be traced to their source if their "natural history" was more systematically studied—the influences upon them of different atmospheric conditions, of heat and light, of the constitution of the subsoil and of the points of the compass.

CHAPTER X

MENTAL ARTIFICIALITIES

WE keenly appreciate the contrast between the natural and the artificial. The one is physical, the other mental. Our feelings and actions are "natural" when they are dictated by the body and its sensory organs, energized by masculine emotion, and directed by feminine motives, whether in their primary phases or as reversed by stresses of masculinity: they are "artificial" when they are suggested by thoughts, influencing or influenced by, these motiving emotions. It is natural to be hungry, enlivened, loving, angry or covetous: it is artificial to be dignified or restrained, conventionally or persuasively polite, and to be enthusiastically or pretentiously idealistic. Courage is natural when it is "physical," artificial when it is "self-imposed." We respect the artificial because it is a manifestation of success. But our respect for it is a *constraint*, and the artificial becomes the ludicrous if its inherent weakness is irresistibly unveiled. We cannot help smiling at the immoralities of an earnest moral propagandist.

Artificiality culminates in imagination, for this creates a world of personalities, things and occurrences that has no objective existence whatever. But it is manifested in many other phases of the unreal. The general, indefinite and abstract ideas that are elaborated by the Mind are artificial. They have only a mental existence although they have been evolved from perceptive experience. There is, for instance, no such real thing as Justice *in the abstract*, although we are pleased and offended by paricular experiences of the harmonious just and the discordant unjust. The embodiment of our ideals in particular persons or things may be quite artificial. The beloved is not as perfect as she appears to her lover: children are not as faultless as their mother sees them: we are not as admirable as we seem to be to ourselves. Dominated as he is by physical motives, no one can be really "free." The respect that is given to a leader may be evoked by quite undeserved prestige. The success that is found in notoriety has no real foundation.

Prominent amongst these artificialities are the *generalizations*—called "beliefs," "rules" or "laws" to which we submit our judgments. To generalize experiences is, as we have seen, an instinctive process of the Mind, originating in the identifying and comparing powers of Intelligence. It generalizes, not only ideas, but connections that occur in experience—either in qualification or in succession. These concepts are of immense importance to our lives and conduct, and are dignified by the name of "laws." A law (etymologically akin to "ligament") is a *link* between a cause and a consequence. They are also called "principles." A man "of high principle" is one whose behaviour conforms to certain "moral laws."

The connections between things and qualities, or between things and causes or consequences, which these laws formulate are of very different kinds. Laws may express facts as they are established by experience—for instance, that arsenic is poisonous, that heat expands materials and that cold condenses moisture. In this case they are "physical," or "natural," laws. They may express sequences as they "seem to be," or "might be"—sequences that would explain courses of events, as, for example, that gravitation is the result of an attraction which masses of material have for one another, that light and sound are progressions of "waves," and that electrical induction is caused by "electrons." Such laws are hypothetical or theoretical. Laws may be probabilities, or "normals," deduced from the calculation of averages. Such arithmetical "means" are, of course, only called "laws" out of compliment. For an average misrepresents the effects of a number of dynamic successions by reducing them to an indefinite singularity. The course of events is generally more dependent upon extremes than upon "means." A single night's hard frost will do far more harm than a low monthly average. Laws may represent sequences as we should like them to be—as that "the voice of the people is the voice of God," that "force is no remedy" (that is to say, that punishment is of no avail), or that "charity covers a multitude of sins." These are "sentimental" generalizations. Laws may express sequences which "ought" to occur. In this case they are "moral laws." Religious generalizations, or laws, are expressed as "creeds." And superstition adds to misleading generalities very largely indeed.

Laws are of great assistance as "ready reckoners": they economize thought. Logic styles them the "premisses" of its reasoning: they are, in fact, the standards from which it makes deductions. The hypothetical laws, or theories, of Science are useful in guiding experiment. But, as we have seen in the last chapter, they hinder advance unless they are promptly discarded when impugned by experience. Laws of the "sentimental" kind gratify our feelings. It dignifies human nature to think of government "of the people, by the people, for the people," and of liberty as "the most precious heritage of mankind"—kind-hearted to hold that "those in need have a *right* to be supported by their fellows." It is pleasanter to think of trade as "free" than as "fettered," and of society as being cemented by persuasion rather than as consolidated by command. But these ideals are, not uncommonly, in flat contradiction to experience; and their influence goes far to explain the extraordinary rises and falls that give human civilization so much dramatic interest. Such sentimental generalities are the mental armoury of a nation's "intellectuals," and are the "slogans" of the political enthusiasts who would wreck the present in order to provide foundation for a Utopian future—the men who ushered in, and were eaten up by the excesses of the French and Russian revolutions. History shows that idealistic revolutions, claiming Liberty and Equality, are hatched out, not in streets, but in class-rooms: they are the products, not of the indigent, but of the "intelligenzia."

Moral laws are of cardinal importance to society. Their ultimate origin is, as I have shown, in our appreciation of mental harmonies. But the degree of this appreciation varies from one individual to another. The harmonious may be only the familiar, and its influence is beset by attacks from the more powerful motives of the desire for pleasure or for profit. It is then of great value that moral laws should be formulated in writings which claim "inspired authority," since this gives them a religious sanction. This is the effect of the Christian Bible, and of the Moslem Koran. In the absence of such an authority morality tends to become an arguable question of advantage and disadvantage, as is illustrated by the Greeks and Romans and by the Hindus of the present day. There is accordingly good reason for the affiliation of Christians and Moslems as "people of the Book." Conduct is more trustworthy when it is influenced by a law than when it is open to discussion from a hedonistic or utilitarian standpoint.

The laws of civil and criminal jurisprudence are similarly artificial "links" between certain actions and certain penalties. They generally take their standards from the morality of the day, and safeguard this morality by enforcing it. But they also create a morality, as have the British laws against *suttee* and infanticide in India. Like other laws, they maintain their existence long after their utility has passed away.

Education begins as a natural, but develops into a highly artificial process. Its germ is in the impulse to *imitate* which is prompted by physical as well as by mental

Intelligence. In the light of mother-love, learning grows into teaching—the instrument for giving continuance to culture by regenerating its accomplishments in the minds of the young. It is an arresting thought that a man's language, religion, manners, dress, beliefs and loyalties are all determined by the fashion of his upbringing. He is born mentally free. But he becomes mentally fettered by his surroundings. He is, as it were, "inoculated" by his elders with the ideas which form their mental capital, so that the acquirements of the past are carried forward into the future. His mind is furnished not by him, but for him. Left to itself, it is improbable that a generation of mankind would rise very much above the level of the brutes. There are very well authenticated accounts of "wolf-children"—children that have been carried off in infancy by she-wolves and suckled by them, and have been captured when too large to take shelter in the wolf's burrow. They all agree in representing them as brutish, and, moreover, as quite unteachable. One[1] of them was in a missionary asylum in the Agra district of India from 1867 to 1895; and his case has been described in a pamphlet which was written in the latter years by the Rev. C. S. Valentine, Principal of the Agra Medical Mission. He was discovered sitting in the company of a wolf at the entrance of a burrow, and was captured under the orders of the District Magistrate, and sent to the asylum. During the years of his stay there he never attained a completely erect position, he never learnt to speak, and his sole accomplishment seems to have been that he used his fingers in eating his food instead of "wolfing" it. Education may be enslaving, but it is also uplifting. It carries on civilization from one generation to another. It must be begun in infancy, and we, therefore, owe it ultimately to our mothers. There is an old saying of the Jesuits, "Give me a child up to six and I care not what you do afterwards to him."

The continuance of civilization must then be compared,

[1] Particulars of other cases are given in a note appended to this chapter.

not to the steady growth of a forest, but the periodic sowings and croppings of cultivated land. If the sowings are interrupted, civilization disappears. So Roman culture perished.

That man can be "inoculated" with ideas in this fashion is obviously due to the detachment of his ideas from particular experiences. He could not be taught "not to steal"—*as a rule*—if his ideas of stealing were inseparably connected with particular objects. The generalization and abstraction of ideas lead to the formation of general and abstract propositions, or laws, such as those which we have just been considering. Education consists very largely in the instilling of these laws or "principles." They become so firmly seated in the mind by habit that any inconsistencies or contradictions that occur are ignored. We avert our eyes from them and dislike, as "heretics," those who call attention to them. "*La bêtise humaine*," which gave Pascal his clearest notion of infinite space, comes from the unquestioning acceptance of generalities, and not from any lack of natural intelligence.

Education may be imitative, authoritative or persuasive. That of the nursery is very largely imitative. Children "imbibe" conduct and "principles" from their surroundings, and retain them as habits. The spontaneously imitative character of a child's early education may very well explain the curious fact that the experiences of our first three or four years take no hold in conscious memory, and cannot be recalled. In this automatic fashion children "absorb" the "atmosphere" of their family, so that trades and pursuits tend to become "hereditary." Bible history shows that there is nothing in the character of the Jews to render them peculiarly prone to money-getting. But, during many centuries, their present was rendered so unpleasant by Christian society that they naturally turned to future profit as the sole means of winning success, and this tendency has been transmitted from generation to generation by imitative assimilation.

The imitative education of our early years is powerfully assisted by admiration. To a child adults are admirable because they are so much larger and stronger than itself, and from this comes a respect for age—and even for antiquity as a *quality* of age—that persists throughout life. Traces of it may be discerned amongst birds and beasts. Admiration, as we have seen, expresses itself in imitation—that is to say, in "approaching" the admired object by assimilating oneself to it.

Authoritative education also commences in the nursery. It supplements the child's imitative propensities by painful or pleasurable inducements. These may be physical—the pain of a slapping or the pleasure of a chocolate, for instance. Or they may be mental—the shame of being blamed or the pride of winning success, praise or a prize. The efficacy of either appeal depends upon the degree of the child's inherited mental sensibility. If this is acute, mental pleasures and pains suffice: thoughts of success and failure are adequate incentives in themselves. But if physical inclinations predominate, appeals to the Mind are of little avail. Discipline must be enforced by the prospect of physical pleasure or pain, and the latter is by far the most effective. For the pleasure of a disobedience will outbalance that of a caress, or a sweetmeat, while it is held in check by the prospect of a whipping. At school and college authority becomes more formal and precise. But it still uses imitation as one of its instruments. For we imitate another's wishes when we give effect to them, and another's ideas when we adopt them. At school a boy acquires, not only memorized knowledge, but tastes, principles, disciplines and loyalties which are of even greater importance. He begins by learning language—that is to say, reading and writing—and arithmetic. These are, of course, primarily *instruments*. But their utility in gaining success promotes them to be *objects* in themselves, and they are, therefore, studied for their own sake. The teaching of Greek and Latin, however, induces very few students to maintain their acquaintance with classical literature in after life. And the utility of the higher mathematics is greatly overrated. For a commission in the Royal Engineers a high standard of mathematical proficiency is required. But their duties seldom involve so much as a sum in algebra. It is urged that the higher mathematics are of benefit in increasing mental capacity quite apart from considerations of their utility. This may be doubted. For the Mind seems to lose practical sense as it becomes more and more fascinated by the artificialities of shadowland.

It is obviously desirable that man should acquire some knowledge of his material surroundings—of geography, natural history and of physical and chemical changes and reactions. In present-day schools Science has gained substantial recognition. But one is not stimulated or advantaged by the unintelligent assimilation of scientific hypotheses—that is to say, by their acceptance in ignorance of the facts from which they have been deduced. It is, indeed, very disconcerting to realize how many very successful men—eminent in practical science as well as in industry and commerce—have had none but the most elementary school instruction. One may reasonably even suspect that high education, while increasing "knowledge," actually blunts the intelligence. The remarkable decline of curiosity from childhood upwards may certainly be ascribed to the lulling—or doping—effect of the prestige of the general rules and dogmas that are inculcated by education. There are schoolmasters who will admit that boys are less intelligent when they leave school than when they come to it. For they are not encouraged to "think for themselves." Inquisitive thought would, in fact, be inconvenient. It is disconcerting—and irritating—to hear accepted authorities called in question.

It is to be noted that education blunts intelligence by running counter to evolution in two important particulars. An idea must obviously exist before a word is invented to express it. Yet we are taught to regard the word as all-important and the idea as simply its "meaning." Again, particular experiences must precede the formation of general rules. But education sets the rules in the forefront, and the particulars, upon which the rules are founded, are cited as "illustrations." Two momentous consequences ensue from this inversion—the immense respect in which words are held, and our readiness to accept generalities without subjecting them to the test of experience.

The most useful of educative studies might be history, since this would open the eyes of the growing generation to the successful and unsuccessful experiences of its predecessors. But history is not taught from this point of view, and is, in the main, an interesting record of wars and persecutions, and of the achievements of men who have won notoriety by their military abilities, their persuasiveness, or their imaginative talents. And, speaking generally, it is highly—and deceptively—coloured by the emotional partialities and prejudices of its writers. Little endeavour is made dispassionately to trace successions of cause and effect, and emphasize their lessons. Its uselessness as a guide to political conduct is strikingly illustrated by the Peace of Versailles.

The principal *taste* acquired at school is that for athletics, and certain forms of sport. This adds very greatly to the pleasure of life by giving it an object, which, however ephemeral, is undeniably exciting. The pleasure that might be gained by artistic appreciation and execution receives less attention. Religious influences apart, morality is taught as adherence to certain general principles, amongst which "good form" is of great importance. Habits of discipline are acquired, and, in particular the subordination of oneself in "team-work" which is so useful in a democratic State. Of equal importance are the "loyalties" that are instilled—loyalties not only to the Head of the State, or the Party, but to those who are accepted authorities or have been enshrined as national heroes. It becomes "treasonable" to question the conclusions of Newton, or the authorship of the plays that are attributed to Shakespeare. Such loyalties delayed for two centuries the general acceptance of Copernicus' discovery that the earth moved round the sun. They have a very remarkable effect in blinding us to the errors of our political chiefs, so that they are ignored rather than forgiven.

Education becomes *persuasive* in the hands of politicians and journalists. The texts from which they preach are generalities that are often quite delusive. The arguments with which they support them may be material, such as a rise of wages. They may appeal to our self-esteem, to our patriotic appreciation of the dignity of our country, or to the liberty that is in fact relief from feelings of inferiority, and are generally sugared with compliments. Rarely do they venture to draw lessons from past experiences. For these would very often be decidedly unpleasant.

These phases of persuasive propaganda all rest upon an underlying artificiality—the transfer of thought from one person to another by means of spoken or written words. By their conveyance of ideas words are instruments for the "insinuation" of thoughts, and consequently for the provocation of emotions and motives. The process resembles telepathy, but is actually one of "propagation." We may criticize and disagree with the thoughts that are thus bred in us, as we may with hasty perceptions and conclusions of our own. But our general attitude is one of acceptance, especially if we are attracted by the spice of sex-appeal or adventure. So we are "led away" by an interesting novel. Religious or moral discourses must be exciting in order to be convincing. The influence of words may be redeeming as well as amusing. But it may also be poisonous, and it has, therefore, great dangers.

Words are, indeed, so powerful that we come to regard them as mysterious "things in themselves," and not as mere "idea-carriers." We appreciate good "literary expression" although in darkness as to what it expresses. In magniloquence, words become attractive through their size, quite apart from their meaning. Indeed, it requires an effort to realize the metaphorical adaptations that are involved in a vast number of the words in common use—for example, "generality," "generosity," "deliberation," "intelligence" and "value." But, when realized, their use becomes attractive as a "conceit." So language becomes "affected," or "euphuistic"—a tendency that was at its height three and a half centuries ago, and materially influenced the diction of Shakespeare. This affectation, or "preciosity," infects manners also, pressing them to become "genteel." We are, however, delighted when gentility loses its bridal veil and gives us unexpected glimpses of underlying vulgarities.

This brings us face to face with the artificiality of Pretence—commonly called "artful." We all acknowledge sincerity to be a virtue, and resent any imputations of insincerity. But the most casual reflection upon one's daily experiences suffice to show how largely "make-believe" enters into the atmosphere of social life. Dogs are capable of "shamming," but only in a small way. Man has far greater capacities of pretence. Owing to the detachment of his ideas from their originating experiences, he can think of conduct or language apart from the motives that they *naturally* serve, and can "affectedly" make use of them for the accomplishment of an entirely different purpose. He can make assumptions—persuasively dignifying or amusing others and even himself—which suggest "make-believe," or "humbug," in speech and action. Hence comes his capacity for "acting,"[1] pretending, for imposing upon others and for deceiving them. This supplies the politeness which lubricates social intercourse, and smooths out friction that would otherwise constantly disturb it. Its instruments are insincere compliments, and insincere disavowals of them. Assurances of success, superiority or consideration are amongst life's greatest pleasures. Is not

[1] It is remarkable that we should use the same word—"acting"—for doing things and for pretending to do them.

Christianity so comforting because it is so complimentary? "If you please" and "thank you" commonly express obligations that are merely pretended. But they imply a gratifying consideration and are therefore conciliatory. Such politenesses cease to be insincere when they become habitual. But they continue to be expressions which are not "felt." How many of those who sign themselves "Your obedient servant," or merely "Yours sincerely," *feel* what they write? Without these pretences, cultured society could not exist. Those who dispense with them—schoolboys, for instance—are constantly quarrelling. And since they serve to stiffen our own dignity as well as to soften the antagonism of others, life may become a course of histrionics, only broken by realities at meal-times and bedtime. Yet we remain susceptible to the harmonious influence of Sincerity, and honour it, although "more in the breach than in the observance."

The emotional sensibility which renders politeness and compliments so soothing is the natural fruit of our ideas of our own—and of human—dignity. In our hearts we are doubtful of its actuality: much religious teaching denies it and enjoins the humility of repentance; and our assumption of its existence is very largely pretended. Indeed, were our confidence in it quite assured, we should not be so easily disturbed by brusqueness of manner, slights and criticisms. The idea is incompatible with the humbler of our daily necessities, and with the humorous appreciation of realities which gives spice to gossip and takes us behind the scenes of dignified histories. Yet—save for the feminine prickings of love, pain and fear—there is nothing that influences us more profoundly. It burdens us, so to speak, with an instrument upon which any other person can play as he wills, making harmonious or discordant music to delude or disturb us.

The pretence of a deferential sympathy is, therefore, the most valuable instrument of skilful salesmanship. Nowadays we have all become "commercially-minded," and are not struck by the insincerity of blatant advertisement, and the humiliating attitude that it involves. Fifty years ago boastful "publicity" was regarded as demeaning. Now it is accepted as an important element of national life. And it is not, of course, only in commerce that "make-believe" is a valuable instrument of success. Without some measure of it, could the professional classes maintain their income, or democratic politicians retain their credit? Is *Punch* alone in scenting an air of unreality in parliamentary business—in catching a humorous resemblance to the "play-acting" of a troupe of children, surrounded by a ring of spectators, and desperately afraid of offending any considerable number of them? All things together, it is not too much to say that pretence is the corner-stone of cultured civilization. It is far pleasanter than reality. But it has its dangers. We may speak on the higher plane, but must generally act on the lower plane to be successful. And we cannot disarm reality by disowning it. Power, Loyalty, Art, Morality and International Comity lose stability as well as force of appeal, when they rest upon the slippery surface of a sham.

"Pretending" vanishes before a surge of violent emotion. Hence the cold-blooded peoples of the North are better able to preserve artificiality of manners than the more emotional Southerners. Albion is called "perfide" because her children can keep up a mask of respectable pretence longer than her critics.

Note on Wolf-Children

The first authentic account of wolf-children in India is that given by Major-General Sir William Sleeman in his *Rambles Through Oudh*, published in 1849. In the course of an official tour through this province—at a time when it was still under Native rule—his attention was attracted by the large number of wolves which infested some localities, and from time to time carried off young children. It had happened, he was informed, that the infants had not been killed, but been nurtured by she-wolves, and had been subsequently rescued when grown too large to enter the burrows. He heard of six cases in which this had occurred within the memory of his informants. Two of these rescued waifs he saw himself, one of them having been for some years under the observation of an English officer (Captain Nicholetts of the 1st Oudh Infantry), who had given the boy shelter in his household. Neither of them showed any traces of human manners. They ran on all-fours: they had no articulate speech: they preferred the society of dogs to that of men and would permit dogs to share their food with them.

Eighteen years later, in 1867, another of these unfortunates was seen by my friend, Mr. W. C. Bennett (of the Indian Civil Service), in the Partabgarh Lunatic Asylum—also in Oudh. Mr. Bennett informed me of his behaviour that his posture was semi-erect: he shuffled about on his "hind-legs," occasionally touching the ground with his hands: he made no use of articulate words: he had no sense of decency, and he preferred raw to cooked meat.

More recently still, two wolf-children have come under observation in the Agra district. One of them was in the Secundra Missionary Asylum up to 1895. His case has been referred to in the text of this chapter. Another was in the Government Lunatic Asylum from 1891 to 1913. The official record of his admission states "that he was taken from a wolf's den." I have been informed by the officer who was for four years in immediate charge of him that "he could only walk erect on quite level ground: his position in walking resembled that of a monkey, except that his head was thrown well back: he never learnt to speak."

There is a still more recent case in point. Through the kindness of Sir Malcolm Hailey—Governor of the United Provinces of India—I have received copies of official records concerning a girl who strayed into the outskirts of the town of Budaon in April 1932. She was naked and had no sense of decency. She attacked with her nails those who interfered with her, or crawled away on all-fours to hide herself. It was obvious from her appearance that this was her ordinary method of progression: she had callosities on the palms of her hands, knee-caps and toe-joints, and the muscles of her forearms and calves were withered. Indeed she could not walk upright: nor could she speak. She would eat nothing but raw meat, and disgusted those who tried to help her by eating a dead rat which was lying in the street, and by seizing a passing kid by its ears with her teeth. In the orphanage to which she was committed, she has learnt to eat vegetable food, to walk upright with assistance, and to understand some simple phrases. Her connection with a wolf foster-mother has not been directly established. But it is an obvious inference that she has been nurtured by a four-legged carniverous animal.

CHAPTER XI

THE PROCESS OF THINKING

"THINKING," as we have seen in Chapter IV, is evolved from the process of perception: an accompaniment of "conscious-making" ideas grows into independent existence. We perceive by ascribing certain conditions to certain objects. The process of thought follows similar lines. But the ideas with which it deals are usually "generals," "indefinites" or "abstracts" in place of particulars, and its objects are called "subjects." In listening, or reading, perception is recombined with thought. We hear or see *words*, and these words are idea-carrying symbols which take the place of the objects of ordinary perception. Through close memorial association, they reproduce in us their "meanings," and we link these meanings into reflective sequences—that is to say, we "understand" what we hear or read—by appreciating the memorial or intelligent connections—and experiencing the feelings—that suggested them to their originators. In conversation this "imitative" thought, as it may be called, alternates with original thought as we hear and reply. Imitative thought grows immensely in importance with the spread of public speaking, newspapers and books. But its source is in original thought, and it is with this that we will commence.

We usually think in words. But wordless thought is quite possible. A dog has no words; but it would be absurd to hold that it does not think. Words immensely facilitate the use of general, indefinite or abstract ideas by acting as their material labels. The word "before," for instance, enables us to think easily of one thing as occurring in advance of another. But the conception of a "being before" must have preceded the invention of a label for it, and, beyond doubt, can occur to a dog. And it is, of course, the use of words that enables us to communicate our thoughts to others.

The course of thought is very difficult to follow and analyse. For it is interrupted if we attempt to watch it in ourselves. And, if we endeavour to unravel written or printed thought, we lose its meaning in following its shuttle-like oscillations; and these, on the other hand, elude us if we attend to its meaning. These difficulties are, moreover, greatly increased by the versatility of which thought is capable in its phrasing, or "make-up." Thus we can think that "the weather has changed," or "has suffered a change," or that "a change has come about in the weather." The Mind can throw thoughts into various phases because its instruments—its individualizations and its descriptive and ascriptive attachments—are its own creations. Accordingly, the same thought may be given different presentments. Activities or qualities that suggest themselves may be used either descriptively or ascriptively. Speaking generally, the "make-up" of a thought is suggested by the idea that is to be particularly emphasized or accentuated. But phrasing is greatly influenced by custom, and an appreciation of rhythm and "elegance" of style.

Since the Mind is a combination of Emotion and Thought, emotions and motives enter into its workings as well as ideas. The two elements act upon, and are acted upon by, one another. Ideas kindle masculine emotion, and these draw feminine motives in their train. When a motive is concerned with the present—as a like or dislike—thought is appreciative or imaginative: it is prospective, or purposeful—arousing a want or urging a *pursuit*—when the motive is concerned with the future. If two objects are in view, we are led to a *choice*: we choose that which seems to be most pleasurable—or least displeasurable—unless we are impelled to face an unpleasantness, in order to obtain a pleasure, satisfaction, or relief that lies beyond it. In the first case we appear to make "an effort of will." In both cases we "make up our minds." But over and above these exercises of so-called "will-power," we owe to our emotional endowment the elastically resistant *stability* which rejects incongruous or discordant impressions or notions, and keeps thought "to the point." Failing this support, we should be as "impressionable" as one under hypnotic influence. It enables us to negative, or contradict, thoughts, whether self-presented or suggested, which conflict with our beliefs, prejudices or convictions. This annulment of an ascription is primarily emotional, and this is commonly the case with the contradictions of ordinary conversation. But, like all emotional activities, it can pass into a purposeful phase, and can be used as the conclusion of a reasoning inference, as a method of phrasing, or to deceive another.

The "feelings" which thus enter into thought may have the effect of diverting its current into new channels. This increases the difficulty of observing its course. An idea that is reproduced, memorially or intelligently, may excite a new motive which switches thought off on to another line. Thought may, then, be compared to the unrolling of a cinema film in the composition of which we ourselves take part. Its ideas stir us, as do the pictures, and their stirrings constantly present new pictures. Its presentments are changed by the feelings that their predecessors have provoked.

These feelings themselves enter into thought. We are as conscious of them as we are of the ideas that excite them. Thought such as "I think," "I am glad," "I hope," "I believe," "I doubt" are part and parcel of the current. They differ from "I am looking," or "I hear," only in being intuitive, not sensory, perceptions. During self-suggested thought sensory perception is an abeyance. But intuitive perception persists. The ideas that it presents must, however, be distinguished from purely *reflective* ideas of feelings. Thus, if in thought comes the fear of another's anger, the fear is an emotional reality, which exists apart from thought, but there is only a mental idea of the anger.

Emotional feelings may also affect the character of thought by throwing it into imaginative or sentimental phases. Our ideas become picturesquely fanciful. We fall under the influence of sentimental hopes, beliefs or convictions, which move us more strongly than common sense deductions from experience. They can only be discarded by an effort, and this must be stimulated by the prospect of a pleasure, or advantage, of some kind, or of a misfortune that can only be averted by their abandonment. The pleasing ideal of Truth, as a moral harmony, is but very rarely a sufficient inducement.

Passing now to the current of ideas that ripples over the depths of emotion, and stirs them in passing, it is a striking fact that their course is in extraordinary contrast to that of our experiences of Life and Nature. These are all of *successions* in which something follows a cause, an origin, a generator or at least a predecessor. They are processions in time, and time is marked by the changes that they occasion. A consequence is later in time than its cause. Motion is a succession of movements that can be used to measure time: the processes of generation and growth are timed successions. The ascriptions of thought also occur in succession: one follows another. And here we must distinguish between the "ruling" ascriptions that are the "gist" of our thoughts and subsidiary ascriptions that are used to *describe* the subject and the conditions that are ascribed to it. These subsidiary ascriptions are of very various kinds. They may, for instance, particularize the subject or the condition by *relating* it to something else in time or place ("who," "when"), by *specifying* it ("that"), by *comparing* it ("as," "than"), by imagination ("as if"), by inference ("since," "therefore"), by *explanation* ("because"), by objection, limitation or elimination ("but," "although"), by conjoining something else. ("and") or by an alternative ("or"). These subsidiary ascriptions are merely descriptive details which add to the particularity of the ruling ascription. This is ordinarily ended by a full stop, a colon or a semi-colon—or by the introduction of something that is conjoined with, or alternative to, the ruling ascription.

In thought that is simply reminiscent or narrative, ruling ascriptions very commonly follow one another in time—that is to say, in the order in which the happenings or perceptions that they present actually occurred. But this regularity is frequently broken by "untimely" backward and forward excursions. And, in thought of other kinds, there may be no trace of successions in time. "I think" may be followed by a retrospective back-swing—that "I was wrong to go," or by a prospective swing-forwards—that "I shall do well to go." Yet both these glimpses into the past and the future are actually in the present: they are "presentments." Similar swings occur in the process of inference—backwards to the standard (whether this be experience or an artificial generalization) and forwards to the conclusion. Being derived from perception, thought oscillates spatially, not in time: its backward and forward swings may then be very aptly compared with those of a weaver's shuttle. Verbs, as we have seen, represent past and future time as directions in space.

There is still more irregularity in the ordering of the *descriptive* details and ascriptions that particularize the subject, and the condition that is ascribed to it. The fashion of their grouping differs in different languages according as it is prose or poetry. The verb of the ascription may be placed early or late in the sentence: pronouns may replace personal endings, prepositions be used instead of case-endings: adjectives may precede or follow their nouns, or may be divorced from them except for the *liaison* of a similarity in gender: timed peculiarities may be expressed by participles or by relative ascriptions—the "desired object" becoming the "object which is desired." The origin of these diversities can be traced to the process of perception, and, in particular, to perception by tactile movement. We perceive a thing as a present whole by successively detecting some of its various qualities, and, having perceived it as a whole, we proceed to detect other qualities. That is to say, we synthetically build up a whole out of its parts, and then analytically dissect it into further detail. In this fashion we *successively* convert a general or indefinite object into a definite or particular object. But the object remains throughout in the present. This synthetical "building up" of a perception is reflected in a very common "turn of expression"—the use of "it" or "there" (in French combined as "il y") to signify "the perceived," that is described in the words which follow.

We are, then, liable to confuse dynamic changes with progressive discoveries that are made in static perception—"some trees have grown" with "I now see there are some trees"—and this leads us to synchronize a cause with its consequence or effect. This error has already been abundantly illustrated. A vast number of words express successions in time as static occurrences, "becoming," for instance, as contrasted with "being." Successions, are, of course, involved in "growing," "moving" and "thinking." In "grateful thanks" the gratitude that *caused* the thanks is associated with them as their *quality*. Active conditions are confused with the passive conditions that are their consequences. "Connection," for example, may mean an active "connecting" or the passive "being connected" that is its result. So the effect of a force is regarded as its "co-efficient." This assimilation of successions in time with the progressions of perceptive detection involves the confusion of Time with Space; and this confusion, it seems, is the foundation of the Theory of Relativity.

Apart from the influence of feelings, the current of self-suggested thought is linked into continuity by Memory and Intelligence—the marvellous reproductive processes through which one idea generates another that is connected with it either by past experience or by the bond of an analogy. These processes, as we have seen in Chapter I, are physical as well as mental: they direct the course of growth and development as well as that of thought. But it is thought that reveals their existence to us—although only in spasmodic flashlights that enable us to detect ourselves. In reminiscent thought, Memory acts alone: imaginative thought is an effervescence of Intelligence. In the process of reasoning inference, each of them takes a part of its own.

Inference, as we have seen, is primarily a faculty of reading from the past into the present. Intelligence and Memory—the masculine and the feminine—co-operate in its working. For it is intelligently that a present occurrence or situation is assimilated with one in past experience, and memorially that a lesson comes forward from it. The faculty, it may be repeated, is an instrument of bodily as well as of mental life. It is "absent-mindedly" that we apprehend the distance of things by their visual perspective, appropriately direct the course of our movements—as in eating, for instance—graduate our strength to various actions and so balance our bodies as to resist the assaults of gravitational pressure. We are unconscious of these physical inferences. And mental inferences that have become habitual run so rapidly as to elude consciousness.

The process develops into conscious "reasoning," or "argument," when it is impeded by a doubt, and when the standard from which it draws its lesson is a generalization that has only a mental existence, such as those that are employed in Classificative and Quantitative reasoning. Doubts are blanks which bar the completion of an ascription, and they, consequently, fall into three classes according as they affect either the *subject* of a halting ascription ("Who was there?"), or the *condition* which is to be ascribed to a subject ("Where was he?"), or the existence of a particular *ascriptive union* between a known subject and condition or attribute ("Was he there?"). In the first two cases the doubt is expressed in language by interrogative pronouns, relatives and connectives: in the third case by putting the doubtful ascriptive union in the foreground, or by the use of the connective "whether."

A doubt is resolved by the discovery of a link. This may be either the testimony of others, the suggestion of "probability" or a material clue. Testimony becomes regularized as "evidence" in the Law Courts. Its value varies with its "credit," and this has fluctuated from time to time. There were days when two witnesses sufficed to prove anything; but there are now authorities of judicial experience who regard all oral testimony with suspicion unless it is corroborated by material clues. In arguing from probability we are trusting to experience. For a thing is more or less probable according to the number of times it has occurred when it has had a chance of occurring. Degrees of probability are in fact *averages*. Material clues are illustrated by the discoveries through which detective stories elucidate their mysteries.

When an ascription has thus been completed as a "conclusion," the link that has been used presents itself as its "reason." The main, or standard, reason is a general experience that is too obvious to need accentuation. If, for instance, a doubt as to the presence of someone on a certain occasion is resolved by the discovery of his umbrella there, this is given as the reason for concluding that he was "therefore" present. In the background is the standard reason that the presence of a possession implies that of its possessor. The linking reason may *follow* the conclusion, with the introduction of a "because," if it is less striking than the discovery to which it led.

Similar lines are followed in Classificative and Quantitative reasoning. In classing a flower or an insect, we find linking clues in its physical organization: in calculating the price of a material we go by a unit rate and its quantity. These are reliable guides. We are less fortunate when we draw conclusions from generalizations that take the form of *rules*, since these are so frequently suggested by emotion, not based upon experience. To one on the verge of bankruptcy religion may dictate that "The Lord will provide"; optimism to the hope that "all will come right in the end"; under the influence of egotistical self-assurance he may "refuse to believe" that things are desperate. The extraordinary vagaries of human history—the ups and downs and periodic downfalls of civilization may very generally be traced to the use of sentimental instead of practical (or empirical) standards of inference. It is unfortunate that while we reason "sensibly" in settling such questions as the catching of a train, we so commonly take sentiment as our guide in matters of grave concern. It is by the mental development of sentimental prejudices that man can conclude that respect for a superior is incompatible with self-respect, that liberty is incompatible with self-discipline, that public opinion may take the place of conscience, and that notoriety is the acme of success.

The process of inference runs so naturally that any deviations from its course are exceptions that impress themselves upon thought. They are accentuated by such words as "although," "but" and "however." "Although" discredits an ascription as a standard for inference. In "although he was uneducated he was intelligent," the generalization is invalidated that education is necessary to the development of intelligence. "But" and "however" accentuate an inconsequence—as in "she was black but comely." Hence "but" is familiarly employed to introduce an objection to an argument, or to limit the inference that is drawn from a standard.

Reasoning is assisted very greatly by assumptions, suppositions or hypotheses. These are possibilities (introduced by an "if," or, as possibilities of inaction, by an "unless") that can serve as standards, or links, in drawing conclusions. Their evolutionary origin may be practical or sentimental. In the first case they are derived, under feminine promptings, from the vicissitudes of experience—particularly in the realization of "prospective" ideas ("if I should meet her"). They are invaluable guides in forming conclusions by either Consequential (common sense), Classificative, or Quantitative reasoning ("if it is hot, it will burn you," "if it has six legs, it is an insect," "if its price is 2s. 3d. a yard, its cost will be 11s. 3d."). They play a leading part in the balancing of courses, and in the choice of a less attractive to win a more attractive ("if I do not start at once, I shall be late," "if you do that again, you will be punished"). In Rudyard Kipling's *If*, they are possibilities of self-control which contribute to the formation of a manly character.

These thoughts of possibilities may, however, spring from a sentimental or imaginative source. They may even involve the imaginative particularization, or personification, of ideas ("if life were but a dream," "if I were you"). In this case their origin is in masculine emotion. But, as has been stressed in the chapter preceding, emotional actions or thoughts can be reproduced deliberately or purposefully. This is, indeed, one of the most important steps in the evolution of the Mind. We can deliberately imagine a nightmare. Such deliberately imagined suppositions may be used in process of reasoning, in lieu of general rules. As "speculative" theories they are used very extensively by science in forming conclusions as to the character of unknown causes and consequences — as to the nature of electricity, or the origin of the Universe, for example. And speculative suppositions of a more emotional kind are the inspiration of gambling, whether on race-courses or in commerce.

Courses of thought can be classified according to the motiving topics around which they weave their ascriptions

—memorial, analogical, inferential, sentimental or hypothetical—or which they illustrate by picturesque imagery. Their classification will involve a brief excursion over ground that has been already surveyed. Topics may be differentiated as of either feminine or masculine suggestion. But, in fact, the two promptings are generally combined in varying proportions. They may take the form either of a "clinging" like, or a "shrinking" dislike, or of the "searching" purpose of a desire or a want. That is to say, they may be appreciative or purposeful, and in both cases are of feminine origin. The one may appear to be of *present*, and the other of *future*, concern. But since the course of thinking is out of relation with successions in time, thoughts cannot be classified by their timing. Imaginative thought, for instance, may be quite purposeless. But it can fancy long successions of future happenings. Consequently both likes and desires present themselves as "static" conditions. But they can be modified by intensification. When the topic which arouses them is strongly tinged with masculine emotion—or is the product of masculine emotion—a like becomes spiritualized into admiration, a desire into ambition. Following this distinction, thoughts can, then, be classified according as they are predominantly of feminine or masculine origin, and again according as they are practically or emotionally appreciative or purposeful.

But here we are met by another complication. Behind thought, which, on its face, is merely appreciative or admiring, there may lie a very practical purpose—that of convincing, instructing, interesting or amusing others. Thoughts of this kind are the equipment of the preacher, politician, journalist, author and artist. But they begin in the admonitions, praisings and blamings of the nursery and class-room, and develop themselves in the course of gossipy or critical conversation. In the lack of a better term we may style thoughts of this kind "propagative." Their end may be to win the belief, the esteem, the amused approval, or the money of their "communicants."

We have already seen that the methods of behaviour and speech to which our thoughts urge us are merely the material instruments of the Mind, and are of quite subsidiary importance when compared with the thoughts, emotions and motives which instigate them. How various are the methods in which love, anger, or ambition can be expressed or prosecuted!

During youth and middle age the most imperious of feminine suggestions are those connected with sexuality and maternal care—urges that are spiritualized by masculine emotion into the idealistic passion of admiring love. Thoughts of food, of comfort, and of working or trading as means of livelihood are also of this practical kind, whether they provoke feelings of like or of desire. Feminine "common sense" appreciates the fact that there is no dependence upon a future which is not secured by the observance of moral rules. These, as we have seen, originate as ideas of harmonies in succession. But they are so useful that they are eagerly adopted as instruments of practical wisdom. Curiosity, also, has its ultimate origin in a revulsion from a feminine shrink, and the discovery of the unknown prompts the practical inquisitiveness of childhood, and the learnings of the nursery, as well as the scientific studies, observations, and researches of later years. Under emotional influences, however, curiosity gives place to the imaginative inventiveness of religious, scientific and philosophical speculation.

Masculine suggestions, on the other hand, are most simply illustrated by thoughts of the playful and emulative amusements that are provided by the games and gamblings which occupy so large a part of both childish and adult life: in their emulative phases they are miniatures of the struggle for success—of oneself or one's "side"—which is in man's case identical with the Struggle for Life. To realize the importance of sport as a topic of thought it suffices to regard the space which newspapers devote to racing, cricket, football, and Stock Exchange fluctuations. The revulsive pleasures of humour and wit are hardly topics of thought in themselves, except in the authorship of such publications as *Punch*. They are illuminating flashes rather than themes of reflection.

We are under masculine influence when thinking of "ideals"—whether social, moral or æsthetic—and are subject to the admiring or purposeful enthusiasms that they provoke. But ideas of *success* intrude themselves here. For by idealistic behaviour—by being kind, charitable, virtuous or elegant—we also win success, social or self-conscious, and it is difficult to decide which of these attractions is the most alluring. Our admiration for Art, for instance, is very largely admiration for the skill that is involved in its execution, and this is, of course, a manifestation of success. Nevertheless, in thinking of the charm of a landscape, a symphony, a picture, a poem, or a cathedral, one feels that Beauty touches the mind as a harmony in itself, quite apart from any merit in the method of its creation.

Of success in itself each man is to himself the most inspiring illustration, for it is through his success in trying, learning and appearing that he has artificially progressed from the blank incompetence of his infancy. The egotistical self-admiration of pride, and purposeful ambition to win new titles to it, are accordingly obsessing themes of reflection. The instruments by which we can gain success are constantly before us. Amongst them is the stylishness in dress and appearance which engross so large a share of women's attention. Other instruments are riches, popularity, notoriety and "social success" generally. Egotistical ambition takes a more romantic phase when its instruments are of an adventurous, heroic or warlike order. Admiring thought becomes *altruistic* when it is attracted by the idealized success of others, in their dignity, power or fame. It ranges from parents, teachers, leaders and commanders to kings and divinities, evolving into the kindred feelings of faith and respect, as we realize our debt to them in the preservation of future interests.

"Gossipy" thought and conversation fluctuate between the egotistic and the altruistic. It may be frankly or subtly admiring or depreciative and in the latter case is attractive because in "running down" others we, by implication, exalt ourselves. Gossip takes a more artificial and dignified form as criticism—literary, artistic and political. In the general lack of absolute standards of value, criticism is appreciative or depreciative according as its objective is liked or disliked—that is to say, harmonizes or jars with the critic's sensibilities or with the public opinion of the day. In either case it is interesting, and it is greatly to the credit of democratic government that it offers this distraction to its citizens with each morning's newspaper.

Masculine influence attains its height in imaginative thought: emotion then sharpens its provocations by giving picturesque forms to them. In this guise, they may present themselves as revealed supernatural realities of tremendous import. Religious thought—appreciative or purposeful—has, therefore, occupied a very large share of the attention of mankind, and has exercised a momentous influence upon the course of history. Imaginative thought becomes "fictive" when its artificiality is confessed. In this form it offers mankind a delightful refuge from the realities of life. In its earliest form it is the "story-tale" of the nursery: it has developed into the novel through the legend, or saga, and into the drama, through the miracle play. It may draw its materials from the objective life of behaviour and circumstance, or from the subjective life of thought and feeling.

Music is a development of imaginative thought. Its images are drawn from auditory instead of visual or tactile experience. But they occur in thought before they are expressed in sound. The attraction of music in its various phases illustrates man's natural—indeed *physical*—appreciation of the harmonious, and the changes which fashion can produce in its sensibilities.

Art implies skill in execution as well as mental inspiration and by nothing is this better illustrated than by the artificial complexities of literary expression. Language is of inestimable value to us, and there is an irrepressible tendency to adorn what we admire. So it becomes, in relation to thought, what variations are to a musical theme—complicated with decorative embellishments that disguise its substance. The impressiveness of a thought is enforced by its accentuation, and a vast number of "turns of expression" have this in view. Our innate appreciation of harmony inclines us to rhythm, rhyme and alliteration—the elegancies of poetical composition. Literary language does not, then, simply represent the theme of the course of thought that dictates it, but presents this theme with the ornamentation of a "descant." In the expression of thought two currents indisputably run together—one of ideas, the other of "word-ideas," connected with one another by substantial identities. For one may think in one language and express himself in another. So far it is true that we think in words. But we can also think without words, as do beasts and birds. This is definitely proved by the very common experience of having ideas for which words are not immediately forthcoming, and must be hunted. Multiple currents in thought are no more "unthinkable" than those which are involved in radio-reception.

CHAPTER XII

LANGUAGE

Speech and hearing, writing and reading, illustrate very strikingly the process of repetitive or memorial reproduction, and the lightning rapidity with which it runs. The immaterial idea of something generates, in material utterance or writing, the word which signifies it; and a word which is heard or seen generates in mind the idea that is its "meaning." The reproductive succession is, indeed, more complicated than this. For, before we express an idea of anything, an idea of the word which signifies it must come to mind: this is evident from the fact that we often have to "cudgel the brain" in order to get a word to express an idea that is before us. It is this "word-idea" which reproduces the expression of the word in speech or writing. Similarly, when the sound of a word strikes the ear—or its sight strikes the eye—an idea of the word must be formed in consciousness before an idea of its meaning is reproduced. There must clearly be a current of "word-ideas," as well as of "thing-ideas," running, so to speak, side by side. Language is so much more complicated than thought that ideas of words must constitute a separate mental stream, swayed by thought as by a ground-current, but eddying and rippling over it. Those who have command of several languages must have in potentiality several of these streams, actuated at first hand if they "think" in these languages, at second hand if they use them by a process of translation.

Language, as the instrument of "thought-transfer," is of such inestimable value to us that we are inclined to regard it as an "inspired"—or, at least, as an "instinctive" capacity—a notion that is strengthened by the fact that no one recollects "learning to speak." It is as difficult to realize that it has been artificially elaborated—and is elaborated in each generation—out of spontaneous cries and mutterings—as to feel convinced that we have family connections with the apes. Yet there can be no doubt that it is an acquired dexterity, to be compared with piano-playing. Otherwise a man's language would not be simply determined by the surroundings of his childhood. English children in India learn Hindustani as easily as their own language. There is no hereditary aptitude except to utter cries of satisfaction and distress. These elementary utterances are of physical, not mental origin, although we become conscious of them. Utterance comes under mental guidance when a child is learning to speak. By a retrograde development, it relapses into the autosuggestive—or even the physical—plane, so that we are quite unconscious of the movements of the tongue and lips in speaking, and must make an effort of attention in order to follow them in detail.

There can be no doubt of the urge to express feelings by utterances, and, through their provocative qualities, ideas are in fact "feelings" of a kind. If we listen critically to conversation that is passing around us, we must be struck by the large admixture of exclamations and expletives that it includes—by the large number of inarticulate noises that are made—not merely to express assent or dissent, but to warn, scold, or soothe another, and are therefore on the same plane as the "conversation" of birds. This close connection between feelings and utterances would of itself prompt the use of utterances to express striking sensations and ideas. If one utterance can signify a pain, another can be used to signify the *cause* of a pain—to give a name of it. The tendency to give names to things is very evident in a nursery. Children are not contented until they have named their pets and playthings—that is to say, until they have adopted words for them.

Words are the sonorous consequences of movements of the chest, throat and mouth which differ from the gestures of deaf and dumb language in that they appeal to the ears instead of to the eyes. We commonly think of the vocal chords—the vibratile membranes of the larynx—as the origin of the voice. But as a matter of fact, we have four "voices"—those of whistling, whispering, speaking and singing, and to the two first of these the vocal chords make no contribution. They result from the "sonority" that is set up in a stream of air when it meets with resistant obstacles, and their pitch varies with the rapidity of the stream, with its density, and with the character and shape of the obstacles that resist it.[1] These are the factors which determine the "voices of the wind." Air is also set into sonority by the vibration of substances that are in contact with it. So it sounds under the vibration of the vocal chords—as it does under the vibration of a tuning-fork—and takes the quality of speech or song according, for the most part, to the degree of their tension. It follows that when speaking or singing we are using two sources of sound—one of resistance to the air-stream, and the other of substantial vibration—and hence vowels and diphthongs can become exceedingly varied. Moreover, the power and quality of the voice are affected by surface undulations that are set up in the skin of the throat and mouth, as they are round the bell of a trumpet, and are comparable with the undulations which give sonority to the diaphragm of a telephone, or of a "loud-speaker."[2] It seems probable that the "singing" voice, in particular, owes much to its reinforcement by these undulations. These variously originating sounds are formed into words by "consonantal" interruptions that are imposed upon them during their passage through the mouth.

The science of Phonetics has distinguished and classified

[1] We can satisfy ourselves of this by blowing into differently shaped vessels.

[2] Undulations differ from vibrations in that they are not stilled by pressure.

in immense detail the various consonantal sounds that are used by the different languages of mankind. We can, however, tabulate them with comparative simplicity if we confine ourselves to the chief languages of Europe. The formation of their consonants can in all cases be traced to movements of the lips and tongue. The lips act one against the other. The tongue acts against the palate, varying in its effect according as it applies itself to the fore or hind palate. The approaches of the lips to one another, and of the tongue to the palate, may be "stopped" or "breathed"—that is to say, they may block, or merely constrict the passage of the breath. Articulation is further diversified by the *character* of the movements of the lips and tongue. These may be approaches followed by recoils, sharply jerked recoils, or simple pressures followed by releases; and are again varied according as they are forcible pushes or light touches.

Character of movements	Articulated By					
	Lip against lip		Tongue against fore palate		Tongue against hind palate	
	Stopped	Breathed	Stopped	Breathed	Stopped	Breathed
Approach and recoil:						
by a push	B	VV	D	TH (*this*)	G	CH (*loch*)
by a touch	P	F	T TZ (*zeit*)	TH (*thin*)	K	C (Latin)
Jerked recoil:						
from a push from a touch	V	W	CH (*child*) J	SH Y	Z	ZH J (*jeu*)
Pressure:						
by a push by a touch	M	FF	N L	S R	N (*bien*) LL (*fille*)	CH (*ich*) R (*rue*)

Each of these three methods of articulation—by lip against lip, by tongue against fore palate, and by tongue against hind palate—is accordingly subject to about a dozen variations, and different languages of the same original stock may be distinguished by particular variations of their own. For instance, the English (and Scandinavian)[1] *t*, *d* and *th* are represented in German by *tz*, *t* and *d* respectively: "the tide" (time) is "die zeit." These shifts of pronunciation may have the effect of completely changing a word. There is no apparent relationship between the Latin "filio" and the Spanish "hijo." The letter H, it may be added, simply represents a movement of expiration. This is troublesome, and is very easily dropped, leaving the letter standing as its cenotaph.

It is noticeable that the alphabetical names of all the consonants that are formed by *pressures* commence with a vowel (eM instead of Be). This is so with none of the others except F, and this letter involves pressure if strongly pronounced.

We customarily regard words as arbitrary symbols of the ideas that they express. But a number of them have been "adaptively" invented—perhaps by physical as well as mental intelligence. They are analogically imitative or adapted—that is to say, they possess some analogy of sound, movement or *feeling* with their meanings. An utterance is not merely a *sound*. It also involves movements, and the tactile sensations that are their consequences. "Bark," for instance, plainly imitates the sound of barking, "suck" as plainly the movements that are involved in suction, and "rough" the *feel* of roughness. Judging from modern slang, the appreciation of such analogies contributed very largely to the origin of language. But words have very commonly lost all trace of their origins in the process of vulgarizing liquefaction through which crystallized languages have passed to their recrystallization—as Latin passed to French, for example. And, of course, the fact remains that a very large proportion of the things of which we speak can have no analogical connection with any sounds, movements or feelings of which the throat, tongue and lips are capable, so that the words that were adopted

[1] Ulfila's fourth-century translation of the New Testament into Gothic shows that this language had Scandinavian affinities. "Theckyen" (our "thatch") takes the place of "decken."

to signify them must have been "nicknames," such as are commonly invented in schools and nurseries. No analogies of sound, movement, or sensation are traceable between the words "house," "ox" and "dog," or "one," "two," "three," and the things for which they stand. Judging from present experience, a nickname would come into general use if it was invented or favoured by one who was powerful or popular.

While, however, it is impossible to trace the origin of the bulk of our vocabulary to any appropriate mental adaptation, the fact remains that a very large number of words have been intelligently invented, or have been extended in meaning by analogical associations. This is particularly evident with words of English, Scandinavian or Teutonic origin that are in common, or vulgar use. The simplest of these inventions is the imitation of a sound by an utterance—such as is within the capacity of a parrot or a mocking-bird. We owe to this process such words as crash, hiss, shriek, whisper and rattle. There may be some connection between certain vowel *sounds* and certain states of mind. "Ah" seems naturally to express surprise, and "oh" attention or calling to attention. But in the development of a language vowels are interchangeable. The "swoot" of Chaucer's days has now become "sweet." But they are usefully employed to indicate grammatical differences, as in "strike," "stricken," "struck," "strake," "stroke" and "streak."

The naming of things by the imitation of *movements* is less easy to follow. But it has contributed to vocabularies much more generously than the imitation of sounds. The tongue can make shift to copy, or "adapt," the movements of other organs. Indeed, by unconscious intelligence, it tends to imitate them involuntarily: a child, learning to write, will automatically follow the movements of its fingers with its tongue. The English language has turned this clue to very good purpose. Words such as "push," "pull," "press," "pinch," "jump," "stop," "flap," "bite" and "spit" will be found to mimic these movements if they are pronounced slowly and the action of the lips and tongue is watched. Such analogies may be discovered, as we have seen, at a deeper level—between utterances and the *feelings* that accompany, or follow, certain movements. Thus the consonanted combinations "str" and "sw" are used to express effort—as in "strength," "strike" and "swim"—because energy is involved in pronouncing them: the words "rough" and "smooth," "hard" and "soft" imitate the "feeling" of surfaces and substances.

There are some less obvious analogies between movements of the mouth and conditions of experience: "good" and "bad" mimic, respectively, the movements of swallowing and rejecting: "yes" and "no" express affirmation and negation by an opening and a shutting of the throat by the tongue.[1] The most curious of these analogies between ideas and feelings of movement are to be found in the use of the syllables LEG (or LIK) and GEN (or KIN) to express connectings and producings of various kinds. In pronouncing the former we use the tongue to connect the fore with the hind palate, and it can, therefore, be analogically taken to illustrate the process of *linking*. We use it in the words "link," "lick," "like" (in the two senses of resembling and favouring) and "likely." In Greek and Latin the syllable originates words that express picking, speaking, reading and thinking—all of which are linkings; and it enters into a large number of words which we have borrowed from the classics, such as "ligament," "logic," "legal," "analogy," "election," "recollection," "intelligence," "obligation" and "religion." The meaning of all these words implies a notion of linking: "obligation" links conduct with rectitude: "religion" links the seen with the unseen. In pronouncing the syllable GEN (or KIN) the hind palate is connected with the fore palate in a contrary direction: the movement runs outwards and is

[1] As a nod is affirmative and a shake of the head negative because these movements are connected with those of swallowing food and of rejecting it.

analogous to the process of birth. It figures in "generation," "preg(e)nant," "gender," "genitive," "origin" and, perhaps, "organ." In its Scandinavian form — as KIN—it occurs in "kind," and, perhaps, "kindle."

A word that has been invented to express an idea can have its use metaphorically (i.e. analogically) extended so as to express numerous other ideas. This extension comes about through the identification of a resemblance of *quality* between a named idea, and another idea, when the name of the first is bestowed upon the second. Metaphor is the origin of the "different meanings" which words bear in a dictionary. Owing to the static character of thought, a thing's cause or consequence can be viewed as its quality. Consequently, a word can be extended from one thing to another because one of them "leads up to" or "follows" the other. Metaphors can accordingly be distinguished according as they arise from *links in character*, or *links in succession*. Grammarian brings the two together under the cryptic title of "synecdoche."

Metaphorical extensions through a characteristic possession are illustrated by the use of "redbreast" as the name of a robin. An apartment is similarly styled a "room" because it has the quality of space. The title "Senate" is applied to a council of elders. A "lady"[1] is a *free* woman —from "ledig," equivalent to "frau." A notion of "sending" is involved in "permit" and "admit," and one of "giving place" in "allow." In "accusing" and "excusing" an idea of causality is metaphorically attached to or detached from oneself or another. We have seen that the verbs by which we ascribe living conditions to other persons and things are drawn from ourselves and are therefore applied to them by analogy. And these subjective living conditions are generally expressed by objective analogies. Words are extended metaphorically from the physical to the mental world: to "understand" is to *view*

[1] Fancifully derived by some authorities from "hlaf-diga"—the loaf-cutter.

from beneath: to "deliberate" is to *weigh*: a "thing" means an idea as well as an object. We may be "struck" by an idea as well as by a missile or by the sun: "running" may be applied to a stream, a machine, the course of a month or to a thought. How numerous are the possible uses of the little word "do"! Different languages may, of course, use the same analogy. "Ram," "belier" and "aries" all signify a battering-ram as well as the animal. The analogy between a blow and air-blast is appreciated in French ("soufflet" and "souffler") as well as in English: that between a perfumed dandy and a nutmeg gives French its "muscadin" and English its "knut."

Metaphorical extensions through *links in succession* are commonly called "associative," and may appear to be made under the influence of memory rather than of intelligence. It is, no doubt, by memory that a dog connects certain words that it hears from its master with certain activities of its own—that it "sits up" when ordered to do so. But extensions of meaning through links in succession can be classed as analogical when a thing's cause or consequence is regarded as amongst its *qualities*—that is to say, is viewed statically instead of dynamically. Extensions of meaning in backward succession are illustrated by the use of the imitative utterances "cuckoo" and "peewit" for the birds that utter these cries: by the use of "saw" and "hammer" for the tools that make these noises, and of "tin" for the metal that sounds "tinny." It is probable that "foot" (or "pad") has a similar origin. "Putrid" and "filthy" extend the movements of expectoration to its *cause*, as "pure" does to its *consequence*. A drink is called a "cocktail" by the backward extension of a canine analogy to its inspiriting effect. "Grace" primarily meaning *thanks* comes to mean the favour that provokes the thanks: "innocence" to mean the purity that is the origin of harmlessness, so that "innocuous" has been imported to signify harmlessness in itself. "Frail" originally meant *breakable*, but came to be used for the delicacy which makes a thing breakable, so that it was necessary to import "fragile," directly from Latin, to express the original meaning.

The forward extension of meanings—i.e. from cause or origin to consequence or product—is illustrated by the naming of "muslin" from Mosul, and of "damask" from Damascus. A "kiss" and a "bite" (or "bit") are the *consequences* of the action of kissing and biting: "connection" means the attachment that results from a connecting, as well as the process of connecting: "building" the *product* as well as the process of construction: "pressure" the *consequence* as well as the action of pressing. "Kind" came to mean the good-feeling that follows upon *kinship*, and "dear" (with the French "cher") the affectionate regard which is kindled by the expensive. Anger of a certain kind is called "indignation" because it is provoked by *unworthiness*. The consequence of "help" is escape, and the word is used in this sense in such phrases as "I could not help it." The history of the word "mercy" is a remarkable illustration of forward extension. As the Latin "merces" it meant a ransom: mercy is the consequence of a ransom, and thankfulness—the French "merci"—the consequence of mercy. "Presently" has lost its original sense of *now*, and means a time that *follows* the present: there is a similar slip of succession in the French *tout à l'heure*.

The most difficult ideas to express in language are perhaps those of the various ties which connect a series of ideas into a sentence. Analogy has immensely assisted their invention. Prepositions that express spatial relations can be used for relations in time because there is an analogy between a distance, or direction, and a period. Thus "always" means "wherever one may look." "For" (or "fore") means "looking in front" and is used in relation to time in "for ever." It enters into several verbs to give them *timed* meanings. One who looks forward does not see the past, and "forgive," "forget" and "forsake" signify behaviour that has no reference to the past. "By"—meaning "next in succession to"—figures metaphorically in "good-bye," "bye-law," "before," "besides," "because," "believe" (by like), "by the by" and a "bye" in games. "If" (gif) means "given that." "Yet" (get) is probably akin to "go-to," signifying a check to an obvious inference: "still" (stop) has a similar meaning. "But" (by-out) signifies "in succession from outside" and not from the word or sentence preceding. The syllable "ver" seems to signify repetitive succession—as in the beating of a drum. Hence "never" means "in no succession," "every," "each in turn," "however," "in the way of succession," "nevertheless," "not invalidated by succession." The same root appears to be used in "very":[1] "very beautiful" is "beautiful, beautiful, beautiful"—a repetition which may also be signified by "too"—meaning *twice*.

Analogies will, further, account for some of the syllables that are incorporated with words to give them special meanings. "Re" is a "spring-back" of the tongue, and is largely used to indicate reactions of different kinds. The syllable "dom" (as in "domain" and "Christendom") contributes an idea of *power*. The suffix "ness," attached to a quality, indicates the abstract condition of *possessing* it—as in "faithfulness." This expedient illustrates the ingenuity with which our forbears adapted the material to signify the abstract. For *ness* is certainly akin to "nose," as in *Dungeness*, the possession of this feature being taken as analogical to the possession of a quality. Not less ingenious is the use of the suffixes "ship" and "hood" to indicate correlatives—as in "sonship" and "fatherhood." For these words primitively mean a basket (skip) and its cover, which not inaptly typify a correlative relationship, since one involves the other and is its contrary.

[1] The origin is commonly taken to be the Latin "vero." This is doubtful, for there is no French equivalent. But "vero" is not improbably from the same root.

The comparative study of languages shows that mankind has been influenced by two contrary systems in connecting the words of a sentence into a continuous string. One system runs from the "particular" to the "general" which the preceding "particular" defines: the other runs from the "general" to the "particular." If we liken the "general" to the roof of a house and "particulars" to the rooms which it covers, the first of these systems runs upwards, the second downwards, and they can be styled, respectively, *anatropic* and *catatropic*. In anatropic sequence adjectives precede their nouns; qualifying details precede what they define and are connected with it by case-endings or postpositions; and the verbal ascription — the most "general" feature of the sentence—is relegated to its end. The catatropic sequence runs contrarily to this: adjectives follow their nouns; particularizing details are added by prepositions to the things that they define; and the verb comes early in the sentence. The difference in order can be illustrated by changing the arrangement of this sentence to that which it would take in Hindustani, for instance. It would run, "this-sentence-of the-order-changing-by the-difference illustrated can-be." It is noteworthy that the harmonies of a musical composition may be catatropically developed from a treble theme, or be anatropically built up from a ground-bass.

A people is disposed to copy the language of its conquerors, and the vicissitudes of conquest have very generally resulted in the "crossing" of these two tendencies. But there are languages that have practically remained "true" to one type or the other. The first, or "anatropic," system is very well illustrated by Turkish and Hindustani; the second, or catatropic, by Arabic and the tongues called "Semitic."[1] Greek and Latin are "polytropic" hybrids; they used both case-endings and prepositions, and adjectives

[1] A title is particularized by the name of the person who bears it: in Turkish and Hindustani the name anatropically precedes, in Arabic the name catatropically follows, the title.

might precede or follow their nouns; the verb was not necessarily harnessed to the end of a sentence. The growing influence of Aramaic (or Arabic) upon Greek can be traced in the language of the New Testament: prepositions came into more general use, and the position of the verb was advanced. Latin underwent a similar change: that of the *Imitatio Christi* had lost the "classical" style, and approached Arabic in the catatropic "lay-out" of its sentences. It is not improbable that this change owed something to the influence of the Moslem Universities of Spain in the eighth and ninth centuries. French has followed out this development: case-endings have vanished, adjectives generally follow their nouns. The evolution of English has taken a similar line. But remnants of the older system remain in the possessive case and in the placing of adjectives before the noun that they qualify. In German these relics are still more in evidence.

In the days before writing was invented languages were much more fluid than they have since become. Each of the tribes into which a horde divided itself might consequently develop, not a mere *patois,* but a language of its own. So it has come about that languages, which are, in reality, closely akin, have hardly a word in common—a contrast which actually occurs amongst the frontier tribes of the Assam Hills, where each group of villages is isolated by vendettas from those around it, and has developed a speech which is unintelligible to its neighbours. A conquest may reverse this particularizing tendency. The language of the conquerors has a prestige which leads to its spread, and also to its literary elaboration. This may produce an artificial, or "classical," language, which may be very different from that of conversation. One may be well acquainted with colloquial Arabic and be quite unable to understand it in its literary form. Indeed Arabic grammarians will insist that some of the most useful—and ancient—words in ordinary use *cannot* be written. There is a similar contrast between modern Greek as spoken and as used in journalism. This generalizing tendency may again be reversed by revivals of patriotic sentiment which is capable of resuscitating languages—such as Erse and Czech —that were almost as dead as Cornish.

The easiest route for the evolution of writing was the graphic or pictorial representation, not of words, but of the ideas that were their meanings—or of things which could stand for their meanings by analogies, however far-fetched. It is obvious that to draw an idea—or a thing—in itself involves the adaptive appreciation of an analogy. For the drawing has but a remote resemblance to its object: it is a miniature in flat outline which would be meaningless were it not substantiated by ideas of solidity and distance that are associated with perspective. The hieroglyphics of Egypt, the cuneiform of Mesopotamia, and the ideographs of China can all be traced to a "photographic" origin. The designs could be abbreviated and simplified. But until words were analysed into syllables and letters it would be necessary to have a separate sign for each word in the language.

Syllables have been isolated from words, and letters from syllables, by precisely such a process as has led to the formation of our general and abstract ideas—that is to say, by comparison, followed by the unification (or identification) of samenesses, and the elimination, or abstraction, of differences. To give a fanciful illustration. The syllable *ca* can be isolated from the word "cabin" because it also occurs in the word "camel," and the *c* can be isolated from *ca* because it also occurs in the syllable *co*. The resulting letters may have been derived from the signs that represented words which commenced with them. We get the word "alphabet" from the Semitic names for *alif* (an ox) and *beth* (a house).

There is, however, another evolutionary route which has contributed to the development of writing—that of denoting utterances in themselves by marks, instead of attempting to depict their meanings. Utterances involve movements, and there is an associative connection in succession between a movement and a mark that is made by it—which may be considered as an analogy between them. For a mark is the consequence of a movement, and a movement is the cause of a mark. The marks that were used could be purely arbitrary—like the Ogham letters which resemble the Morse telegraphic signals in being dots and dashes. Designed in this fashion letters could represent movements of articulation. B, for instance, signifies a push and P a touch of the lips, D a push and T a touch of the tongue. There is a curious fact which seems to confirm this supposition. The utterance of the simplest vowels involves no articulating movement, and the marks for them would therefore stand outside the consonantal series. It is remarkable that in Arabic the signs for the short vowels are in a class apart from the other letters, and are inserted as supplements, either above or below the line.

Man sets a higher value upon the artificial than the natural because the artificial represents *success*, whereas the natural seems to "come of itself." For instance, modern taste has more admiration for "made-up" than for natural complexions. Language is incomparably more artificial than conduct, and grows in esteem with advancing culture: it is admired as it is elaborated, and is elaborated because it is admired. From being an instrument it becomes an Art. The vulgar slangy survivals of a degraded vocabulary are remodelled, repolished and rearranged: a ship, as it were, is reconstructed from the broken pieces of a predecessor. Harmonious rhythms, rhymes, alliterations, contrasts and cadences give a pleasure akin to that of music—that is to say, they excite emotional interest. Its phrases may be as meaningless—or as surprising—as those of much modern music. But they serve to arouse an agreeable sense of admiring confusion. Thought, however forcible, or useful, is unattractive unless it is presented with graces of rhetorical or literary style. Moreover, language which conveys no logical message—possesses, indeed, no definite meaning—

can charm us by complimentary or sentimental implications that tickle the feelings. Its influence extends further than this. It gives persuasive *power* to those who can command it, so that it becomes a means of controlling a people that has lost respect for authority. Public speakers and newspaper articles are, therefore, the accepted instruments of democratic government. With unsophisticated peoples, oratory is of little account: they suspect that it is a deceptive ruse for the concealment of motives, and hold that

> Words are like leaves, and where they most abound,
> Much fruit or sense is seldom to be found.

The dignity and reality of their political meetings, or *durbars*, would be lessened by speeches that were more than brief formalities. But, with the spread of education and the growth of an "intelligentzia," oratorical and literary skill becomes a power. And it gives a delightful feeling of pride to those who can exercise it. One reason why democracy is so popular is that it affords so many opportunities for public speaking. Its appeal may be to the shallowest of sentiments or the most blatant self-complacency. But it is so convincing that it can efface all recollections of a politician's mistakes. Eloquence, like the ink of the cuttlefish, becomes an invaluable instrument for the veiling of incompetence.

CHAPTER XIII

THE MIND AND ECONOMIC LIFE

THE economic life of a nation is generally regarded as typically "material." But, in fact, it is dominated by the immaterial in the form of ideas of the future and of the "credit" which brings future prospects into present use. It is because this point is not adequately appreciated that political economy is so unsatisfying a science, presenting conclusions which are often mutually contradictory, and are incapable of explaining the origin of such a depression as that which is now afflicting us, or of suggesting logical remedies for it. Its study has not been able to protect civilization from extraordinary vicissitudes of fortune, nor to safeguard human judgment from orgies of extravagance, from flushes of over-production, or from such short-sighted blunders as the Treaty of Versailles. Things are not understood when the material is allowed to overshadow the immaterial, and no sufficient consideration is given to the influence of the Mind.

Prosperity—as the word itself indicates—springs from the utilization of *future* prospects. Economic civilization grows by the development of *future* "potentialities" that can be exchanged for possessions, services or enjoyments in the *present*: that is to say, by the establishment of *assurances* which can be exchanged for *advantages*. Future prospects give "credit" when they inspire trust: "credit" is, in fact, their value expressed in terms of money. And money itself is really a form of credit: its use is in the future: apart from what it *promises* a pound-note is of no value. There is, consequently, distress and unemployment when future prospects become overclouded by uncertainty or have been exhausted by extravagant borrowing, or by war. If they dissolve into mist, man can only rely upon the possession of land for his food, of houses for his shelter and of gold or silver for his purchases. During centuries this was the condition of the Indian peasant.

The future can, however, only be built up through the present—through present enterprise, work and savings. Present *consumption* is also necessary: the "circulation" of exchanges occurs between the resources of Capital, the wages of labour, and purchases for enjoyment. Consequently distress and unemployment result if there is a decrease of expenditure in purchases and wages. Present and future interests, then, are both involved in the maintenance of prosperity. But, as between themselves, they are antagonistic, and draw us in contrary directions. For they play upon different sides of our character. The spendthrift masculine would sacrifice the future to the present in the pursuit of pleasure: the careful feminine would sacrifice the present to the future by working and saving. Economic prosperity is, then, only obtainable by a course which balances these rival temptations, and steers between them.

These difficulties are complicated by the fact that future prospects *consciously* exist for us only in idea. We are conscious of them because the Mind makes analogical deductions from the recollections of the past. Memory assures us that the past was once the present, and that the present was once the future. We consequently infer that there is a "to-morrow" which will in time become "to-day." From a deeper level than that of consciousness, the feminine side of our nature, as we have seen, urges us to pursue what is in the future, instead of abandoning ourselves to the present. But in conscious life this urge takes the form of prospective *ideas* of future gains. These may be either pleasurable or profitable. They may incite us either to spend or to save. As the offspring of the Mind, ideas of the future may be born of optimistic imaginings as well as of reasonable inferences. There is consequently an emotional pitfall in the course of our economic life.

It is, then, as a mental existence that the Future consciously affects us—that is to say, as a prospect which is foreshadowed by ourselves. In man's original habitat—equatorial "Islands of the Blest," where fruit and edible roots are in season all the year round—the morrow's meals were assured by Nature. But as soon as he migrated to less generous regions, he became obliged to *produce* for his support. This was impossible without some preliminary expenditure—if only in planting and sowing—which could only be met by saving, or by borrowing from another's savings. So originated Capital—the fruit of labour in the past, and of saving in the present. Man "thrives" by "thrift" because thrift is the simplest means of establishing a future. Capital not merely assures the future, but creates it. If Capital is lacking, the future is a blank. That is to say, although Nature offers future crops and Commerce future profits, present possessions of some sort are necessary to turn these offers to account. Moreover, present possessions provide a means of obtaining things, or services, by exchange; and open to other persons a method of livelihood by rendering services.

Accordingly, exchange becomes the motive of industrial and commercial life. Its incentive is the gaining of something that is *valuable*. "Value" is an idea of *comparative* utility, pleasure or profit which can overcome one's reluctance to part with something in exchange for something else. That is to say, it is an idea of comparative "worth" (or "valour"), which may differ very considerably in amount as formed in the minds of a seller and a buyer. Value is materialized when it is embodied in possessions, or in the rendering of services of various kinds. Prospective value is materialized in money. This was invented, in the first place, as an instrument for giving a present exchange-value to prospects which exist, but are not materialized—a claim for repayment or for earned wages, for instance. It fulfils this purpose by *circulating* from hand to hand. It is, then, a "vehicle" of exchange, and its efficiency immensely exceeds its amount, just as the efficiency of the cars of a railway system exceeds their number. In this capacity, its function is "dynamic." But its function becomes "static" when used as a measure of value and as a means of accumulating and storing it. The value of money may be, and generally is, purely conventional. But an exception must be made in the case of gold. This, for some inexplicable reason, is universally desired in itself, as well as a guarantee of future purchasing power.

From the use of money as measuring exchange value, the Mind has elaborated an idea of "money-value" *in the abstract*—a mental measure of value which can be used for the valorization of future prospects whose material existence is, at most, some form of "security"—prospects which can only be *possessed* in mental anticipation. Thus mentally realized, these anticipations can be brought into comparison with possessions or with money, so that one can be exchanged for the other. Thus a future annual income of £5 can be appraised at a present value of £100: the potentialities of a mine may be equivalent to a present value of many thousands of pounds. A tradesman's "goodwill" may add very largely indeed to the selling value of his business. This valorization of future prospects brings them into present use, and immensely increases a community's resources.

It leads to a further evolution. The future can be increased (as a family is through its children) by its subdivision into various grades of proximity. In the transaction of a purchase, a possession or enjoyment is exchanged for a future potentiality, whether in the form of money, a cheque or the incurring of a debt; but in the two first cases the future is near, in the third it is more or less remote. It is still more distant in the case of a money loan, when a near future, in the form of cash, is sacrificed in order to gain a remote return as periodical payments of interest. The discounting of a bill of exchange similarly involves the sacrifice of near in order to gain distant potentialities, at a profit. Future prospects, then, become differentiated into various degrees of proximity and distance, with the remarkable effect of increasing them in amount. For the lender can himself borrow on the strength of the interest that is owed to him. A properly secured loan may, then, be likened to a double-crested fountain, part of whose water falls behind—representing the loan advanced—and part in front, in the increased borrowing power that it gives to the lender. The loan may then add substantially to general purchasing power. The case is similar with a farmer who invests money in cultivation, or with a manufacturer who expends it on a factory: they gain borrowing power by the future prospects that they have opened out, and, by their borrowing, they can create a new "segment" of future. Economic life resembles a skyscraper. It grows in amplitude by the addition of stories. But each story depends for stability upon the one below it. If one crumbles, it drags others with it, and the construction may, then, rapidly dissolve into ruin.

Unless supported by some *security* future prospects are, however, merely hypothetical. Nature offers some security in her crop returns, and Commerce in its yield of profits. These can be reinforced by insurance—the sacrifice of near potentialities in return for the promise of larger ones should losses demand them. Repayment of a loan may be secured by the exaction of a pledge in pawn, or of a mortgage. But, ordinarily, much reliance is placed upon "common honesty"; and this is the only guarantee for the payment of foreign debts. A reputation for honesty is, therefore, one of a nation's most useful assets. In the case of home debts, behind honesty stands the law; and written are more valuable than oral engagements because they are less easily disputed. The State gains security for the collection of its taxes by its *power* to enforce payment. This is, generally speaking, the safest of all securities, and States can, therefore, borrow on much better terms than private individuals or companies. Indeed, at times when confidence in the future has been shaken, State loans may almost monopolize investments.

Security of a less substantial kind is that offered by "financial prestige"—that is to say, by confidence in the resources of Banks and Financial Corporations. Carefully fostered by the magnificence of their buildings, it encourages the public to take loans (or "credits") from them, even at high rates of interest, without much regard for the actual possessions—or substantial assets—which would secure their ability to make advances as required. In this matter, however, banks are placed in a strong position by the use of cheques in payment. For they can acquit themselves of an obligation to pay money to another bank on a customer's account by setting against it a claim to receive money from the bank on another customer's account; and, by the use of a Central Clearing House, different banks can pool their obligations and claims, so that a vast number of obligations can be discharged without the use of any money whatever. Payments are made, in fact, by the bartering of cheques. In this fashion money-value amounting to hundreds of millions of pounds may be *daily* transferred by book-entries —an activity which puts the nation's cash currency, or gold reserves, into insignificance.

By banking agency, then, an immense amount of money-values is created, for which a general feeling of confidence is the only security. During the years 1921 to 1929 the American banks, by lending and borrowing, increased the amount of credit money-value in the country by nearly 4,000 millions of pounds. They grossly over-estimated future potentialities, and a general crash followed. For the credit-currency of a country is to its money-currency as a balloon is to the basket that it carries. The basket may be unshrinkable, but the balloon may lose gas until it collapses. There is such a loss of public confidence on the discovery that a mass of money-values has been created which greatly exceeds the security given by realizable potentialities.

The "currency" that acts as the wheels of industry and commerce is very commonly taken to be the money in circulation. But, in truth, by far the greater proportion of it is money-value that has no material existence. Vast sums, as we have seen, are represented by banking cross-entries. As a matter of fact the industries of a town can probably be run continuously with the money that suffices them for the period of a month. At each week-end, employers draw money from the bank by cheque for disbursement in wages. This soon finds its way back into the bank from the tradesmen with whom it is spent in purchases. There it generates money-value for its depositor, as a credit account, which takes its place and releases it for further transactions. Banks are, therefore, centres for the recirculation of money that has been used before. Money, in fact, provides commercial activities with wheels that are transferable, and can be used over and over again in different connections. The "chariot" of these activities is the money-value that they command. Accordingly, if future prospects fade, the currency shrinks very greatly although the amount of money in circulation remains unchanged. Prices fall—that is to say, money-value rises because it is less abundant. It is to be observed that, since money-value depends so greatly upon the state of credit, and this is subject to wide fluctuations, the valuation of goods in money involves their comparison with a fluctuating standard. Statistics comparing prices at different periods are, therefore, not very reliable.

The value of the money-currency is, nevertheless, of great importance, since this determines the money-value of credit potentialities. If the money-currency is largely added to—or "inflated"—the value of money falls, and prices rise. Hence the issue of token, or paper-money is generally limited by some ratio to a stock of gold, or realizable assets. It is, however, to be remarked that by increasing the money in circulation a Government may materially add to a country's resources in credit-capital. For, *so long as its redundancy is not suspected*, new money creates credit by serving as a present token of future possibilities—without, moreover, making any charges for this service. There is, however, a temptation to issue money in gross excess, since this enables a State to meet its obligations by using a printing-press—an expedient which is particularly attractive during a time of war. The experience of the last war seems to show that, up to a point, the currency may be inflated without much effect upon prices, but that, if this point be passed, there is a rapid progressive fall in money-value, due to failing confidence, and the need of meeting its effects by further inflation. For money-value sympathetically adjusts itself to the value of money. Lenders who have sacrificed money for prospective money-value may be ruined. On the other hand, those who have fettered their future by borrowing are freed from their obligations, since they can discharge them by making payments that cost them much less. Currency debasement is tantamount to repudiation. It involves gross injustice and grievous hardship. But it may be the only means of restoring a future that has been hopelessly overdrawn.

The money-currency may, on the other hand, be "deflated" by the State. Money and money-values then rise in general potentialities—that is to say, prices fall. This enhances the potentialities of those who receive fixed remunerations in wages and salaries, and in particular of banks and of creditors generally. They profit at the community's expense. Those who have borrowed money before the contraction are penalized; and agriculture and industry may, therefore, suffer severely, as illustrated by world conditions at the present time. By the careful limitation of issues, the home-value of the pound has been maintained much above its foreign value.

Currency is used to convert *possible* possessions and enjoyments into *actualities* through their purchase—that is to say, it implements the desires that lead to the Consumption by which Production and Distribution are supported. This brings us to the consideration of these activities. They rest upon the future prospects that are represented by Capital. This may be owned, borrowed, or loaned. Owned capital is material: it consists of money and equipment that are the fruits of work, profit and saving. Borrowed and loanable capital may also be material: but for the most part its existence is due to "credit." It is the money value of future prospects, and often rests upon nothing more substantial than the financial prestige of the borrower or lender—upon a reputation that may have no valid foundation, and vanishes altogether during the pessimism of a "slump."

The growth of substantial capital by a capitalist's savings depends very greatly upon the rate of wages, being most considerable when wages are low. There was rapid accumulation in the days of slavery, and in later years when labour was commonly "sweated." The Bolshevik Government of Russia is now rapidly creating real capital by conscripting labour and paying merely subsistence wages. The creation of credit-capital is conditioned by mental—or "psychological"—factors, and is therefore liable to great fluctuations—and, indeed, to catastrophic reversals—as future prospects arouse confidence or distrust. "Mental" capital of this kind plays a part of immense importance at the present day, and industry and commerce are overfed at some times, and starved at others, as its amount rises or falls.

Capital may be defined as a stock of potentialities in money, money-value, or plant that is used for the earning of potentialities from others, either by rendering them gratifying services or by providing them with gratifying possessions. These potentialities are earned as the price of the gratifications, and are distributed amongst those who have contributed in furnishing or providing them. The surplus that remains after paying expenses is taken by Capital as its net profit.

Services are almost as multifarious as possessions, ranging from domestic help to professional assistance, entertainments of all kinds and railway passenger transport. An obvious distinction between a service and a possession is that the one is immaterial, the other material: the one generally affects only the present, whereas the other affords a future. But, in respect of durability, it is difficult to choose between a tune on the violin and a jam tartlet. And, indeed, much capital may have been expended in training the violinist and in presenting him to an audience. From the economic point of view, however, material possessions and services stand far apart. It is possessions that furnish the necessities of life—food, clothes and shelter: they are, then, the fundamentals of economic exchange. A possession, however ephemeral, gives a *future*, both to him who has it and to him who takes it in exchange. A service gives a future to him who renders it, but to its recipient is merely a present advantage. Hence people cannot live by "taking in one another's washing." Expenditure upon services consequently involves a contraction of the range and variety of exchanges—that is to say, a lessening of the creation of "values" or "wealth." For "value" arises out of opportunities for making exchanges. Moreover, material possessions are far more effective than services as the begetters of credit. A man can borrow more readily on his assets than on his talents. To pawn goods is, indeed, the simplest method of raising money. Credit plays so essential a part in commercial life that the industrial development of a community is checked if it spends largely upon services —either in maintaining dependants or in remunerating lawyers, doctors or entertainers. And it must be realized that "services" include those rendered by us in charity to others—as well as those that are received by us from others. It is remarkable that excessive expenditure in these directions should characterize the early as well as the late stages of economic civilization. In the former—as in India—resources are taxed by the maintenance of hosts of dependants: in the latter by extravagant expenditure upon professional services, public charity, and entertainments of various kinds. In both cases the growth of economic "values"—that is to say, of wealth—is checked.

And there is another point of very great importance. Material possessions are portable and transferable, with the result that their prices are more widely distributed than the remuneration of services. The *value* of a material thing depends upon its accessibility. It exists because it is produced. But to have value it must be transported, and it generally passes through a large number of hands before it is exposed for retail sale. Its value grows as its accessibility increases: a pound of tea which may be worth less than a shilling in Ceylon sells for three shillings at the English grocer's. It reaches its destination through a series of transfers. It follows that *distributive* enterprise and its instruments—ships, railways and shops—employ capital as *profitably* as the production of things by agriculture, mining and factories. For if productive industry creates things, it is distributive industry that creates local *values*. By these transportations and transfers, the potentialities that are represented by the prices of material things are spread more widely than those that are earned by services. This conclusion must not be pressed too far. The services rendered by railway passenger transport maintain multitudes of people. But, speaking generally, commerce spreads its net wider than service. This is an important factor in economic life. For widely distributed earnings mean widely distributed purchasing potentialities and sale-receipts, and these again provide wages for earning, as well as savings on capital account.

The resources of Capital consist of fixed "plant"—whether land, mines or factories—of technical assistance, and of labour. Labour, or "work," is its ultimate instrument. However great be its use of machinery, the human element must be in the background, and the machinery itself was constructed by labour. The wages of labour are paid in money currency, which circulates through the hands of employers, workmen, shopkeepers and banks, and thence back again to the employers to begin a new round.

Production, distribution and retail selling (including investments in these enterprises) all spring from the desire for the money, or money-value, that can be gained from purchasers. It is obvious that unless goods were purchased they would not be produced or distributed. Purchasers are mostly actuated by the desire for pleasure or satisfaction: were they only made under the pressure of actual necessity, their amount would be comparatively insignificant. The demand for pleasure is, then, the force that ultimately energizes the economic life of civilized communities. It gains in strength as tastes in pleasure grow and multiply. The purchasing public includes the whole community—producers, distributors and retailers and investors in their businesses, those who can make charges upon others that are secured by law, those who earn money, or money-value, by rendering services of all kinds, and those who live upon salaries, doles and interest that are provided by the taxes. The money, or money-value, which they expend in purchasing, is the incentive that inspires the enterprises of producing, distributing and selling, and maintains them in interlaced activity. A wilt spreads along the line if goods remain unsold because the demand for them has been overestimated, or because there has been a change of fashion. And there is wilting from the other extremity of the line if constantly recurring losses of capital are not replaced by the investment of income. This default may be the consequence of a contraction of credit that reduces incomes, or of over-expenditure upon services and pleasures, or of the taxation of income that would otherwise be invested.

The demand for *pleasure* is, then, the ultimate origin of production, distribution and sale. But these enterprises are actuated, in themselves, by the desire for prospective *gain*—or profit, in the form of money, or money-value. Labour would not work without wages, and without profits there would be no production, distribution or selling. These gains are made by sharing the money, or money-value, that is received from purchases: and each claimant's share can, therefore, be increased by reducing the shares of the others. There is, consequently, a standing distrust, or antagonism, not only between Labour and Capital, but between the different Capital interests that are engaged in producing, distributing and selling. The relations between Labour and Capital are frequently disturbed by strikes and lock-outs that shake the stability of the prospects upon which credit depends. Competition between producers, distributors and retailers may be less aggressively hostile. But it very commonly leads to a scandalous disproportion between the remuneration of producers and that enjoyed by the intermediaries who place products upon the market. For the nearer is the capitalist to the purchase-money, the wider are his opportunities for retaining it. Making every possible allowance for increases in wage rates, it seems preposterous that bread should be twice as expensive as it was before 1914, whereas wheat costs only half as much. There is an extraordinarily large difference between the price of Indian tea in England, and that received by tea-growers in India. Why should cocoa-nibs command a price of two shillings a pound in Bristol when the West Indian producers receive only a penny farthing? It may be argued that the accumulation of capital by the investment of profits is more rapid when profits are engrossed by a few hands than when they are evenly distributed. But experience shows that when wages run fairly high Capital may receive large accessions from working-class savings.

The taxes are the price which the State exacts for its services, in securing future prospects as well as present conditions. There can be no trust in a future that cannot be foreseen, and the maintenance of law and order is, therefore, a prime necessity for economic prosperity. State expenditure upon the maintenance of its armed forces, police and magistracy, and upon its administrative services is, therefore, essential to economic stability. Trade communications must be maintained. The future must, moreover, profit from the past through the education of the rising generation. The public health must not decline. In so far as the proceeds of taxation are spent upon these objects—without extravagant exaggeration of their requirements—they secure the future and the existence of credit, and rank with the outlay of industrial capital.

States are, however, pressed to spend very extravagantly in order to preserve popular interest and contentment, in pursuit of idealistic aspirations, and for their own aggrandisement and glorification. Democratic government is recklessly extravagant: it amuses the public, but charges exorbitantly for the entertainment. Public establishments are increased, social services are extended, and public works are undertaken on a scale which the country cannot afford. The Coliseum, the Acropolis and the Pyramids testify to the decline of civilizations which they were intended to adorn for ever. So Spain and Portugal dissipated the riches which they drew from America and India. When economic resources have become exhausted, agriculture alone may survive. For, in the growth of crops, Nature gives much in return for little.

This review emphasizes the immense influence which Emotion exercises upon economics. It gives an imaginative drapery to events which are actually a chain of causes and consequences. Hence originate the booms and slumps which distract industrial and commercial life. There is a boom when there is an optimistic appreciation of future possibilities, and, therefore, an eagerness to regard them in terms of money-value. This arises, not only from feelings of confidence in the regularity of future events, but from hopes that they will *improve*—a state of mind which is illustrated by the extension of purchase on the instalment system with its resulting widespread indebtedness. Banks afford these hopes opportunities for fulfilment, since they can float new loans upon assets that consist very largely of paper claims to receive interest upon loans that they have already granted. Credits are given for speculative adventures in company promoting. Discount is granted on bills of exchange that represent no substantial assets. Loans may, indeed, be made to debtors in order to enable them to pay outstanding interest, since it is hoped by this means to avert total loss through their bankruptcy. A seller may even lend a purchaser the money wherewith to pay for his purchases, in the hope that the price will be made good by the interest that will be demandable from the purchaser for ever.

The over-valuation of future prospects naturally leads to extravagant expenditure, maintained by private and public borrowing—whether for purposes of enjoyment, amusement, general administration, public assistance, social services, or ostentation. Savings which alone give the future a *substantial* existence are dissipated upon purposes of the moment. How prodigal has been the expenditure upon motoring! How immense are the sums spent upon amusements, compared with those that contented our grandparents! It is, indeed, a question whether the dense populations of highly civilized countries are not outgrowing the future potentialities upon which their existence depends.

So it comes that booms are reversed into slumps. Even in times of fair prosperity the future is being constantly undermined by the erosion of its resources. Capital is lost owing to seasonal calamities, changes of fashion, over-production, cut-throat competition, defaults on a small, and bankruptcies, embezzlements and swindlings on a large scale. Future values rock under Stock Exchange transactions which are gambling pure and simple, although they are not called so. To these must be added the very serious losses that result from the depreciation of the currency of debtor countries. Recovery from these erosions is thrown back by strikes, by growing taxation that takes the heart out of profits, by apprehensions of war and by such uncertainties as attend our present policy in regard to India. The situation becomes desperate when there is added the realization that the future has been overvalued, and does not contain the potentialities that have been ascribed to it. The optimistic balloon collapses from loss of its sustaining gas. Confronted with these troubles, we frantically search for explanations that will excuse our own improvidence—like a boy, who having eaten green apples, with the punishment of a stomach-ache, attributes his anguish to "bad luck" or the "course of events."

In these circumstances the future must be revalued by a reduction of the obligations with which it has been loaded. Recovery is, of course, delayed if the revaluation is not shared by the community—if, for instance, "sheltered wages" protect the working classes from its effects, and salaries, pensions and interest on State and commercial loans are not reduced. Moses realized the inherent extravagance of mankind in ordaining a jubilee of debt remission every seventh year. In an Indian province a general readjustment of debts to amounts that could be paid off in seven years was miraculously effective in restoring heart to a people that had been worn out by successive famine: and a reduction of interest rates has recently been enforced in Australia. Such direct interference is, however, anathema to creditors, the *rentier* class and banking interests, and preference has generally been given to the indirect method of reducing future obligations by the inflation, devaluation or debasement of the currency. Since the time of Solon, history abounds with illustrations of this expedient. It has the advantage of distributing a loss of future prospects throughout the community. But, for a time, it severely dislocates commercial life. The future must, however, be rehabilitated if prosperity is to be recovered, and it is, indeed, a question whether our enormous internal War debt should not be made terminable by gradual reduction of interest. It is economically ruinous that the sins of the fathers should be visited upon the children to the third and fourth generation. It may be argued that the debt actually *provides* a future for those who have invested in it. But this is by forestalling the future, not by contributing to it, since it involves taxation that lessens profits.

The aim in view being to regenerate a future that has been in great measure consumed, the incurring of fresh debts is, of course, to be avoided except for purposes that are certainly remunerative. But this is complicated by the necessity for providing employment or maintenance for the workless—a need which can only be met by borrowing on the part of the State. This increases the burden of taxation. There is, however, this much to be said, that the State, with its taxing powers behind it, can raise loans on much better terms than private individuals, and that taxes have at least the advantage of distributing widely the economies that are needed for recovery.

Prevention is, however, better than cure, and the State might reasonably interfere to prevent the thoughtless forestalling of the future. Some control should be exercised over the issue by banks of "paper" capital, and over Stock Exchange speculation. It was by acting on these lines that M. Poincaré succeeded in raising the value of the franc from half the depth to which it had fallen. It has been recognized that fluctuations of international exchanges can be brought under control if the State itself invades the market, supported by an Exchange Stabilization fund. There is, moreover, a good deal to be said for State interference to limit the excessive demands of retailers, and even to check extravagant private expenditure by sumptuary laws much further-reaching than D.O.R.A. But such measures cannot be expected of politicians whose fortunes depend upon their avoidance of unpopularity.

CHAPTER XIV

IDEALISM AND COMMON SENSE

It is a very trite reflection that life is a tissue of contradictions. Its elemental texture is a web of two interwoven inconsistencies—of feminine urges to have regard for the future, and of masculine enthusiasms for the pleasures of the present. These inconsistencies grow and multiply under the influence of the Mind. Another's inferiority, for instance, may render us pitiful instead of disdainful if it calls up, by correlative association, an idea of our own superiority. Another's authority may be resented instead of respected, if our admiration fails to extinguish our jealousy. These contradictions become particularly startling when we are acted upon by *ideals*. For, by setting up standards that represent only *certain phases* of experience, they revolutionize our responses to experiences in general—our "valuation" of life's incidents. They may compel us to admire what is physically contemptible, and to contemn what is physically attractive. Nor is this all. Ideal standards are in some cases contradictory of one another. Forgiveness, for instance, is really inconsistent with Justice: Liberty is incompatible with Obedience: Superiority out of accord with Equality, Victory with Forbearance.

Common sense argues from causes to their consequences and is, therefore, our guide to *future* happenings. It appreciates the *useful*. We recognize its predominantly feminine character in calling it "mother-wit." There is the strongest possible contrast between it and masculine

Idealism. For, by intensifying the pleasures of the present, idealistic enthusiasm weakens the influence of the future. Ideals thrust aside prudent inferences from the past to the future—the wisdom that argues "by their fruits ye shall know them." We regard Idealism as something of higher rank than a form of pleasure. But there can be no doubt of its joys, if we observe the effects of an "ideal" upon its votaries. Through thought it throws them into such an ecstasy of emotional exaltation, as alcohol may do through the body. We call its effects "spiritual" instead of "spirituous." But to realize the similarity of the two we have only to call to mind the self-abandoning raptures of religious revivalism, or to reflect upon the transports of popular enthusiasm which went hand in hand with the cruelties of the French and Russian Revolutions. And, these extravagances apart, enthusiasts are blissfully insensible to the consequences of their ideals in human suffering and mortality. They avert their eyes from the massacres of Russia, the miseries of China, the bloodshed, prosecutions and executions in India, which have been the instruments or effects of idealistic politics: they regard these evils, indeed, as almost irrelevant—just as religious fanatics lost pity for those whom they martyred. Our Indian policy is now risking the happiness of millions of mankind in order to gratify some intellectual aspirations. Velocity—the triumph of the motor-car—has become in these days a popular ideal; and thoughts of the thousands who are killed and injured on the roads merely lead to self-excusing expedients.

Ideals, as already explained, are mental abstractions, or quintessences, of harmonious, and therefore admirable, experiences. They affect us emotionally but may possess a practical value. Peace, for instance, appeals to feminine prudence, as does war to masculine excitement. Ideals affect us through sensibilities to their influence. Those that represent phases of success make an irresistible appeal to all mankind. The influence of other kinds vary from one individual to another, but can be strengthened by the familiarity that comes of practice. *For a time*, their appeal may be very greatly intensified by the emotional effect of the words of a propagandist, prophet or apostle. So Peter the Hermit initiated the Crusades by insisting upon the justice of revenging insults to the Majesty of Christ and Christianity: Jack Cade, Rousseau and Lenin were the prophets of the fundamental Equality of mankind: Muhammad of the fraternal Unity of the faithful: in these days Mahatma Gandhi has been the apostle of Indian Independence. It seems marvellous that a single individual should exert such an influence upon his fellows. But, in order to fire the zeal of multitudes, an idealistic leader has only to fan into a flame a spark which is already alive, as a potentiality, in the minds of those who listen to him. The flame spreads rapidly by sympathetic imitation, each man's enthusiasm increasing his fellow's and being increased by it. By this imitative infection it becomes "epidemic." But its practical influence is short-lived unless it is accompanied by an increase of sensibility to the kind of harmony that it represents; and this (as already noted) can only come about through the familiarity of consistent *practice*.

Ideals give a "spiritual" value to the present, and introduce into feeling an element which we appreciate as "nobility." For they appeal, not to physical, but to mental emotion. Life that was directed solely by Common Sense would be little above that of the social insects. Nevertheless, civilization depends upon future as well as upon present values; and, indeed, although for a time we may shut our eyes to the future, the feminine element within us will not permit us entirely to forget it. The light of experience may be dull. But it is our only beacon towards future prosperity. There comes a revulsion and Idealism falls into disrepute. History is a succession of these oscillations; and we shall be assisted in understanding its vicissitudes if we briefly pass our ideals in review, and compare the aspirations that they beget with the exigencies of the future that are presented to us by Common Sense. This will involve some recapitulation of Chapters V, VI and VII. But the subject is of such importance as to deserve it.

It may be mentioned again that ideals can be associated with persons or things as their *qualities*. When an ideal has thus been "materialized," our admiring enthusiasm goes out to its possessor. So Buddha is honoured as the type of self-discipline: St. Francis is admired for his loving-kindness, Nelson as the sea-hero, and Rheims Cathedral as an expression of Gothic architectural beauty. Our acceptance of another as the personification of an ideal may be based upon fashion in public estimation: so we may admire the glory of Success as embodied in the owner of a Rolls-Royce car. It may be based upon a belief that has been inoculated by education: we credit historical personages with the virtues that history attributes to them.

One of the most glowing of our ideals is that of International Peace. We endeavour to attain it by rhetorical exhortations, conferences, and the limitation of armaments. But experience shows that war can only be checked by the elimination of its causes in aggressiveness on one side, and a sense of injury, insult or injustice on the other; and that unless supported by the fear of penal consequences, pacific idealism is mere sentimentality. Appeals to international goodwill cannot prevail against ambition, apprehension or the resentment of injustice. To obviate heat we must avoid friction. This can be commercial as well as political, and the patriotic self-interest which is now penalizing foreign goods to promote home production, however reasonable in itself, cannot but add to the possibilities of international disagreement.

Aggressivement might be repressed if nations would whole-heartedly unite in punishing it. The use of a punitive military force would be very dangerous. For war fever is catching—*αυτὸς γαρ ἐφέλκεται ἄνδρα σίδηρος*. It might be possible to punish an offending nation by fining it, or by blocking its external trade. But this course would be beset with difficulties, amongst which would be the feeling that to fine would be as unworthy of the occasion as the waters of Jordan seemed to Naaman the Syrian. And, in order to secure peace, the past must be regarded, as well as the present and future. The humiliating provisions of the Treaty of Versailles keep the fires of resentment burning, and our protestations of goodwill stop short of the rendition of Tanganyika.

Unless, then, measures for the preservation of international amity are much more practical than they are at present, Common Sense endorses the text that "when a strong man armed keeps his house, his goods are in peace." A nation best protects itself from the aggression of others by maintaining such a defensive force as would render aggression exceedingly expensive. It can undoubtedly be imbued with pacifism by propaganda, or by the over-valuation of comfort, luxuries and amusements. But history shows that this is a very dangerous frame of mind. Rome fell because her people would not fight for her.

Social ideals are typified by the Loving-kindness of "fellowship"—the love of our "kind," with which, as human beings, we are mentally identified and united. It is transcendentally idealized as Love that is extended to those who do not merit it. On the feminine side, our affections are inclined to be exclusive within the family, or social, *clique*. Masculine enthusiam, under the influence of an analogy, is willing to receive mankind generally into the sympathetic comradeship of "brotherhood," and, in dealing with them, to forgive offences instead of punishing them, to use persuasion instead of command, conciliation instead of forceful authority, and to give alms in charity without recompense in exchange.

It is only by winnowing the Gospel narratives that this attitude of sympathetic forbearance can be taken as fundamental to Christianity. The texts that enjoin it shed an atmosphere of benevolence that would lighten present hardships. But their observance is quite incompatible with the interests of the future. What would become of its prospects if we forgave criminals their trespasses, "turned the other cheek" to violence, and gave all our belongings to the poor? We should certainly be "taking no thought for the morrow."

To begin with the ideal of Forgiveness. It shrinks sympathetically from the infliction of pain. We justify it by such unpractical maxims as that "force is no remedy," or that "it is all done by kindness," ignoring the outstanding fact that pain—in hunger, thirst and lust—is the fundamental urge that ensures life's continuance. Whipping is the most humane—as well as the most ancient—punishment for young offenders, and there is very good evidence to show that in adults it checks criminal tendencies that can survive imprisonment. Its indiscriminate use in the past is no argument against its discriminate use in the present. Imprisonment is now regarded rather as an apprenticeship in morality than as a deterrent of immorality. And there is a tendency—encouraged by the newspapers—to sympathize with the romantic side of crime, and to search for excuses. This is exceedingly dangerous. There are signs that juvenile crime is increasing, and that professional criminals are gaining in audacity. Experience shows that the appeal of sentimental exhortations is of little practical avail. How infructuous they have been in checking reckless motor driving, and the littering of picnic places!

It is more complimentary to be guided by persuasion than by command. This gives democratic government its attractiveness. Democracy will be referred to in the chapter following. But it may be noted here that experience does not show that it necessarily renders a people happier in the present, or more prosperous in the future. Are not Portugal, Italy, Germany and America more contented under their dictators than they were during the preceding days of democratic confusion? A regiment under a strict, but just, colonel is commonly likened to a happy family. For the prestige of a commander gives an admiring pleasure that is hardly provoked by political oratory. And it excites the stabilizing feeling of loyalty. In these days it is being eliminated from home as well as political life. Fathers are content to sink their parental prestige in relations of "good fellowship" with their children, and children resent parental orders. Is the effect upon the younger generation such as would give us confidence in their ability to meet future difficulties with enterprise and industry?

The social idealist would meet antagonism with conciliation. But this is effective only when it is attributable to a desire for justice—not to apprehension. Otherwise, it merely sharpens aggressiveness, as we have learnt from the course of events in South Africa, Ireland, India, and from domestic strikes without number. By compliments and manifestations of sympathy democracy endeavours to secure itself against international wars and proletarian revolts. The uncertainty of these instruments has been accentuated in recent years by the Great War and the General Strike. They may be effective in fair weather. But they fail in dealing with the storms which are constantly threatening social life. Whatever Christian idealism may maintain, weakness is despicable to the majority of mankind, and is an active incentive to insolence and aggressiveness. The conciliatory abasement of the flag endangers our future: for we live by commerce, and commerce only follows the flag when it is an emblem of power. As a commercial emblem, it excites no such respect. One cannot idealize the huckstering of the market. Individuals and nations gain a future by strivings and overmasterings: they lose it by concessions and compromises.

Charity is amongst the first of social virtues, and affords its bestowers an agreeable glow of patronizing superiority. But its effects upon its recipients may be pernicious unless it is discriminating and does not discourage industry.

According to the tenets of Hinduism, charity that discriminates does not "earn merit." This idea seems to be spreading to England. It is an extraordinary thing that this country stands almost alone in requiring no work whatever from the recipients of the "dole." There is ample employment available in the reclamation of marshy and the trenching of good land, and in town improvements and scavenging. Philanthropic efforts to provide instructive occupation for a microscopic minority, however gratifying in themselves, are no substitutes for regulations that would insist that the acceptance of relief by the able-bodied should involve some self-sacrifice. A man's character is a most valuable asset, and charity that undermines it threatens the future.

If social ideals are widely propagated and insisted upon, their influence becomes epidemic as that of "public opinion." Charity becomes fashionable, and is dispensed without feelings of real sympathy: conciliation must be used by employers of labour and politicians because it is "the thing to do"; and it becomes "bad form" to insist upon the adequate punishment of offenders, or to deprecate an excessive multiplication of public amusements. An attitude such as that of parents who "spoil" their children becomes harmonious, because it is in accord with public feeling. But its effect upon the morality of the future is, of course, none the less harmful. And it "eats up" the resources of the future by recklessly borrowing for its sentimental extravagances.

The ideals of *fundamental* morality—such as of Justice, Honesty and Truth—are as useful in securing the future as they are ennobling in the present. They make a *natural* appeal to human sensibility. Justice inspires such a respect as is not given to benevolence, or brotherly manners, for it raises no suspicions of self-interest or of "saving one's own soul." It is the stablest basis of governing authority, and the only reliable guarantee of its continuance. Without Honesty a commercial future would not exist. Men's universal appreciation of these ideals provides an unassailable argument for those who are convinced of his inherent goodness. But sensibilities to their harmonies may be blunted by discordant habitudes, or be vitiated by propaganda and example. This applies to both "fine" morality and fine art, and it is possible to hold that both decline together. A nation's future is largely dependent upon its mass morality. Rectitude, Honesty and Truth may not "pay" in particular cases. But they secure the future against the shocks of disillusionment which leads to revolution. Moral ideals, in fact, serve us rather as guardians of the future than as ministering to the present, and for this reason do not arouse very great enthusiasm. They are respectable, but not so inspiring as are social ideals—that of "uplifting" others, for example. We lay more stress upon kindness than upon justice. But justice is the more impressive as it is the rarer of the two.[1]

For the ideals of *conventional* morality our admiration must be less unqualified. Laws maintain internal peace, and the acquittance of obligations by their discharge. But they may be glaringly unjust, although supported by public opinion. Custom is a conservative force of immense power. From before the beginnings of history it has maintained monogamy in Europe and polygamy in Asia. Its traditional views and practices may be drawn from fanciful analogies, and may be exceedingly cruel. They may serve to provide public amusements at recurrent intervals. They may be gratifying because they preserve distinguishing peculiarities. The meticulous rules of their Law have given the Jews an enduring individuality that has outlived that of any nation in Europe; and the rigid observances and prejudices of the Indian caste system has, it seems, at times

[1] God sends the rain—as rain it must—
Upon the just and the unjust:
It gives less trouble to the unjust fellah
Because he has the just man's umbrella.

protected the people from lapsing into barbarism. Custom may, however, act as a restraint that cripples development, and in Europe and America it is rapidly giving way before the influence of a changing fashion. But in Asia it is still a dominant force.

It is difficult to appraise the *moral* effect of religious ideals — their effects are obscured by the admiration and hopes that they inspire. It may, perhaps, be said that they give more illumination to rules of conventional than to the promptings of fundamental morality. The artificial is more esteemed than the natural. Religious enthusiasm may, in fact, lull the promptings of Conscience by its self-exalting pleasure; and hence conversion to Christianity may actually be demoralizing. There are few who will deny that a sceptic may be as just, honest and truthful as a religious man: he is, indeed, more likely to be so, since he has nothing wherewith to salve a violated conscience. Experience shows that religion is disposed to endorse the morality of the day. If this is philanthropic, it is encouraged: if it is distorted by sectarian or warlike animosity it is endorsed. Speaking generally, religion is a conservative force, and governments that have tried to banish it have soon recalled it as a sedative of anarchistic discontent.

Æsthetic idealism—the influence of Beauty, physical, moral or intellectual, shows its power most masterfully when it transfigures sexual attraction into romantic love. Having regard to the future and to the stability of the family, should marriage be based upon Romance or upon Common Sense—that is to say, upon a consideration of prudential motives? The English incline to the former, the French to the latter—and indisputably the more ancient—view. It is impossible to decide upon their relative merits without an amount of detailed knowledge that is unattainable. But there is this to be said for Romance as a bond of conjugal affection—that, when it grows cold, there remains an attaching fragrance in its ashes. Time may trample out the enthusiasm of the past—

> . . . mais sur nos fleurs fanées
> Vous ne marchez jamais.

Apart from its effect upon love, the æsthetic idealization of Beauty gives future as well as present pleasure through its *creative* effects—its embodiment by artists as a quality of their imaginative works. Æsthetic appreciation adds immensely to the pleasures of the present: artistic creativeness also stores the future with pleasures. Æsthetic enjoyments have, it is true, a future in that they may be recalled by memory. But the artist provides more vivid and enduring provocatives. By his work in architecture, sculpture, painting, designing, music, poetry and fiction, he endows the world with beauties that rival those which Nature offers us. And gardening must be added to this list of the fine arts. It is, indeed, England's typical contribution to the beautiful—affording an inspiring interest in a present which can bear flowers and fruit in the future.

Life is an unceasing battle between the appeal of our Peaceful, Social, Moral and Æsthetic ideals, and feminine suggestions that are dictated by sensual and prudential self-interest. Ideals of Success introduce another army into the conflict. They may reinforce one side or the other. We may find success in selfishness or in self-denial; in pride, in benevolence or in command. And they are of contradictory tendencies in themselves. They may inspire, at one time, cries of anarchistic independence, and, at another, shouts of respectful loyalty. This results from the capacity for affecting us either egotistically or altruistically. Their influence, as well as their origin, has been touched upon in Chapter VII. But it is of such immense importance that some repetition may be excused.

Their *egotistic* influence manifests itself particularly in the self-admiration of Pride, Vanity, or Self-conceit—the product of a consciousness of our own myriad successes, and the triumphs that they have given us. Its effect in giving an active, self-assertive complexion to phraseology has been already remarked. It is a notable fact that ideas of self-importance are intensified by the successes of education: they are stronger in the University than in the school (where, indeed, they are repressed by frankness of language and manners), and become a dazzling obsession amongst the intellectual classes. There have sprung from them some conceptions that have been of immense political importance—that there is no natural inferiority between one man and another, and, consequently, that man has a natural "right" to freedom from compulsion. There has followed the idealization of the social Equality of democracy, and of social and political Liberty. These two ideals, being of common origin, are bracketed together in revolutionary propaganda. But they are in truth quite distinct. We are as much bound by the vote of a hostile majority as by the order of a dictator. Trade Unionism is democratic: but what is more slavish than that a man should be prevented from working when he wishes to work? There is social equality in Russia. But there is hardly a pretence of freedom. It is to the Athenians that we owe this misleading identification of democracy with liberty. The Owl of Athens laid an egg which has hatched out into the "Bird of Freedom."

Death conflicts with these ideals. It is not merely a painful severance of interests and affections: it is an offence against human dignity—a dishonour which visions of personal immortality, or of such immortality as can be conferred by fame, or by memorial monuments—may enable us to repudiate. Imagination may suggest that personal continuity may be secured through one's son; and the dread of sonlessness stamped itself very markedly upon the Greeks and Romans, and is still endorsed by religion in India and China.

The delight of self-esteem grows with the mental influence of education. It undermines the power of authority, and Governments must find a substitute in the persuasive arts that constitute successful "salesmanship." It lays us open to the inveigling effect of compliments, and complimentary apologies, because they harmonize so delightfully with this sensibility. Express or implied, they are the introductory, if not the ruling note, of persuasive oratory: their payment, deprecation and repayment provides polite conversation with much of its stock in trade: they lubricate the course of commerce, and of religious, historical and critical expositions—and even those of science. They are the recognized instruments of international diplomacy, as they are of political propaganda and commercial business. It cannot be claimed that they have any *progressive* influence, except as rewards that encourage accomplishment. The shame of repentance may be more fruitful—a truth that has received religious endorsement.

Turning now from egotistic self-likings to egotistic pursuits, or desires, it will be well to rehearse some of the rather complicated distinctions that have already been drawn in Chapter VII. Desires of success—that is to say, ambitions—are to be distinguished, in the first place, according as they are *subjective* or *objective*—according, that is to say, as they affect the relations of ourselves to ourselves, or the relations of ourselves to others. And, within each of these two classes, they are to be further distinguished according as they are *practical* or emotional, and as they have for their object something to be accomplished as merely the gratification of personal vanity.

The *subjective* ambition to conquer oneself is one of the most striking and most useful of human qualities, although its evolutionary origin is simply a desire for victorious success, and the sense of triumph that follows it. *Practical* self-control enables us to struggle against the present temptation of an immediate satisfaction in order to gain the satisfaction of a success that lies beyond it—as that of duty accomplished and conscience appeased. This immensely reinforces the influence of moral harmonies and the "duties" that are their offspring. It enables one to do justice "against himself," and to fight down fear by moral courage. For the thought of a triumph over self can outweigh other prospective pleasures. So, from the creeping roots of Evolution, man is able to raise the "white flower of a blameless life." Self-control also reinforces prudent care for the future, endowing industry with conscientious strength that can withstand the tiresomeness of work. In this case feminine care is reinforced by an idea of masculine origin. These thoughts of self-conquest are very potent elements in the process of selecting and rejecting which we apostrophize as "The Will." Self-control is the one security against emotional storms, on the one hand, and engulfing material quicksands on the other. It is the guardian of the "Golden Mean."

As an object in itself, the *emotional* self-discipline of Asceticism is more impressive than useful. It was a cardinal principle of Buddhist morality. It entered into Christianity as a doctrine of the Essenes, and was stressed by the introspection of St. Paul, who picturesquely described himself as "buffeting his body, and leading it about as a slave": it bore dramatic fruit in the thousands of anchorites who followed St. Antony into the deserts of the Egyptian Thebaid, in the monastic life and in the observance of fasting. It inspires the *bushido* of Japan. It was the keynote of the Stoic philosophy: Epictetus held that, without self-restraint, life was merely the periodic filling and emptying of a bag: Marcus Aurelius found himself continually engaged in a wrestling match with himself. It was the moving spirit of Puritanism, and of the evangelical suspicion of pleasure for its own sake that was in repute during Victorian days. Asceticism is an evolutionary exaggeration of self-control converting an instrumental safeguard of the future into an object in itself. We may smile at its eccentricities. But one must respect it as the source of a *reserve* of power—an "accumulator" or "storage battery"[1]—from which useful self-control can gather strength.

When subjective ambition is contrarified in the fear of Shame it gains in controlling power. But it is pessimistic. Saints, Stoics and Puritans are not types of light-heartedness. It is, therefore, unattractive, and has, in these days, fallen into deep disrepute as a motive of conduct. Reproaches that would awaken it are libellous outside the nursery, the school, and the Church service. A "broken and contrite heart" is quite out of fashion.

In *objective* life Ambition in its *practical* phases has been the spirit of civilizing progress, continually endowing the future with new possibilities. For, in this phase, Ambition is under the influence of practical feminine inclination. If it is stifled by conservative custom—as in India during many generations—the future is merely a *replica* of the past. As an emotional—purely masculine—desire for success in itself, it adds immensely to the gaiety of present life through games and gambling. "Sport" has its useful side. It tends to improve physique: it teaches the subordination of self to one's team, and the maintenance of kindly feelings towards antagonists. But, as a spectacular or gambling amusement, it lacks these advantages and may be very demoralizing. For it breeds passions that may deaden all sympathy with suffering. As the spirit of war—the emotional desire for victory—it threatens the future with destruction, as it has destroyed civilizations in the past. Conquest may, however, be reconstructive if the emotional desire for glory passes into a practical wish for improvement. It cannot be denied, for instance, that British domination in India has restored to the people a future that has been wrecked by the disorders that followed the collapse of the Mogul Empire. The future profits but little from the "inferential" ambition which seeks success through popularity.

[1] Hence "charge your battery" would be a useful moral slogan.

Yet it must be admitted that the desire for respectability is a powerful safeguard of conventional morality.

When egotistic Pride and Ambition are altruistically extended to the country or community to which one belongs, they act as a cementing flux that produces social solidarity. They give cohesion to the members of a State, a political party, and an army at war. This is also the effect of ideals of successful superiority in their purely altruistic developments—that is to say, when they are attached to others and stimulate loyal Admiration, Respect and Faith. For men are united when they are drawn by these feelings towards the same personality—religious or civil—and the same institutions. The influence of these feelings is generally conservative: it is by deference to authority that civilization preserves what it has won in the past, and transmits this to the future. They begin in the home—as respect for parental authority—in particular for that of one's mother. If some ancient fables are to be trusted, women take more delight than men in the exercise of power. If this is true, we may congratulate ourselves upon it. For the well-being of the future depends upon the civilization of the rising generation, and this mainly proceeds from maternal authority. Experience has shown that if children are neglected, they do not rise above the level of quadrupeds. From the home these feelings of respectful loyalty spread to the teacher, the chief and the king, to the heroes of the past and to the guardian institutions of the State. They are the motives which give Religion their compelling force, and invest religious Churches with their controlling authority.

History shows, however, that this uncalculating devotion may be a sensibility through which man can be drawn into frenzies of destructive extravagances. Devotion has focused the zeal that has animated religious wars and persecutions —the romantic cruelty of the Crusades, the extermination of the Albigenses and sectarian strife that reduced the population of Germany by nearly a half. It cost France the expatriation of multitudes of most useful Huguenot citizens. It consolidated the marauding hosts of Attila, Tamerlane, and of Napoleon, and in the Great War it drew uncomprehendingly hundreds of thousands of young men to mutilation and death. It must be confessed that conscientious objectors have the wherewithal to defend themselves.

When another's Power has not been actually experienced and affects us only as his *prestige*, his authority rests upon an idea which may be overthrown by the suffering of injustice that shatters Faith, through weakness that negatives Power, or through the educative spread of ideas of self-assertive independence that rejects submission to authority as demeaning. A revolution follows. History shows that weakness—" strength by limping sway disabled "—has been the most general cause of political upheavals. The French revolution would not have occurred had Louis XVI been capable of determined action.

On a general review of our idealistic enthusiasms, we must, then, conclude that, having regard to the interests of the future, only two can be accepted without qualifications. Those of the fundamentally Moral and Æsthetic kinds can be whole-heartedly endorsed. Ideas that are fundamentally moral—such as those of Justice, Honesty, Truth, Duty and Gratitude—introduce harmonies into experiences of the present, and also stabilize prospects of the future. Ideals of Beauty draw our eyes from the turbid current of life, and fringe its banks with charms which glorify their scenery, although actually springing from our own sensibilities. And, when embodied by artistic skill, these ideals create an artificial environment that may be far more pleasing than the actual. Social ideals temper the harshness of a purely practical outlook, and soften the hardships that it involves. They must be viewed, however, through the shadow that is cast upon them by their demoralizing effect upon their beneficiaries. They may draw man's eyes heavenwards. But he must keep his feet on the ground. Personified by ourselves, ideals of Success, Power, Dignity and Honour endow us with a serviceable self-respect, and also with a vanity which lays us cruelly open to the machinations of others. They beget inspiring but elusive visions of Liberty and Equality. But they also energize life with Ambition—the spring-head of the stream of activity that has civilized mankind. Turned in subjectively upon ourselves, these ideals move us to Self-restraint—the most peculiar and ennobling of our faculties. It can be carried to excess in a self-sanctifying asceticism. But it stabilizes the future as well as the present, and is amongst the most valuable of our capacities. Personified by others, Power and Dignity command our Respect and Obedience—conservative forces, like that of Custom, which preserve civilization as already attained, but may prevent it from advancing, and be inhuman in repressing change of any kind. These feelings may, however, be excited by power that is aggressive, revolutionary or ascetic, and may actually destroy the achievements which under other orientation they protect.

Swung hither and thither by these contrary forces, man can steer a safe course only by keeping a watchful eye upon the Golden Mean, and the hand of self-restraint upon the tiller. What losses of life and resources Europe would have escaped had Lord Lansdowne's counsels of moderation been accepted in 1917! It is only by self-control that we can weather the distracting storms of emotional enthusiasm, and can avoid currents of money-grubbing prudence that would draw our lives into monotonous, soul-deadening routine. But, for this, our "resistance battery" must be well charged.

CHAPTER XV

LIBERTY AND DISCIPLINE

Liberty is the self-expression of masculine excitement: Discipline—the practice of Obedience—accords with a feminine impulse. For we obey another by imitating his wishes, and imitation is a mental phase of physical clinging. We are carried along by another's wishes as a child by its nurse. That obedience is, in fact, imitation was realized by the author of the *Imitatio Christi*. By a confusion of consequence and cause—of the passive with the active—the word discipline is often used to express the control to which obedience is rendered—in the sense of "disciplining" instead of "being disciplined." In this chapter it is used in the latter of these senses.

The contrast between Liberty and Discipline is, then, as sharp as that between Idealism and Common Sense. Liberty is a condition in which we "express ourselves" by behaving, thinking, speaking or writing as we please—acting in accordance with our sensibilities and with the ideas that present themselves from time to time. Moralists will object that this is not "true liberty," but *licence*, implying that a man must be bound by one leg in order to be free. This is a contradiction in terms; and, to avoid it, I take "liberty" to signify what is the obvious meaning of the word. Discipline, on the contrary, is a condition of restraint. It may result from one or other of four causes. It may be imposed upon one by oneself; or it may be compelled either by the force of circumstances, by the influence of public opinion, or by an enforcing authority.

Liberty is, accordingly, not to be confused with Democracy. For this constrains a minority by the wishes of a majority: it substitutes persuasion for command only so far as the majority is concerned. It is popular because, through the competition of its rival parties, it affords amusing interest to the public, and because it soothes people's vanity. Voters are *consulted*, and this satisfies *amour propre*. And the educated classes are conciliated by the offer of unlimited opportunities for persuasive eloquence. But this may, of course, mislead the judgment as effectively as force constrains behaviour.

Now it is obvious that the more substantial liberty of unrestrained "self-expression" is also, in great measure, imaginary. For life is subject to imperious necessities. We must eat and drink in order to live, and there are other less respectable physical demands which must be obeyed. Love is a tyrant. Social life necessitates the legal restraint of conduct which would cause injury or loss to others. One can, however, exercise liberty by breaking the laws. There is liberty of behaviour in giving full rein to self-indulgence —sensual or sentimental, and in working, or incurring debts, as one pleases. There is liberty of thought in the free development of our opinions, beliefs and imaginative creativeness; liberty of expression in freely communicating our thoughts to others, through speech, writing, or artistic representation. Phases of liberty may, then, be distinguished as of behaviour, of thought and of communicative expression.

Law-breaking—or criminal liberty—is of course inconsistent with social life: it wrecks, not only the peace and enjoyment of the community in the present, but its future prospects. There is something exciting in tales of crime which renders reports of it interesting, and may even dispose us, very unfortunately, to sympathize with the criminal, to hunt for romance behind the scenes, to find excuses for him in human nature, and even to rejoice in his acquittal. Hence crime provides "good copy" for journalism, and criminals are assured of the dignity of notoriety. But to palliate crime is exceedingly dangerous. It weakens the law in its perennial conflict with lawlessness. And an increase in criminality, especially amongst the young, is a sure sign of national decadence.

Liberty of the self-indulgent, sensual kind has been defended even by strict moralists,[1] when it is "at one's own risk and peril." It is admitted that this freedom can only be conceded to adults and must be denied to the young. But there are phases of human behaviour which render it doubtful whether man ever outgrows the irresponsibility of childhood. It is difficult to regard, as other than childish, the ceremonies of Free Masonry and the Order of Ancient Buffaloes. And, having regard to the imitative propensities of mankind, it cannot be held that the libertinism of individuals is not dangerous to society in the example which it sets—especially when it offers temptations to excess. Sensual liberty has, accordingly, been condemned by every religion of repute. For a prophet would belie his name were he not concerned with the future; and it is obvious that the lure of to-day's appetites and amusements diverts men's eyes from the difficulties that are presented to him by to-morrow.

The most primitive and urgent attraction of the senses is that of sex, and, amongst peoples who have not elaborated the tastes of the palate or the capacities of amusement, the purchasable pleasures of femininity represent almost the only form of sensual indulgence. With the progress of material civilization, the attractions of food and drink are developed, and there comes about a passion for frequent amusement, the gossipy and complimentary intercourse of society and the self-ostentation of dress. It becomes ridiculous to be prudent. The satires of Juvenal give a lively picture of the social demoralization which these tendencies had brought about in the Roman life of the second century. His descriptions may be exaggerated. But a satire would lose all point if it were not in general accord

[1] As by John Stuart Mill in his defence of Liberty.

with actualities. At a later period—just before the fall of Rome—the historian Ammianus presented even darker scenes of general profligacy. The unrestrained pursuit of sensual pleasure and of amusement was not confined to the richer classes, amongst whom it may, perhaps, be regarded as a normal extravagance. It had spread to the mass of the people, vitiating the life of the community as a whole. Rome fell. For people who have lost the power of withstanding themselves cannot withstand the attacks of enemies. Amongst the outstanding facts of history is the failure of the *noblesse* in France and Russia to offer a united front to the revolutions that ruined them. Luxury had undermined their fortitude, and licence their discipline.

It would be absurd to draw a parallel between the demoralization of Roman manners, and our own social conditions of the present day. Yet there are some disconcerting signs to show that our feet are set on the path that leads to decadence. During the last half-century an astonishing change has come about in moral outlook. The puritanical dislike of pleasure and amusement for their own sake has completely disappeared, and the young are now frankly advised to "express themselves." Gone also is the respect for economy—for the solid as compared with the showy—which built up the commercial prosperity of Victorian days. Ideals of "propriety" in dress, of decorum in manners, are ridiculed. There is a relaxation of sexual restraint which renders divorce interesting, if not fashionable. More than a tenth of the population subsists upon outside support. Industry and commerce are languishing under a load of debt, contracted in extravagant anticipation of the future. Yet throughout the whole community there is an inordinate passion for amusement. The interests of life are centred upon cinemas, "dog-dromes," football matches, motoring and the spectacular breaking of records in velocity. The art of amusing others, which with unsophisticated peoples is of very low social repute, is artificially exalted by civilized minds to the heroic level of the gladiator, the toreador, the actor, the athlete and the film star. It is, however, fortunate for England that under the bracing influence of a chilly and uncertain climate, revulsions may occur which can restore public feeling to sanity. Our past history offers many instances of evangelical revivals.

The liberty of sentimental idealism has been discussed in the chapter preceding, and its dangers have been exposed. History shows that civilizations are in danger when they idealistically glorify sensual pleasure, emotional excitement, self-assertive liberty, or submissive pacificism. It will suffice here to remark that Idealism, in overriding the warnings of Common Sense, can call logic to its assistance by formulating pleasurable generalizations (or rules), which are fallacious but, being mental creations, are deemed to rank higher than the grim lessons of experience. It is, for instance, more agreeable to believe that a majority vote is right, than to gather from the past that it has been generally wrong. So again it was comforting to hold the old Liberal doctrine that the settlement of wages, prices and rates of interest should be left to individual freedom. But in regard to the settlement of wages the interests of employers and employed are antagonistic. Employers are individually the stronger, and justice was not obtainable by a policy of *laissez-faire*. The working classes have redeemed themselves from sweated toil by forming combinations which, by the use of strikes, have lessened working hours, and raised wages to an extent which is often incompatible with the prices at which products can be sold. One evil has given place to another. And experience is demonstrating that prices cannot be left to adjust themselves in the liberty of free—or "cut-throat"—competition. Goods owe their *value* to their distributor, and he is entitled to substantial profits. But the difference between the price that he can command and that received by the producer is often scandalously great. Capitalists can protect themselves by forming "rings," or "combines." But those who lack capital, or the enterprise and knowledge that are needed for self-protection, suffer severely. In the interest of justice—and of peace—it is desirable that wages and prices should be subject to the interference of some non-political authority, representing both parties, such as, it seems, Signor Mussolini is endeavouring to introduce into the industrial and commercial life of Italy. Bitter experience has demonstrated that there should be some control over the power of banks and financial corporations to overdraw future possibilities by the flotation of speculative capital. And it seems just that the State should interfere to reduce agreed-upon rates of interest, when money-value has risen substantially.

It is unquestioned in these days that there should be liberty of *thought*—that is to say, freedom in forming opinions and beliefs, and the creations of imaginative Art. As a matter of fact, however, the Mind is narrowly controlled in these matters by education and public opinion. Those who can free themselves from these influences are "heretics." In the days of religious persecution it was an offence to *think* heretically. It is now recognized that thoughts must be expressed in order to be punishable. Liberty has gained ground. But we must not jump to the conclusion that the free play of the intellect necessarily advances wisdom. Reason, unrestrained by Common Sense, may lead to very erroneous conclusions. The theoretical generalizations of philosophers, from the days of Plato onwards, have served to nourish speculative interest, and gratify self-complacency. But it cannot be said that they have brought us much nearer to the real understanding of Life and Nature.

Free speech and a free Press are held to be amongst the greatest of modern privileges. Our enjoyment of them is, however, subject to many limitations. We may—truthfully or untruthfully—praise or advertise whom or what we will. But the law of libel penalizes the publication of what is true when it is to the injury or discredit of another. The law of copyright forbids the literary use of another's thoughts or words. In both cases the object is to protect "vested interests." These are also attacked when an established religion, or the State, is criticized in a hostile spirit; and such criticisms are still held in some countries to be blasphemous or seditious and are severely penalized. We repress Communist propaganda, but generally allow much latitude in religious and political discussion. With us revolutionary arguments have not so subversive an effect as with more emotional peoples. What with us is a safety-valve, with them may detonate an explosion. An uncontrolled Press has beyond doubt been very harmful in India: it has unsettled convictions and has offered nothing substantial to replace them.

Freedom of publication is also restricted by the force of public opinion. Editors and publishers hesitate to give currency to views that run counter to the accepted conclusions of the day, unless they are emotionally exciting through their mystery or incomprehensibility. This may have delayed the spread of some novel scientific and philosophic doctrines. But it may reasonably be doubted whether our understanding has suffered thereby. The astonishing advance of practical science has proceeded not from theory but from experiment.

Freedom of publication, or of artistic exhibition, is also subject to limitations in the interests of public morality—not so severely, however, as when vested interests are threatened. The sale of obscenities can be stopped: but much is permitted. Theatrical representations and cinema films are subject to censorship: but it is by no means strict, and there is an influential body of opinion in favour of greater stringency.

We turn now to Discipline. This is generally taken to be the antithesis of Liberty. But, in fact, it is only through the disciplining of our sensibilities that we can hope to attain real Liberty and Equality. For it is by the tyranny of our sensibilities that we are enslaved: and it is their disparity, between individuals, that renders one superior in character to another. Their origins and natures have been sketched in Chapter II and have come under remark elsewhere. They can be disciplined because they are so largely dependent upon the force of habit—that is to say, upon memorial familiarity. Those that are innate in us can be weakened by disuse as they can be strengthened by indulgence. Self-conceit can be shrivelled by rebuke as it can be swollen by compliments. And the multitude of our artificial, or acquired, tastes—as those for various foods, drinks, intoxicants and amusements—are the fruits of experience, and can, therefore, be intensified or lessened by practice. Sensibilities can, in fact, be "cultivated" by being fostered, trained or repressed. Repression is a disagreeable process and can only be executed under the pressure of discipline.

This, as already remarked, may be impressed upon a man by himself, by his circumstances, by public opinion, or by enforcing authority. Self-imposed discipline is that of self-control—*practical*, when it protects future interests by the repression of sensibilities to present enjoyment or uncalculating idealism, *emotional*, when it represses selfish sensibilities in the interest of social, moral, or æsthetic harmonies. It acts through the "inhibition"—a sense of the "disallowed"—which it is now fashionable to regard as an evil instead of a protective safeguard. Fear is held to be degrading, whereas it is in the front rank of life's guardians. This has been frankly recognized in the past. "The fear of the Lord is the beginning of wisdom."

The capacity of self-control can undoubtedly be strengthened by the accumulation of a reserve of power through the deliberate practice of ascetic formalities, or "acts of supererogation," which in themselves are childish—as, for instance, by resolutely getting up from a chair simply to thwart a desire to remain seated. The regular performance of gymnastic exercises is useful to this end, quite apart from their physical utility: they are more disciplining than games because they are not pleasurable. They are approved instruments in the *Yoga* of Hindu philosophy. Decorum, however conventional—even in the wearing of a stiff collar—has its use in reinforcing the power of "keeping oneself in hand."

Self-control is the essence of the quality which we vaguely describe as "strength of character." A "man of strong character" is one who can withstand himself, and can, therefore, counteract the insinuations of dislike or spite and the temptations of egotistic vanity. He gifts himself with patience and perseverance. He is neither overheated by idealism, nor over-chilled by a calculating prudence. Amidst the swirling currents of life, he can avoid Scylla on the one hand, and Charybdis on the other. The saving value of this self-control becomes the more conspicuous when it is surrounded by a rising tide of self-indulgence. Yet it is surprising to find one of the most forcible of its appreciations in the lines of such a cynic as Juvenal.[1] With diffidence I venture to express their meaning—

Pray for sound health, in Body and in Mind,
  For a courageous heart that smiles at death,
Can find in life's full stop that Nature's kind,
  And faces troubles with unbated breath—
Is slow to anger, envies not the rich,
  Like Hercules, fights evils that befall us,
And shuns delights, e'en of such pompous pitch
  As glorified the Court of Sardanapalus.

I only show thee what thou hast. The gate
  To Peace is Virtue: through this one arrives.
No Luck needs he who's wise. Almighty Fate!
  'Tis we who make thee Mistress of our Lives.

Such being the inestimable value of self-control, it is surprising that education does not lay more stress upon self-discipline as a means of cultivating it. Self-control is generally taken to come to man "as a grace." But experi-

[1] At the end of Satire X.

ence seems to show that there is more hope for it in practice than in prayer.

The discipline which comes from the pressure of circumstances is sometimes belittled as the "virtue of necessity." But it has a very healthful effect upon mankind. For working, even of necessity, involves the self-control of patience and perseverance, and develops the self-repressive tendencies that are the essence of "virtue." It is easy to find fault with those that are richer than oneself. But, making every allowance for this foible, it is difficult to avoid the conclusion—driven home so forcibly in the Gospels—that unassuming virtue is commoner amongst the working classes than amongst the wealthy. Any acquaintance with the life of industrial families brings to light evidences of self-sacrifice which is rarely met with in the higher ranks of society. It was necessity that first taught man to work, and, in cases which offer little scope for ambition, it is necessity that keeps men working. From this point of view, it seems clear that disasters may have an energizing effect upon mankind, and this explains the rapidity with which their losses are recovered.

Industry is, however, cheerless[1] unless it is brightened by ambition—by the hope of success. In this respect agriculture and gardening are the most inspiriting of pursuits, since Nature gives so much in return for so little. A gardener, speaking generally, is more cheerful—although less "temperamental"—than an artist. His successes are not only greater in relation to his labour, but are less open to belittlement by hostile criticism. From this point of view the introduction of machinery must have a depressing effect upon the spirits of our industrial population. For no such success can be obtained by serving the action of a machine as by the exercise of a handicraft; and the subdivision of manufactures into a number of merely contributory pro-

[1] As when one "works to get enough to eat, to have the strength to work, to get enough to eat, to have the strength to work"—and so on, in deadening repetition.

cesses denies to the artisan the satisfaction with which he could regard a product that was completed by himself. Work becomes dreary, and the factory-hand searches for outside amusement far more avidly than did the craftsman of the past. The satisfaction of personal ambition is also lacking when industry is so severely mechanized as it is under the Russian Soviet system.

The influence of "public opinion" is so compelling that no one who is subject to it can boast of freedom. It is an urge pressing us to assimilate, or adapt, ourselves *imitatively* to others who attract us in like or admiration, or are mentally unified with us as our "fellows." The urge is, therefore, instrumented by intelligence, although its hold is tightened by memorial familiarity. It affects our behaviour as Custom (or "good form"), our minds as Popular Sentiment—in epidemics of enthusiasm; and, as Fashion—cut adrift from tradition—it constantly changes dress, manners, forms of pleasure and amusements. Custom is safeguarded by the fear of disgrace: it is, then, severely disciplinary. The hold of Fashion is on the other hand, riveted by the desire for distinction. Popular Sentiment owes much to idealism, including such idealized successes as female suffrage. But a desire for distinction enters into it very largely, noticeable in "society" charities, and in movements for "social uplift."

Customary observances may be suggested by common sense, as when they maintain a certain standard of sexual morality. But they are more commonly prompted by imaginative fancies, or a desire for the "hall-mark" of peculiarity. Their character has already been discussed. They may take the form of "taboos." Amongst the Jews and Hindus they prescribe the character of one's food; and during more than twelve centuries they have maintained amongst Moslems an abstinence from alcohol which it has been impossible to enforce in the United States. Before the beginnings of history, custom had made Europe monogamous, Asia polygamous. Popular Sentiment sustains religious creeds. It inspires peoples with patriotism—also with "war fever," and a pathetic longing for peace. It has been the propagating force of the religious, moral and sympathetic enthusiasms that have fired crusades, reformed religions, repressed immorality, abolished slavery, maintained hospitals and charities, extended the suffrage, and inspires the movements for "social uplift" that are so popular at the present day. These enthusiasms, it is true, cannot exert discipline until they are supported by law. But their votaries are not "free" when they are "carried away" by them. Nor can liberty be claimed by the devotees of fashion. They submit to the commercialized versatility of "arbiters of elegance."

Finally, of the discipline that is imposed by a governing authority. This commences in the nursery and school, and can never be relaxed in the direction of military and police forces, or in the control of a ship, since it is only through discipline that unity of action can be preserved. A government may be democratic or dictatorial—that is to say, *commanding*, although its commands may be guided by consultation. The sustaining gas of democratic government is the breath of popular favour: its motive power is derived from the superiority, not of strength, character or intelligence, but of a numerical majority, awarded by party feeling, or won by persuasive argument. It is popular because it recognizes the supreme importance of personal vanity, and beatifies its indulgence as "liberty." Its inducements are, then, words not deeds, and experience counts for little by the side of eloquence. In its armoury conciliation ranks high above compulsion. It can introduce reforms only when they have gained a secure footing in public opinion; and it is necessarily timid in carrying them into execution, since reforms are generally obstructed by "vested interests," and these must be treated very delicately by a government that exists through favour.

A democratic government must be a party government, except on the rare occasions when public opinion is almost unanimous; and its aspirations must always be curbed by apprehensions of an increase in its opponent's popularity. Party feeling easily degenerates into a hostility that is ready to use violence. England has offered democracy its best chance of success, since the English can soften political rivalry with the good nature of a game, as they stiffen a game with the seriousness due to politics. But the spirit of "fair play" is not in itself a substitute for administrative efficiency. The British Parliament, for instance, is still discussing the problem of "slum-clearance," whereas in Germany slums were eliminated twenty years ago. It has been unable to interfere effectively for the control of exorbitant retail prices; and the working classes owe their wages and conditions more to aggressive Trades Unionism and strikes than to government action.

Its distrust of compulsion renders democracy inefficient in organization and control. It was only by sheer weight of numbers that democratic nations won the Great War. Strikes and "red" insurrections are dangers against which it must fight with its hands tied. It can only meet them by concessions, which imperil the future by encouraging fresh demands and by adding to taxation. Future must yield to present interests. And the future is extravagantly exploited to provide for the costliness of democratic methods, in the multiplicity of its ministers and councillors, in its consultations and conferences, and in the large advisory and clerical establishments that it must maintain. Its officials must lack the self-denying energy which is given by personal responsibility—by the stimulating pride that a man feels in accomplishment. There has consequently arisen a disquieting suspicion that democratic government cannot withstand violent social upheavals, or cope with the flood of economic difficulties that arises from the thoughtlessness of industrial and commercial life. It may work well enough in smooth water. But, amidst the troubles of social disorganization and economic collapse, Germany and America have now turned to dictatorships, hoping for such success as has been won by General Camorna in Portugal, by Ghazi Kemal Pasha in Turkey, and by Signor Mussolini in Italy. In our admiration for parliamentary government we have tried to force it upon Egypt, and are extending it to Malta, Ceylon and India. But history shows that it is—even in normal times—incompatible with the emotional excitability of peoples who live in warm, sunny climates. With them it hardly rises above the dignity of a rowdy football match. Their emotional disposition cannot be conciliated by compromise. They will "take" but not "give."

It is claimed by democracy that it creates a feeling of "responsibility." It certainly is "responsible government" in that its elected representatives are "answerable" to their constituents. But responsibility to public opinion is very generally, not a steadying, but a demoralizing force. How many of the statesmen who assented to the vindictive extravagances of the Treaty of Versailles would have done so had they been able to follow the duty which they owed to themselves instead of the angry passions of the multitude? It is this feeling of responsibility to oneself that marks the "gentleman"; and there is some excuse for the shocking cynicism of those who deny that democratic politicians have any claim to this title.

It is commonly held at the present day that man has a natural dislike to controlling authority—a natural desire to share in the direction of State affairs by subjecting it to the influence of a public opinion to which he himself contributes. But this conclusion is not supported by history. This shows that castes, tribes, sects and nations have been incessantly searching for a control that is at once strong and just; and that democratic aspirations have sprung, not from the spontaneous wishes of the multitude, but from the ambitions of comparatively few men who, finding that their only chances of gaining power and distinction lay in the swaying of public feeling by persuasive eloquence, instigated public opinion to demand opportunities for rewarding their efforts. This conclusion is most emphatically endorsed by the development of the Indian Congress movement, during the past half-century, from a surface ripple into a tidal current. As a matter of fact, the majority of mankind feel lost without a leader. Communities which term themselves socialistic are as a general rule dominated by one, or a few, of their number, and popular revolutionary governments tend to crystallize into autocracies.

Nor is this surprising. For the future is of such economic importance that present enthusiasm must ultimately yield to the need of preserving its security. This is endangered not only by the jealous or criminal aggression of one man upon another, but by waves of popular sentiment which shake future prospects by the incalculability of their consequences, and consume them by thoughtless extravagance. Men come to feel the need of an authority which is not subservient to public opinion, but can antagonize and control it. The *idea* that such an authority exists is a reassuring force even although the hands that hold it may be inactive or unworthy. There can be no doubt that the *prestige* of a king and a royal family adds to a nation's stability and to the maintenance of credit. For the idea of overshadowing authority gives confidence and a feeling of security. And, indeed, it is only when authority is independent of public opinion that it can still the vagaries of sentiment by opposing to them the dictates of conscience and common sense as to what is humane, generous, just or politic.

The idea of another's *power* is, then, fascinatingly attractive. For power implies protective ability. Mankind, almost automatically, ranges itself on the side of "big battalions." And there is an equally strong tendency to desert the weak. Illustrations of this abound. The mutiny that occurred in the fleet three years ago was to the French an alarming sign of weakness in a much respected power. They withdrew their gold from England in such quantities that we were forced off the gold standard.

Democracy has, in fact, served as a *pis aller* in man's

search for systems of government. This search for trustworthy objects of fidelity and obedience has been one long course of disappointments. There is confidence in the "strong man" who is elected as their chief by those who know his strength. But admiration for him is extended to his family, and accepts the hereditary transmission of his office to descendants who are quite unworthy of it. A curious experiment was made by the Italian city-states of the twelfth and fifteenth centuries. They imported foreigners as governors (podestas, or senators), in order to protect themselves from the injustice of local favouritism. A similar security was enjoyed by the people of India under the Indian Civil Service. As a safeguard, chiefship may be bestowed upon two men—consuls—each acting as watch-dog upon the other. But, if they hold office by periodic election, they become subject to public opinion and are swept away by it when they should be serving as a restraining dyke. A Senate of "elder statesmen" possesses the prudence that comes of experience, and, if hereditary, a prestige that enables it to resist popular clamour. The House of Lords has undoubtedly been a stabilizing force in our history. But if its powers are shackled or its numbers indefinitely increased by a popular government, there is a serious decline in its value and influence.

In actual experience loyalty to a controlling authority gives deeper and more abiding happiness than a sense of liberty. For the one allays apprehension of the future which is a deeply seated feminine urge, whereas the other gratifies a self-esteem that is merely a figment of the Mind. Moreover, respect for a leader—personal or ideal—is the only force that can effectively repress individual jealousies, and create an enduring spirit of united good fellowship. History shows that, sooner or later, democratic artificialities go down before the practical efficiency of a leader, dreams of liberty being thrown contemptuously aside.

It is, then, no matter for surprise that man should have sought a solution of his difficulties in Theocracy, rejoicing to feel that "The Lord is King." The Hebrews were governed during many years by prophets as interpreters of the Divine commands, with executive "Judges," who were specially appointed in times of difficulty. But their prophets failed them: "the sons of Eli lay with the women who assembled at the doors of the tabernacle," and the authority of temporary Judges was too spasmodic to be effective. Kingship seemed to be a more reliable alternative. The theocratic idea may express itself in a controlling Church. Such have been the Christian Churches of the Byzantine Empire and of Rome. But can we forget the murderous sectarian persecutions of the earlier centuries, the demoralization of the Papacy, the futility of the Crusades, the extermination of the Albigenses and the cruelties of the Inquisition?

These are gloomy reflections. Has experience taught us nothing as to the methods of government? Historians are agreed that the peoples of the Roman Empire were at their happiest during the second century of our era under a succession of emperors each of which had been *adopted* by his predecessor in years of maturity. And it is reasonable to conclude that a ruler who is at all interested in his duties will take care to select a successor who will not ruin his achievements. The end of prosperity came when Marcus Aurelius—a Stoic who could resist himself but not his wife —accepted the succession of his blackguardly son Commodus. We may, then, infer that a dictatorship, continued by the adoption of men who had shown their merit, has much promise. But to grasp dictatorial authority it is not enough that a man should be strong and capable. He must have aroused enthusiasm by some spectacular success: there must be a widespread *idea* that he is strong and capable. The Roman emperors gained this by deifying themselves. Kingship has been buttressed by the doctrine of Divine Right. A general—such as Napoleon, Cromwell and Kemal Pasha—can gain confidence by his victories. Signor Mussolini gained heroic stature by daring to oppose and overcome a government. Mr. Roosevelt and Herr Hitler have made themselves evangels of national resurrection.

There is also much to be said for a Council of Elder Statesmen, sharing legislative authority with the executive Chief of the State. It was under senatorial control that Rome became mistress of the Mediterranean. But, if its members hold office by periodic election this must not be of the popular kind. They must represent the leading interests of the country—religious, land-holding, professional, commercial, industrial and labouring—not heterogeneous masses of its population. And, under such a common-sense government, the various departments of State authority would be entrusted to men with experience of them. Ability to talk about them is all that Democracy requires.

TABULAR VIEW OF THE EVOLUTION OF HUMAN IMPULSES

Their origin in a harmonious* (or pleasing) idea.

A surge of masculine expansive (or pleasurable) emotion.

- If provocative idea is realistically pleasing.
  - In the present.
    - A feminine motive of clinging attachment or like.
    - (The enjoyment of physical pleasures and of amusements.)
  - Prospectively.
    - A feminine motive of searchful pursuit (*practical* in industry, trade or thrift, *emotional* in desire for pleasures and amusements.)
- If provocative idea is idealistically pleasing.
  - In the present.
    - A feminine motive of admiration.
      - For religious, social, moral and æsthetic ideals. (Loving enthusiasms.)
      - For ideals derived from success.
        - Egoistic. (Pride, vanity, self-assertion, self-complacency.)
        - Ego-altruistic. (Patriotic and party-feeling.)
        - Altruistic. (Love, respect, faith and obedience.)
  - Prospectively.
    - A feminine motive of ambition.
      - For religious, moral, social and æsthetic ideals. (Their cult, observance and spread.)
      - For ideals derived from success.
        - Egoistic.
          - Subjective.
            - Practical. (Self-control.)
            - Emotional. (Asceticism.)
          - Objective.
            - Practical. (Discovery, invention, direction, artistic creation.)
            - Emotional. (Emulation, war, sport, distinction—hunting.)
        - Ego-altruistic. (Patriotic or party aspirations.)
        - Altruistic. (Fighting, or suffering for a respected leader.)

* Discordantly provocative ideas act in contrary fashions.

INDEX